The Company They Keep

Life Inside the U.S. Army Special Forces

ANNA SIMONS

THE FREE PRESS

New York   London   Toronto   Sydney   Singapore

THE FREE PRESS
A Division of Simon & Schuster Inc.
1230 Avenue of the Americas
New York, NY 10020

The Free Press and colophon are trademarks
of Simon & Schuster Inc.

Designed by Carla Bolte

Manufactured in the United States of America
10   9   8   7   6   5   4   3   2   1

Library of Congress Cataloging-in-Publication Data
Simons, Anna.
   The company they keep: life inside the U.S. Special Forces /
Anna Simons.
     p. cm.
   Includes index.
   1. United States. Army. Special Forces—Military life.
I. Title.
U766.S59   1996
356'.1671'0973—dc20   96-38870
                                    CIP

ISBN 0-684-82816-2

For John T. Jordan, Jr.

Contents

Author's Note

SF NOMENCLATURE IS SPECIFIC AND STANDARD. EACH TEAM IN every group carries a different three-numeral number. The first numeral designates the ODA's Group. The second and third numerals combined indicate the ODA's battalion and company. For instance, ODA 311 is a team in A Company of the First Battalion of 3rd Group. It is a regular (or ruck) team. So would be 312, 313, and 316. In 3rd Group ODA numbers ending in 4 (e.g., 314) generally indicate a HALO (High-Altitude, Low-Opening military free-fall parachute) team, while numbers ending in 5 (e.g., 315) generally indicate a combat diving, or scuba, team. Members on both types of specialty teams have specialized qualifications above and beyond the normal Special Forces skills.

Because I wish to preserve as much as possible the anonymity of the men I describe, I have created my own set of ODA numbers: 304, 305, 306, 307, 308, and 309. Number 304 is a HALO team, and 305 is a scuba team. The numeral 3 correctly places each of these teams in 3rd Group. Otherwise, there is no 0 Battalion. I have likewise dubbed the company, which would normally be known only as A (Alpha), B (Bravo), or C (Charlie) Company, as Z Company.

Finally, I do not use soldiers' real names. Just as most of these men shy away from having their photographs taken for security reasons, many are still working in SF or elsewhere in Special Operations. The last thing I want to do is jeopardize their positions or endanger them in any way.

Prologue

THE THIRD SPECIAL FORCES SOLDIER I MET I WOUND UP MARRYING.
Back in the days when most people still had no idea where Somalia was, four Special Forces soldiers were assigned to the embassy in Mogadishu. They were there at the invitation of the Somali government to help train a portion of the Somali Army, not a particularly unusual assignment. Most men identified as American military advisers around the world are, in fact, Special Forces soldiers. And many, many countries invite them.

I was in Somalia for my Ph.D. research in anthropology, hoping to live with camel nomads somewhere in the country's dry, central reaches. However, Somalia was fast coming unglued in 1988–89, and once such a project was no longer feasible I found myself instead documenting the effects of the dissolution on young Somali civil servants I knew in the capital. This also meant that I spent far more time in Mogadishu than I had intended, although one of the unforeseen consequences of this was that I also got to know these four military advisers. Suddenly, they presented me with a new, foreign culture to consider: Special Forces.

Like most moviegoing Americans I thought I already knew what Green Berets were all about. I knew Rambo was a Green Beret, and I'd seen innumerable action movies in which there were cameo appearances by highly trained, beret-clad killers. But I also felt one small step ahead. For years I had been reading Vietnam War literature, and right before I left for Somalia a good friend introduced me to W.E.B. Griffin's Brotherhood of War series (which unreels a fic-

tionalized history of Special Forces). Thus, when the first military adviser I met introduced himself as a "Special Forces soldier," I was familiar with the term and knew how to translate it and be impressed:
a Green Beret.

Even better, though, was discovering that Sergeant Henry Williams
was a medic. I met Henry at the Thursday night American Embassy
disco, which attracted expatriates from all walks of life, and to which I
was dragged by friends insisting that it was an "interesting" social event,
well worth an anthropologist's time. While the mix of people did render the evening fairly interesting, it became far more so as Henry described the kinds of medical problems he encountered among Somali
nomads. Out near the Somali military camp where he worked he'd already treated dozens of them, mostly for dust- and wind-related eye
and ear infections, though—and this is when he got really animated—
he'd also been able to remove a fair number of abscesses, not a procedure he ever would have been asked to perform as a paramedic back in
the States. At any rate, he offered me extra first-aid supplies, which dou-
bled as an invitation to the soldiers' team house. And so, with that initial
chance meeting, my alter-existence in Somalia began.

At least for the first half year of their yearlong tour in Somalia,
Henry and two fellow sergeants spent the work week 100 kilometers
outside the capital, at a Somali Army base, overseeing the training of
Somali conscripts. The three soldiers usually returned to Mogadishu
only on the weekends. But as conditions deteriorated in the countryside, they too found themselves increasingly stuck in the capital, and
in their three-storied, Ethan Allen–furnished team house—which
proved a boon for me. The more they were around the better I got to
know each of these enlisted men, as well as their captain, who, owing
to the requirements of rank, was quartered in another well-ap-
pointed house nearby.

Within the first few weeks of meeting the members of this four-
man team, referred to by the army as a light infantry technical assistance field team (TAFT), I felt drawn in. For one thing, all four
soldiers were way too generous. They would do anything for anyone.

But also, they were contrary to all the stereotypes, yet still had the ability at times to seem larger than life. For instance, they traveled around in two Land Cruisers with special military license plates, granting them carte blanche on Somalia's roads. In Mogadishu they could drive the wrong direction on one-way streets without consequence, while out in the rural areas they could send goats hurtling through the air while driving at high speeds without having to worry about dealing with a nomad's wrath. Of course, they never intentionally did such things. But occasionally we would sit on their house's flat rooftop and pepper a neighbor's sheep with carefully aimed BBs. This was more to give doves and pigeons a respite than to harm the sheep, which barely reacted to being hit.

BB guns were the least of their armaments. Whenever we went camping they brought M-16s, and once violence descended on Mogadishu in July 1989, high-powered radio equipment was hauled out of a storeroom, so that constant communication could be maintained between team members at the military camp and those who stayed behind in Mogadishu. On a more mundane level, it was impossible ever to sit down in front of their TV and VCR and watch any movie without one of them identifying every weapon used. Running critiques of Hollywood pyrotechnics were also free for the asking. At times I had to wonder what they didn't know, especially as they also exposed me to a whole new language, full of acronyms, and in general proved themselves adept at crossing all sorts of cultural barriers.

Hands down, these soldiers displayed more patience with Somalis than did any of their expatriate compatriots. Usually they also treated Somalis far more decently. They went out of their way to help improve their interpreters' English. They routinely did favors for all members of their staff. And they genuinely tried to make a difference. Yet, at the same time, they could easily be provoked. When it came to matters of integrity and security, they had quick fuses and hot flash points. When they got mad they went just to the edge of violence, rapidly escalating through their personae: diplomat, friend, counterpart, challenger.

The more I saw, the more they made me wonder: were these four individuals truly representative of Special Forces soldiers? In Somalia I had no real way to find out.

Not only did I have to complete my fieldwork and then write my dissertation before I could even think about shifting my focus to Special Forces as a subject, but the Gulf War also intervened. Only when the soldiers were finally back at Ft. Bragg did I marry and move from Cambridge, Massachusetts, to Fayetteville, North Carolina. This is when I also became—in military parlance—a military dependent, or spouse. In anthropological jargon, marriage made me a real participant-observer. Not only was I right where I needed to be to observe SF, but a military ID card and my name (next to my husband's) on the company roster rendered me a participant, too.

To write this book I spent well over a year in the daily company of SF soldiers. In fact, most of my time was spent with a single company. I have dubbed it Z Company. It is a real company that exists in a real battalion in the 3rd Special Forces Group, stationed at Ft. Bragg, North Carolina.

While some of the soldiers in Z Company did initially wonder why an anthropologist would want to "study" them—did I think they were Neanderthals? Was it because I thought they were primitive?—they were hopeful. They were especially encouraging when I said I wanted to demythologize them. They hated all the popular misconceptions, particularly after the Gulf War, as journalists made much of a select few instances of Green Beret heroics. Taken together with the years' worth of Hollywood hype, this latest media fascination with the dramatic misadventures of a few teams actually troubled many long-term SF members, who found themselves increasingly worried that expectations of them may have become too unrealistically inflated.

For this reason alone most men in Z Company were anxious for me to see team life as it really is, though, in reality, they also wound up having little choice. The demands of their jobs soon made them forget that I might hear them swear, complain, pass gas, and be lewd. Moreover, it helped to have John (my husband) reassure them that he didn't behave any differently with me at home. From the outset, John was critical to my being accepted. But also, I was pretty sure after a midnight march on my second visit with the first team I attached myself to—a pitch-dark hike through calf-deep water—that I passed a critical test not even John could have helped me with. I proved no one would have to carry me.

The only occasion on which I really did require special treatment was one grossly hot and humid July night about nine months into my research. The company was on a field training exercise. In the morning, as soon as we arrived at the training area I, like everyone else, strung up a poncho shelter. As proud as I was of the job I did, I didn't realize that the site I chose included a nest of tiny seed ticks. Without my ever seeing them, ticks were suddenly all over me, hundreds of them. It took me most of the day, between moving from firing range to firing range with the teams, to pick off the ones I could see, which only made me wonder about the hundreds more I couldn't see. And, of course, as I tried to rid myself of these tiny brown freckles, all I kept thinking was that there was no way this particular field exercise was worth my getting Lyme disease. Nor did it help that none of the medics could tell me whether these ticks might carry it.

So forgetting valor, I bailed out of the field for the night. I wanted to go home and shuck my clothes and at least give myself a fighting chance to ward off the disease, while the only way to do this gracefully was to admit, yes, I *was* a wimp, although at least one of the soldiers in the team I was following spent his day obsessively picking at his own clothes and checking himself far too often not to have also been consumed.

In this respect, no SF soldier at all approaches Hollywood's hyperindividuals—more animal and automaton than human. SF soldiers themselves recognize that they had better be realistic about their limitations, as well as their strengths. If not, they'll simply set themselves up for disaster. For this reason it's also far more important to SF soldiers that recruits recognize what the organization is really about than that policymakers or even the public understand them. From the standpoint of SF veterans, too many recent recruits have bought into the Green Beret hype and seek to join SF for endless, glorious shoot-'em-up action, rather than to teach first aid in some dusty, uncomfortable village somewhere. This has created unsettling expectations within Special Forces about what SF soldiers should be doing; it doesn't help that family members don't always know what daily life on the teams entails either.

In the soldiers' view not even many SF wives really understand what the unit is all about, although all wives definitely do understand what it means (and costs) to be an SF spouse. Certainly I would not have been any wiser had I not received the active support of 3rd Group's commander, as well as Department of Army permission, to follow the teams through training and exercises. Just sitting in the team rooms was elucidating. I got to see males bonding, teams tightening, tempers exploding, and humor asserting itself. Wives, though they are said to be members of the Special Forces family, still can't really be fitted into this fold. They put in their own hard hours but not the *same* hard hours, and they rarely have the opportunity to become a roving appendage. I was lucky.

During 1991–92, 3rd Group was less fortunate. It was still suffering growing pains when I was at Ft. Bragg. The group had been reactivated only in July 1990, and worse, on the very eve of military downsizing. This meant that money was drying up just as teams yearned to get abroad to train. As a result, I heard a lot of complaining.

Soldiers complained about not getting to deploy often enough, about organizational changes that were creating more and more layers of control, about too much paperwork, and about officers who increasingly placed their own careers above good team training. Mostly, though, veteran SF soldiers feared that everything unique about SF was being gutted as SF was made more and more like the conventional army. As if changes in the types of training allowed were not enough, further proof came in the form of new rules and regulations relating to, among other things, appearance and safety, two areas in which SF soldiers had traditionally received special dispensation as members of an *un*conventional elite. Teams weren't supposed to be so regimented or controlled.

However, as if by magic, even the bitterest complaining would stop if a team was told to get ready to deploy. Then nothing else mattered but the mission at hand. This is when these soldiers would display the traits that truly set them apart from other soldiers. This is when they would both focus as individuals *and* gel into a team.

THIS BOOK DESCRIBES THE PROCESS OF GETTING TEAMS OF TEN, OR eleven, or twelve men to that cold-fusion point. It is a book about teams, *the* defining feature of SF: how they work, play, differ, compete, yet remain interchangeable. By filtering what I saw through an anthropologist's lens, I present a bottom-up view: of daily drama, unglorified training, and the processes of bonding. It is a view from inside the team rooms.

Consequently, I adopt the perspective of soldiers. Sergeants make up at least 85 percent of SF operational troop strength. No officers spend as much time on teams or in team rooms as SF sergeants. Junior officers have their own set of concerns, senior officers yet others, while the further any officer rises above the teams, the more politicized his view. I stay at ground level.

I also stick to life as lived on the teams, not in people's heads. Although I explore the dynamics between individuals, and how these wind up shaping the teams, I don't try to get under the skins of individual soldiers themselves; I can't. Even were I trained to poke through individual psyches, probe innermost thoughts, and reconstruct childhoods, I doubt that such techniques would work well with these soldiers—which should already say much about their talents.

SF soldiers are as skilled at compartmentalizing their feelings— and who they really are—as they are adept at slipping in and out of the woods at night. Intensely private about the personal things that matter the most to them, team members have an unspoken rule that even they do not need to know certain things about one another. In fact, to a large extent this practice is critical to teams being able to work at all. Also, SF soldiers are great at telling others what they think they most want to hear. Perhaps this comes from being in a military hierarchy, where careers are always determined by how you present yourself to superiors. Alternatively, dissimulation might be one of those personality traits Special Forces unconsciously selects for.

But there are two further reasons why I focus on teams. First, this organizational construct distinguishes Special Forces from most other units in the military. Second, it is at the team level where the unconventional nature of SF is both forged and tested. If SF is becoming too conventionalized today, as many of its best soldiers fear, then the team, as an unconventional military organization, may be in jeopardy. If so, then SF itself is doomed—on the cusp of the millennium, with no new world order in sight, as humanitarian crises mount, and as arms flow everywhere. Yet the United States has no other force to match SF capabilities. Such is SF's blessing, and its curse.

Introduction

SF IS ABOUT TRAINING, TRAINING TO TRAIN, AND TRAINING TO TRAIN others. Contrary to screen images or the high drama injected into fiction and nonfiction accounts, the real purpose of Special Forces is instruction. SF soldiers have to be adept at the insurgency and counterinsurgency techniques they teach foreign soldiers, and occasionally as military advisers they *do* get caught in combat situations—as they did in the jungles of Southeast Asia in the 1960s and 1970s and Central America in the 1980s—but far more often they run classes, operate schools, teach from lesson plans, perform medical or engineering services, and build rapport in quieter settings.

While SF soldiers never operate as lone wolves and aren't at all inarticulate—to lay to rest two other myths—they are not closet intellectuals either. Presenting SF soldiers as renaissance men tends to be the work of writers and journalists who upon actually meeting SF soldiers find themselves face-to-face with their own misconceptions. They discover that, though camouflaged and heavily weaponed, these men aren't really such thick-necked, bullheaded, uncivilized brutes. Consequently, short-term visitors to the teams sometimes play up Green Berets as multilingual, widely read, family-oriented, well-adjusted, sensitive 1990s-type males. But this does no justice to SF soldiers either. Certainly it doesn't describe the SF soldiers I know, none of whom can be characterized as philosopher-poets. Perhaps there are officers who would squeeze themselves into such a stereotype. But not many noncommissioned officers (NCOs).

Typically, the distinction between NCOs and officers is that officers have completed college and NCOs have not. Throughout the mil-

1

itary a college education winds up tracking servicemen and -women along different paths of subordination and command, with officers being those in command. But as Special Forces public affairs officers, as well as others of higher rank like to point out, lots of SF sergeants also have attended college. It is a matter of pride for them that they have smart soldiers. What they don't go on to explain, however, is that, having been to college, many of these NCOs could have become officers but didn't. They made a choice. And the choice they made was to stick with labor over management and keeping hands rather than noses dirty. NCOs don't like what officers have to do—kowtow to other officers (though they generally describe the process in far more graphic terms). Also, above the rank of captain there are no officers on Special Forces teams (also known as Operational Detachments Alpha, ODAs, or A-teams). At best captains manage to spend two years on a team. Yet teams are where the action is, which for many men also makes remaining enlisted (and on an A-team) a simple choice.

In choosing team over hierarchy, and SF over any other unit, SF NCOs actually assert a whole series of preferences: for army over family, career over job, discomfort over ease. In many ways, what can be said most broadly about SF NCOs is probably true of many career enlisted soldiers. Staying in the army for twenty or more years usually signifies two things: dedication and feeling trapped at some point. A profound sense of patriotism is implicit in expending all one's youth on the military, while dedication demands loyalty to unit, standards, and all the practices that sustain professionalism. Whether conscious of it or not, the NCOs I know have a huge capacity for sentimentalism, but they are also supremely practical men. At some point in their career, they always consider abandoning the army. They've been fed up, they've wanted out, or another line of work has strongly beckoned. But the army has trapped them. They either have a wife or owe alimony, children or child support payments to think about, a mortgage and bills, or some other responsibility that won't allow them to jump free and clear. So they stay. They may not want to but they do, though being stuck in SF affords them at least one advantage. Life around the teams provides little opportunity for bitterness. It doesn't allow for wallowing. Teammates won't tolerate anything less than serious commitment. In at least one sense, then, all SF soldiers are of a type.

BEYOND THE USUAL MISTAKES ABOUT WHAT KIND OF MEN SF soldiers are, there are other ways in which the Green Beret stereotypes err. First, just calling SF soldiers "Green Berets" is one giveaway that someone doesn't really know them. Most SF soldiers hate the term. As they put it, they wear green berets; they aren't Green Berets. They are Special Forces soldiers.

Technically speaking, being an SF soldier means completing the Special Forces Qualification—or Q Course—and then serving on an ODA. Only soldiers who pass the Q Course can wear the Special Forces tab on the left shoulder of their uniforms. This and not the beret has been the steadiest indicator of whether someone is SF-qualified. Meanwhile, the mark of being in a Special Forces Group is to wear the SF unit patch—a dagger with lightning zigzagging through it—just beneath the Special Forces and Airborne tabs. Nor are these simply subtle indicators. For those knowledgeable about uniforms, which means anyone in the army, tabs and patches are easy to read.

One glance at a soldier's uniform tells another soldier almost everything he needs to know: rank, specialized training, unit, combat experience. There is a whole system of rules dictating what is worn where. Berets are simply one element in the total outfit and signify little more than unit affiliation. Until recently, everyone serving with an SF unit was authorized a green beret, even pregnant clerks. Thus, sporting a green beret around Fayetteville came to mean relatively little to actual ODA members. Indeed, some soldiers went out of their way to avoid wearing berets, preferring patrol caps, they so resented the implied swagger of support personnel who quite intentionally advertised their belonging to an SF Group. In places, however, where SF soldiers were not such a familiar sight, these same ODA members were not quite so self-effacing. Then they wore their berets so members of other branches and services *would* know what they were.

In a lot of ways, negotiating their self-presentation outside SF may be among the most difficult things SF soldiers have to do. Most play down their skills and accomplishments to outsiders, who invariably seem to assume they are shaking hands with a professional killer. If an acquaintanceship is struck, "How many men have you killed?" usually gets asked. Women, particularly, seem to want to know. Consequently every team probably has at least one member who will take advantage of what he knows civilians (and women especially) assume. One sergeant I know used to claim, with a straight face, that he had sixty-three confirmed kills, and he'd always linger on that word "confirmed." He also asserted that, like all SF soldiers, he was trained to fly a commercial airliner in case he needed to evacuate a country quickly, and that he could detect the presence of other people long after they were gone just by sniffing the air.

Martin's teammates would scoff at all this nonsense while he was uttering it, and then mutter about him afterwards. As far as they were concerned he was an embarrassment. Not surprisingly, he never managed to last on any one team very long, although it is revealing that he was also never booted out of SF. Instead, soldiers like Martin generally wound up being shunted from team to team or found themselves kicked upstairs, relegated to teaching assignments around Ft. Bragg. One reason for this was that teams were always more concerned about themselves than the broader unit. So long as the team got rid of whoever didn't fit, they had solved their problem. And the joke would now be on someone else.

THE WHOLE HISTORY AND STRUCTURE OF SF IS BUILT AROUND teams. Organizationally, six A-teams (72 men) and 1 B-team (11 men) build into a Special Forces company; three Special Forces companies (along with a Battalion Headquarters Detachment and a Battalion Support Company) build into a Special Forces battalion; and three Special Forces battalions (along with a Headquarters and Headquarters Company, and a Support Company) build into a Special Forces Group. SF currently consists of five active-duty groups. Each group has a different geographical, linguistic, and cultural orientation, which means each is responsible for responding to events in different regions of the world. Most also call a U.S. base home. For instance, Ft. Bragg is home to 3rd Group—responsible for Africa and the Caribbean—as well as 7th Group—which is oriented toward Latin America. Fifth Group, which saw considerable action in the Gulf War because it covers Southwest Asia and North Africa, is stationed at Ft. Campbell, Kentucky. First Group, which operates in the Pacific and the Far East, is based at Ft. Lewis, Washington, while 10th Group, devoted to Europe, has recently moved from Massachusetts to Colorado.

Despite the implied scattering of the groups, two things should be noted. Numerically, the entire SF community is relatively small, and members of different groups meet and mix whenever they attend schools and special training, which they do throughout their careers. At the same time, daily life rarely extends much beyond the company. Often battalions gather for formations. Occasionally the entire battalion trains together. But even during a battalionwide exercise, responsibilities are split among companies, so that while soldiers may come to recognize other members of their battalion, they don't necessarily come to know them well.

Whole groups, meanwhile, seldom coalesce. When they do it is almost always for something ceremonial, like marking a change in command. Such ceremonies usually take place only once every two years. And when they do there is a lot of grousing. SF soldiers join SF in part to get off of parade grounds. They don't want to be conventional. And yet to be accepted for SF training in unconventional warfare, all SF candidates must have been among the best conventional soldiers the military produces.

Without doubt, SF *is* an elite organization. It is one of several in the armed forces that falls under the Special Operations umbrella. Probably most often SF soldiers are compared to Navy SEALs. SEALs, however, tend to be younger and train for waterborne missions. The Marines have Force Recon and the Air Force has Combat Control Teams. Only SF trains to organize or teach foreign troops.

Not surprisingly, SF's closest connections are actually to other army units. The Q Course draws many of its candidates from among soldiers who are already airborne-qualified and in elite units—82nd Airborne paratroopers and Army Rangers. The teams themselves occasionally shed soldiers to Delta Force, the counterterrorist and

hostage-rescue unit. But anyone—even a band member or a cook—
can apply for SF selection. Whether a soldier is then chosen to be a
candidate for the Q Course depends on his record, psychological
profile, physical ability, and intelligence. Whether he makes it all the
way through the selection process is far trickier. Does he *really* have
what it takes? SF demands far less physical prowess (although that is
important) than it does a careful mix of mental agility and steadi-
ness, skill at basic soldiering, and specialized expertise.

To thrive in SF, individuals have to be able to thrive while caught
in a series of paradoxes.

Like all soldiers, SF members live in a largely military world.
They are commanded by superiors. Also, their status as U.S. citizens is secondary to their role as fighting men. Although SF members fiercely believe in, and would die to protect, a democratic and
constitutional system, they themselves come under military law
twenty-four hours a day, three hundred sixty-five days of the year.
No matter how compelling the call of a girlfriend, a vacation, a sick
child, or an expectant wife, orders always take precedence.

At their most daring, too, SF missions are supposed to be invisible. If they succeed no one necessarily needs to know, while if they
fail the U.S. government might even go so far as to deny knowledge of
the very men it has involved. Many missions conducted during the
Gulf War still remain classified, and many SF casualties there went
unreported in the press. Secrecy itself is part of the SF arsenal. For
the record, it is as if SF does not exist, whether soldiers are on clandestine direct action missions or merely participating in joint training exercises inside the United States. Thus, there is no public
acknowledgment of these men as individuals, and what they are allowed to discuss (even with their own families) is often limited. At the
same time there is widespread public knowledge that Green Berets
do exist. Such public acknowledgment of their existence but not the
extent of their operations, of their abilities but not their specific assignments, means SF soldiers are caught in high-profile anonymity.

This is especially true in a town like Fayetteville. With two active-
duty Special Forces Groups (3rd and 7th), along with the United
States Army John F. Kennedy Special Warfare Center and School (US-

AJFKSWCS) and an array of Special Forces commands garrisoned at Ft. Bragg, there are hundreds of Special Forces soldiers in the area.

TO MANY SOLDIERS, FAYETTEVILLE REPRESENTS THE ARMPIT OF the state. According to their logic, army bases are rarely located in garden spots. Nor is there anything particularly charming about Ft. Bragg's environs of sand hills and pine trees, midway between the North Carolina coast and the foothills of the Smokies. Only two sets of people seem to actually relish Fayetteville's location: golfers and hunters. Southern Pines—a golf mecca—is only just down the road, and the region has traditionally held enough squirrels, birds, and deer between the tobacco fields to have attracted some of the country's wealthiest citizens to hunt.

Otherwise, as far as many soldiers are concerned, Fayetteville is much like any other large military town. It has ample barber shops, pawnshops, used-car lots, and Army/Navy surplus stores, in addition to the requisite collection of nationally recognizable franchises for fast-food, semi-fast-food, auto parts, and computers. Whole chunks of Fayetteville cater to the military.

Yet most NCOs could easily put the lie to Fayetteville's sentimentality, displayed whenever troops are deployed and network television cameras descend to pan across the yellow ribbons and flags put out by the town's merchants. For many soldiers, such tribute is as predictable as clockwork, and perhaps just as mechanical. They understand what inspires the laments about their deployment: whenever they go, there goes their money.

There are a number of reasons why such a gulf yawns between Fayetteville's civilians and soldiers. For one, the soldiers' world is too transient for bonds to form. And Ft. Bragg is too big. But deep down, too, no matter how cheek-by-jowl soldier and citizen live, they still exist on different sides of the civilian/military divide, operating according to different schedules, different laws, and different codes.

Also, those civilians who live the closest to soldiers tend to see the least soldierly side of the armed forces. They see uniformed personnel out of uniform, at play. Making noise. Partying. Acting irresponsibly. Getting into trouble.

As for Americans who don't have soldiers in their midst, the gulf may be even wider. It's not often that many Americans get to mingle with military personnel. If you don't grow up in a military town like Fayetteville or remain close friends with high school or college classmates who enlisted, when do you get an opportunity to meet soldiers? And in those few instances when members of the decision-making elite do interact with members of the military—in graduate programs or in Washington, D.C., for instance—it is seldom NCOs they interact with. The same is too often true of the media, whose members invariably gravitate toward (and are shepherded by) officers.

Many civilians without any direct military connection nevertheless harbor deep-seated prejudices toward soldiers. This is particularly pronounced for people who grew up during the Vietnam era, when out of moral conviction or for reasons having to do with self-preservation, they avoided the draft at the same time they scorned those who couldn't (and didn't). Nor has the abolition of the draft and our now having a volunteer army changed people's attitudes. Rather, what winds up personalizing the army for legions of Americans is who, out of their high school class, joins up. For the college-bound who don't join the service, this represents a sharp and self-flattering divide. Without keeping up with classmates who enlist, there's no way for those who go off to college to know how much the army may change their uniformed peers. Memories wind up freezing the enlistees in an unflattering adolescence. Also, stereotypes remain about what the army does to the spineless people it manages to attract. The military is rigid, too regimented, rule-bound. It brainwashes people. . . .

And without any encounters to contradict these impressions, the stereotype of soldiers (especially enlisted soldiers) persists.

But not even SF soldiers, who should be among the easiest to type, are typeable. After all, SF soldiers are self-select volunteers three times over: for the army, for Airborne training, and for SF. All are males (SF is a combat unit), the minimum rank accepted for selection is sergeant-promotable (E-4), and the reenlistment rate is 99 percent; they're career. Yet beyond such statistics Special Operations psychologists don't feel comfortable characterizing SF soldiers. And at least officially no computer program can crunch the men and discern a common pattern. The only patterns I've detected are that few SF NCOs applied themselves in high school, many have at least one close relative whom they no longer speak to, and few grew up privileged. Otherwise, for every soldier who refuses to sit with his back to a door in Fayetteville restaurants, there are others who scoff at such security precautions. For every three who like golf there are two who prefer fishing. For every one who has a German shepherd another has a Yorkshire terrier and a third breeds mastiffs.

SF soldiers themselves don't indulge in navel-gazing and are brusque about self-analysis. While expert at analyzing all sorts of things and gathering all kinds of information, dwelling on the quirks in their own makeup or the sociology of teams is not among their pastimes. This is not only very military but characteristically NCO on top of that—others are paid to indulge in such thinking, which brings us to the ultimate paradox SF soldiers live: how do they live?

There is no more financial remuneration attached to being in SF than to belonging to any other airborne unit. Rookie policemen in Los Angeles earn more money than do senior army NCOs. Nor does any widespread glory or fame come from being a Special Forces NCO. As the Gulf War demonstrated, NCOs seldom earn the medals officers do. Even in peacetime it often takes an NCO twenty years to be recommended for the same service medal a colonel receives after serving only two, and the NCO is generally awarded this only if he has a good friend willing to chase his paperwork and fight for him after he has retired. So why do SF soldiers work so hard, knowing they may be called on to expose themselves to danger? What drives, sustains, and commits these men?

Ultimately, it is the company they keep. SF soldiers are their own harshest critics. Teams roil with peer pressure. The challenge lies within—within individual soldiers, within teams, within the company, and within the unit. Ego plays a part. But ego usually has to be subordinated. To be good means being good on a team. And being part of a good team is—for these soldiers—as good as it gets.

1 Operational Detachment Alpha 309

IT MUST HAVE BEEN ALL THE DESERT CAMOUFLAGE THAT LENT THE team photograph such a sepialike quality. There stood, or squatted, the men of ODA 309, ready to deploy. Just behind them, like some giant prop and not an instrument of war, was the helicopter that would ferry them across enemy lines into Iraq.

As they showed me the photograph, I tried hard to stare through all the mustaches, which team members grew to foster rapport with their mustachioed Muslim allies. But I still could recognize only six of the eleven men now on the team. Just five months after the Gulf War, here was clear proof that turbulence was indeed taking a considerable toll, as soldiers were moved from team to school to new unit, and ODA 309 had lost and gained and shifted personnel.

Even so, everyone on the team, whether he had been in the Gulf War or not, was well versed in the team's view of that seminal wartime mission: piece of cake, no big deal. In fact, one team member slept on the helicopter ride to the first target site. Essentially— according to ODA 309—it had treated the foray just as it would any training exercise. Adrenalin may have been flowing, but no panic, no alarm, no last-minute uncontrollable fear.

That, only so many months later, was what was readily volunteered. It was not the actual sequence of events involved in getting

11

into Iraq, landing, setting up a hasty defense, scooping soil, and then swooping off, which the team liked to draw attention to. Much more important was having been chosen for such a mission in the first place. *That* was the truly big deal, particularly because only two teams out of the eighteen in the battalion had been picked to operate behind enemy lines before the ground war started. Nor did ODA 309 "just happen" to be one of the two. To hear ODA members tell it, the reason ODA 309 was sent was simple: it was the best.

As for the mission, it was straightforward but critical. The team was transported into Iraq to collect soil samples ahead of the invasion force. Given information about soil type, armor commanders would be able to plot routes for tanks, armored personnel carriers, and other heavy vehicles in the impending ground assault. Team members needed only ten minutes on the ground in two different locations to accomplish their task. In contrast, the other Z Company team sent into Iraq (ODA 307) had a much trickier assignment: reconnaissance. Its mission was to stay behind enemy lines undetected, in a hide site, watching, for days—clearly a longer, harder job. However, either operation, if compromised, could have proved deadly.

Nevertheless, as far as ODA 309 was concerned, it performed incomparably better than 307. It didn't frantically request extraction, nor did anyone on the team panic. According to 309, members of 307 did both. But then, 309 needed something to justify its own view of itself as *the* best team in the company and the battalion, if not the entire group. Never mind that it really didn't get the best mission, or that peers from other teams describe 309 members as having been a good deal more nervous than anyone on the team recollects, or that it wasn't a matter of 309 being especially singled out so much as other teams drawing missions that, in the end, weren't needed.

The collective memory of 309 edited out such details. In fact, the team version, as it developed, was that 309 was so professional and so used to training that the mission seemed to be just that: more training. Of course, by the time this had become a well-honed myth, most team members who had sat on that helicopter entering Iraq—and posed for the photo now leaning against the team-room wall—were no longer with the team.

THE STRUCTURE OF ALL SF A-TEAMS IS THE SAME. THEORETICALLY, each comprises a captain, warrant officer, operations sergeant, assistant operations sergeant, and eight additional NCOs. These eight include two medics, two engineers, two weapons sergeants, and two communications sergeants. Redundancy is the object of this design, so that a warrant officer (or chief) can substitute for the captain, the assistant operations sergeant can stand in for the operations or (team) sergeant, and either medic, engineer, communications, or weapons man will do.

There are lots of reasons for duplication. Some operations call for fewer than twelve men; occasionally a mission might require that the team be split into two equal wholes. Also, the normal routine of army life and NCO careers increasingly demands that soldiers attend certain schools. Training schedules and school schedules rarely jibe. Most often this means that at least one person will be away from the team at any given time; sometimes several soldiers are away. Alternatively, one ODA member might have the exact skills and experience required on a particular mission assigned to another team. In that case he will be detached from his ODA and temporarily reassigned to the team that needs him.

Every team in the company underwent some of this turmoil during the year and a half I was with them. And 309 was no exception.

In fact, the first time I went on a patrol with 309, I followed Carl Phoenix's "ranger eyes"—the two luminescent tabs sewn onto the back of every SF soldier's patrol cap. Because this particular patrol took place well after midnight, these were practically the only things I could make out on Carl. They also wound up being virtually all I saw of him. A few days later he was off to school. Already a communications (or commo) sergeant, he was now being formally cross-trained as an engineer, a procedure that took months.

Other team members came and went to other schools, or with other teams on real-world missions, or simply moved down the hall during training exercises. All this rendered 309's team room fairly kaleidoscopic, but it was never chaotic.

Military rank structure disallows chaos. Instead, it gives each soldier a specific place in an official pecking order. Every soldier has a position, a role, and a series of tasks for which he is responsible. For example, of every two medics (or engineers, commo, or weapons sergeants), one is always senior. Seniority depends on time in grade and is nonnegotiable. This in turn means that competition on teams is never direct. It does not mean that there is no competition, though, or that other significant pecking orders don't develop.

For instance, there is little the army or SF can do about personality. Certain character types can be screened for. But how personalities interact and develop, given the mix of people on a team, is impossible to predict. This is team-dependent, and it, too, is kaleidoscopic.

Theoretically, the captain and team sergeant are in charge. The captain interfaces with the world of officers beyond the team room. The team sergeant is responsible for the NCOs within. Practically, though, there may not be both a captain and a team sergeant. Or there may not be either. Alternatively, whoever is in charge might be ineffectual and easily dominated by more forceful personalities who form a critical mass further down the team. All these permutations could be found in Z Company. Yet if any team came close to approaching the ideal, it was probably 309.

For one, 309 had a team captain as well as a team sergeant. It did not have a warrant officer, but this rarely seemed to matter. The division of labor was such that Captain Tucker took care of much of the team's paperwork, while KC, the team sergeant, orchestrated how the paperwork would be filled in. In other words, KC made the significant personnel decisions, in essence, running the team. And this is what he was supposed to do, being more than ten years Captain Tucker's senior and far more experienced in the army, in the field, and with NCOs.

KC's running of 309 meant that not just the team was in constant training but also Captain Tucker. For Captain Tucker this two-year assignment to an ODA would be his one and only opportunity to work at a team level and learn how teams really operate. Once he left 309, it would be for staff jobs and ever-loftier managerial positions. As a major (the next officer grade beyond captain), he might even wind up back at Z Company, but then he would be returning as its commander, responsible for all six teams in the company, no longer deeply involved with any particular one. Hence, the time Captain Tucker spent in the team room was precious, though not necessarily for the reasons he himself might have cited.

Yes, two years on a team would provide unparalleled opportunities to hone leadership skills, learn field craft, make important decisions, and impress higher command. But as far as NCOs are concerned, nothing is more critical than having officers who understand them. After all, officers send them on missions. More immediately, officers determine whether daily life will be tolerable or not. The most important lesson, then, from the NCO point of view, that young captains need to be taught during their tour with the ODA is to respect NCOs; all else follows from this. If an officer is willing to accept the suggestions of more experienced soldiers, this allows NCOs considerable leverage, influence, control, and also comfort.

Legions of officers never seem to understand this. In theory, many pay lip service to the importance of earning NCOs' confidence and respect. But there is a difference between promoting confidence and projecting it, and many officers seek respect in far too clichéd and one-sided a manner. As one colonel told me (in Hollywoodesque terms), "I don't want to be liked, I want to be feared." Not surprisingly, he was actually hated, although soldiers had to respect his rank, and doubtless this confused him. More confusing still to NCOs under his command was that he had been a sergeant before attending Officer Candidate School. In the NCOs' view, he should have known better. But perhaps the problem was that he thought he already knew. Arrogance doesn't cut it with NCOs. And arrogance is impossible to hide from them.

Yet arrogance is something that officerdom inspires. There are two intertwined ironies here. One is that much of what officers practice is what they have been taught, either by books or by other officers. It is lectured, not learned—secondhand, not firsthand, knowledge. It is strictly theoretical at worst, based on someone else's experience at best. Meanwhile, this is precisely the type of knowledge SF NCOs distrust the most. Experience and common sense count for more, as far as they are concerned, than anything taught by or from a book. Hands-on experience is how and what they teach; it's what they live by.

At the same time, even the most junior captain outranks any NCO. His word is literally their command. Yet how has he earned this position? He's gone to college. As NCOs put it, four years of drinking beer and partying and a piece of paper separate the officers from them. Again, in the NCO lexicon this counts for nothing, yet for those who have been to college (or an academy), one of the things they learned there is the weightiness of this distinction. Implicit in the difference between those who are educated and those who are not is the linkage the wider society makes between education and intelligence. The military turns this to advantage in structuring its hierarchy. With officers controlling the decision-making process, the assumption that higher education denotes intelligence naturally supports officers' believing that only they deserve control.

AT LEAST ON 309, THE LINES OF CONTROL WERE ALWAYS ORDERLY. In the equation that made them unequal, Captain Tucker unabashedly represented book knowledge, while KC epitomized experience. At first glance, other differences might have seemed more pertinent, with KC the son of Southern factory workers and Captain Tucker a New England Yankee. But scratching the surface a little deeper, you could tell that the real differences could get confusing. While Captain Tucker went to private school on scholarship, then to an Ivy League university, KC bought his first house before he graduated from high school. KC watched the news at night and was a dittohead before the term was coined. Captain Tucker favored newsprint and *The Washington Post.* Their different preferences could have created quite a problem, but they never did. In large part this is because KC stressed professionalism in the team room. This meant respect for Captain Tucker. It also meant hard work and minimal complaining all the way around.

The unwritten rule on 309 was that everyone should anticipate what needed to be done and then do it without having to be told. Coherence on the team emerged out of a strong work ethic and came from successful completion of a group task. It never seemed to matter what—individually—was really motivating team members to work. That one team member continually sought KC's approval while another always strove to outdo everyone else and a third had to work hard because he happened to be on a team where his peers valued hard work did not detract from either the team's overall accomplishments or its image. Because a critical mass within the team *was* motivated and could stay motivated, the team remained convinced it was the same team that had been chosen to go into Iraq, despite any subsequent personnel changes.

To keep busy, 309 often practiced patrols. Patrols are infantry meat and potatoes. There is nothing more basic and nothing more standard, yet nothing more necessary than patrolling.

Patrolling is critical to being able to get to a spot in order to conduct surveillance (as part of special reconnaissance) or to set up an ambush or diversion (as direct action). But beyond its military role, a patrol can do three other things for a team. First, it will alert the team sergeant and captain to any deficiencies of individual soldiers. Second, it enables the team to practice coordination. During a patrol, every team member has to worry not only about his own stealth but where his teammates are. This is as much to pass hand signals up and down the line as it is to ensure security. Meanwhile, all this calls for a team to develop its own particular standard operating procedure (SOP), which, if it isn't practiced, can't become rote. Practicing SOP until it becomes fluid, then, accomplishes a third goal: getting the team out of the team room.

And this was always KC's preference. Otherwise everyone would sit around and grow too accustomed to not having to go outside and sweat or freeze. Also, life in the team room tended to produce complaining—and KC hated complaining. So as often as possible (though never as often as he would have preferred), he made sure patrolling was on 309's training schedule. On those mornings, team members would meet in the team room, sling on their web gear, and head for the woods.

So well-wooded is Ft. Bragg that whenever soldiers say they are going into the field on post, they mean they're about to disappear.

Teams can easily get lost. Consequently, no one really has to know whether the team is actually patrolling or only pretending to, though anyone familiar with 309 would never pause to wonder; not only would 309 be patrolling but team members would also probably be sweating, just because. In part, because it was Captain Tucker who plotted the routes. As an officer, he was always on trial. Thus, patrols were never as simple as they appeared. According to KC, patrols were always supposed to be difficult. So Captain Tucker always found himself trying to pick difficult routes.

Difficult or not, day patrols invariably feel slower than night patrols. Not only do soldiers move more deliberately because they are more visible, but there is also more to visually concern them—the ground underfoot, the surroundings off to the sides, and potential hand signals from up ahead or behind. At a closed fist everyone on the team should stop. Upon seeing an uplifted hand tightly circling in the air, the entire team needs to come together. Maybe there is a danger area, in which case scouts and guards have to be sent ahead.

Coordination can be complex. Everyone has to stay alert, and unpleasantness cannot become a distraction. If the plotted route crosses a ridge, then the unit must cross the ridge. This is particularly the case even when a perfectly good dirt road is "just over there." Never mind that over there it's flatter and clearer and easier walking. Dirt roads are danger areas. They are open and you never know when someone else might be traveling on them. Also, footprints are dead giveaways. And roads lead places. Therefore, the enemy knows roads are tempting.

At Ft. Bragg it's not hard to find areas that hold few temptations. There are thickets full of unforgiving brambles and plenty of patches of poison ivy and poison oak. For anybody who has to spend much time in the area, the topography makes two indelible points: first, forget looking for mountains or dramatic land forms. There are none. Second, learn the vegetation. It isn't so much the literal lay of the land as changes in plant type that signal easy versus hard, and dry versus wet. For instance, bamboo can mean easy or wet. Not all wets are the same.

The first damp area Peter takes us across barely wets anyone's feet. I am the sole casualty and that's only because I'm not wearing jungle boots. Had I worn them, my shoe wouldn't have been sucked off in goo. Otherwise, there are enough firm footholds to scuttle across, although no one goes too far out of his way to avoid mud. That would be pointless. It would also be antithetical to training, although the army doesn't pay for laundering; individual soldiers do.

The second draw is why fastidiousness is useless. While Captain Tucker purposely aimed the route through two low points, maps can't account for meteorology, and it's past rainfall that fills depressions. Captain Tucker couldn't have known this second draw would be so unquestionably swampy, with foot-sized islands rooted in the muck, spaced as though we just might be able to use them. Maybe. Peter first.

Peter, on point, is responsible for breaking trail because he missed rendezvousing with the team on a night patrol earlier in the week. Having everyone behind him now, scrutinizing his every move, is part punishment but also quite serious. Peter has to restore his teammates' confidence in him before he slides from simply being the butt of numerous company jokes to becoming an actual liability for 309. *Can* he get through the woods from point A to point B?

At the moment, all anyone really cares about is whether he can get across the points directly in front of him. Will he make it through the stagnant stretch of gunk and still stay dry? Surprisingly but quite effortlessly he does. His boots and feet are wet, but he's safe on the other side by the time it's the next man's turn to follow.

The next man—on compass—is Chris. But Chris doesn't follow Peter's exact route. Instead he must think he's found a better line through the muck than Peter drew, and so chooses a slightly different trajectory. One minute Chris is standing. The next he is attempting to swim.

It's hard to know who's more surprised, Chris or the rest of us. But watching Chris is also instructive: his hands remain above the water, which is where he would want to keep them were he carrying his rifle. But doubtless he also wants to keep them aloft because there is nothing particularly pleasant about the ooze. In fact, its color and consistency indicate it's too soupy for water, which means it also isn't likely to feel refreshing. Wearing long-sleeved battle-dress uniform (BDU) camouflage blouses over olive drab T-shirts, long camouflage (BDU) pants tucked into jungle boots, with web gear strapped on, carrying canteens and survival gear, every-one could certainly do with a cool dip by this point. Not that anyone really wants one, though, watching Chris.

Indeed, faced with Chris trying to wade out of the mess without miring himself even more, everyone laughs. Although we shouldn't make noise, we can't help it. Chris is flailing chest-deep, with Peter already dry on the other side. But the prospect of winding up as gunky as Chris also means at least a portion of the laughter is nerves. Soon that could be any of us. Consequently, everyone be-gins removing wallets and anything made of paper from pants pockets, transferring them to shirt pockets. No one attempts to keep anything else dry. A few comments are made about the per-fectly good road, which is essentially in sight, "just over there." Then pressure to do it the hard way prevails.

Still single file, the team begins to head through. Not surpris-ingly, everyone sticks very close to, if not right on top of, Peter's line through the swamp. Everyone, of course, also gets wet at least to the knees, since with every additional football of weight, the weeds sink a little bit deeper. Nor, as everyone already knew, is the wet just water; it's also stinky slime: the highlight of the patrol.

The rest of the walk back to the team room is a hot and humid slog, especially since the sun is now out in full force and climbing higher all the time. There are no more significant dips, nothing of topographical interest ahead. But no matter how anticlimactic or rote-seeming the rest of the patrol, and no matter how much ten-sion was broken by Chris's plunge, no one can afford to let his guard down. This remains a patrol. Regardless of how familiar or easy the surroundings, it still counts as a behind-the-lines mission in enemy territory. Of course, it's also Ft. Bragg. Therefore, realistically, any enemy can exist only in the minds of team members. The task is to stay vigilant though this is just an exercise in the team's backyard.

Part of what makes for tension in the first place is what still fuels vigilance. No simulation is necessary to feel watched. Everyone *is* being watched—by one another—so that the team drives itself. From Peter all the way down the line there isn't a person on patrol who doesn't take peer pressure seriously, doesn't worry about what KC thinks, and doesn't worry about his performance. To a certain extent simulated opponents would just get in the way.

This is also why, even when everyone recognizes exactly where we are—at the edge of the hardball road leading back to the company building, which is only a few hundred meters away—the entire team still scatters and runs when KC whistles and then yells "incoming." Running is precisely how the team is supposed to react were a real shell to head for its midst. Of course, there are more grins than grimaces as everyone bolts in the direction of the company. From KC especially. Everyone is relaxing, which means joking, just as team members reach the company doors.

There is nothing like the air of cohesion to give 309 an edge. The mud badges everyone wears slathered around his legs also help make it obvious to the rest of the company that 309 has been out training, which sends a variety of messages. Ideally Major Geoffries, the company commander, will be impressed. Doubtless members of other teams will be jealous, while some team leaders will think they see right through what KC and Captain Tucker have done. Team sergeants will recognize that KC is showing 309 off, and other captains will view Captain Tucker as showing them up.

Across teams there is intense competition, especially between captains. This is integral to the military's overall design. Competition among officers provides one method for sorting out who will be promoted, since the hierarchy grows narrower at every level. Not everyone can be forever propelled upward, which is similar to that other reality of there never being enough real-world missions for every team. Nor are the two unrelated situations, given a captain's ultimate goal: to win whatever missions there are. This enhances his career, and presumably explains why he joined SF—to perform.

Meanwhile, the picture is also much broader. "Higher authority"—as it's called in the military—can't care about a captain's career or a team sergeant's reputation. Decision makers can't afford to dwell on individuals to this extent—one measly practice patrol can't matter. But in another sense, what determines a team's reputation is how all the practice patrols add up—added to all the other training. To whose attention this reputation then comes depends on who has made it: the team's captain or its team sergeant. The way the officer-driven chain of command works, commanders are far likelier to be interested in captains than in team sergeants. Officers mentor other officers, socialize with them, politic, backscratch, line up favors, and establish alliances, patron-client ties, and information nets.

Both KC and Captain Tucker understood this, though KC also understood more. While many of the men on 309 regarded KC as the best team sergeant they could have, and KC clearly cultivated his image, he did everything within his power to promote Captain Tucker, too. KC knew that no matter how "hot" 309 might seem to the rank and file, it wouldn't go anywhere, and was certainly un-likely to be sent abroad, without a creditable officer. As it was, NCOs in Z Company were convinced that what the battalion and group commanders thought of the separate teams depended on how well they liked individual captains. Thus, no matter how brilliant KC may have been, the team needed Captain Tucker to make an even more favorable impression. Fortunately, this too played right into KC's talents. He started his spin in the team room first.

KC zeroed in on Captain Tucker's strengths. Captain Tucker often alluded to how smart he was. After all, wasn't he an Ivy League graduate who, 309's team members knew, read all the time? In fact, the team was convinced Captain Tucker remembered everything he read. And why not? He quoted stuff continually and knew all sorts of regulations by heart. The word that KC helped the team spread, then, was that Captain Tucker was indeed an unusu-ally smart officer.

Not everyone in the company bought this. Because Captain Tucker regularly visited the Special Warfare Center library to study journals and newspapers and catch up on the latest developments in sub-Saharan Africa, 3rd Group's area of operations, some con-sidered him an intellectual busybody. This is because, as much as these visits may have served to sate his curiosity, which was quite genuine, his gleanings also allowed him to make innumerable policy-related pronouncements to superiors. Other captains in the company didn't do as much homework in this area as Captain Tucker did. Tellingly, they didn't have to. There are whole offices full of people SF soldiers can call on when they need to find out what is happening in a country where they might deploy. Nonetheless, Captain Tucker's displays of knowledge always threatened to put him ahead.

Consequently, while Captain Tucker may have been making one kind of impression on some of his superiors, he was making an altogether different one among his fellow captains, and an even worse one among certain senior NCOs. At least a few openly questioned how anyone of substance was even taken in. While they regarded all officers as brownnosers—too often ignoring the degree to which they, too, had to please higher-ups—they found Captain Tucker's continual angling too shamelessly transparent. He wasn't smooth or subtle enough but was too much like a ferret, constantly seeking information. His endless questions, which often came in the form of assertions, also bugged them. And what about that whining, wheedling voice?

Captain Tucker couldn't help his voice, the thin edge of a potential wedge that KC never discussed but simply ignored. Still, SF NCOs are mercilessly hypercritical, and no matter how skilled KC was at impression management he couldn't completely protect Captain Tucker. Nor did he go uncriticized himself. Other team sergeants were skeptical. To them Captain Tucker wasn't a genuius and KC didn't walk on water, no matter how many soldiers in the company seemed to think so. But part of the genius in how KC ran 309 *was* to stifle complaining, which—he convinced his team—was unprofessional. Without complaining there could be no visible fissures. Without fissures, critics would have too little to go on. Within the company at large, therefore, 309 *would* be the ideal ODA. Not that KC explained all this to the team.

2 SF: Purpose and Place

KC POSSESSED A GIFT FOR READING PEOPLE AND SOMETHING ELSE
that proved useful for manipulating—or as he preferred to regard
it, motivating—his team: mystique.

At five foot eight inches tall, KC was 309's shortest member. He
trimmed his mustache narrower than it needed to be, which made
it suspiciously Hitleresque. His camouflage fatigues were usually
faded, and he invariably donned his beret as if it were a flying
saucer, not a badge of eliteness. Still, once KC interacted with
someone there was never any doubt about his stature. He always
achieved appropriate distance. If you couldn't hear it in his tone,
you could read it in how he carried himself, posturing aside.

While official and unofficial army regulations alike dictate how
officers should keep themselves apart from their men, team
sergeants, too, must attain a certain degree of separateness if they
want respect. This isn't always easy. As NCOs, they have come up
through the ranks themselves, and no matter how many stripes the
army may place on their sleeves and collars, they still fall on the enlisted side of the divide. Yet by the time a senior NCO is promotable to
team sergeant, he should know how to impress others without being
overbearing. Usually this means he has learned where his strengths
lie, and which communications skills work the best for him.

KC, for instance, used looks: the cold look, the appraising look, the exasperated look, the disconnected look, and the you-know-I'm-watching-you look. These were useful not only because they kept everyone looking *to* KC for approval but because everyone on the team could gauge how KC was regarding others. This was one way to maintain continual peer pressure. Such silent communication also allowed self-criticism to take effect before KC had to start criticizing, which in turn meant fewer arguments. If KC didn't offer an opening for someone to give him an excuse, then he guaranteed himself fewer excuses. Excuses were like complaints: the less said the better.

Interestingly, KC himself practiced "the less said the better" when it came to his own military experience. Everyone on the team knew he had spent some time away from SF, at first doing something with Delta Force and then working for the Department of Defense. That he would obliquely allude to this "classified" work convinced 309 that he had experience (though no one seemed to know in what) that could benefit the team. Perhaps not surprisingly, some senior NCOs wondered about this. Certainly KC was creative; maybe he was embellishing. . . ?

Because some real-world SF missions (such as reconnaissance into Iraq or training of mujahideen on Stinger missiles in Afghanistan) have required secrecy, and because many SF missions still remain classified, an air of mystery can very easily be woven into peoples' reconstructions of their pasts.

This is especially true when individuals have worked "behind the fence" or "on the dark side"—terms that refer to Delta Force assignments. This extremely well-funded hostage-rescue and counterterrorist unit, which paralleled and then supplanted SF's own Blue Light program, continues to draw many of its members and support staff from ODAs. Thus, despite the secrecy with which it surrounds itself, Delta Force is not so much of a mystery to SF NCOs who maintain friendships with former teammates now assigned to Delta Force's fancy compound set deep in Ft. Bragg's woods.

Even if veteran SF NCOs don't know details about the sorts of security missions dark-side units engage in, they have extensive experience at putting two and two together. The Special Operations community is not so tight-lipped as security experts would probably prefer. It is very hard to prevent men, each of whom may hear different bits and pieces of information from different sources, from putting these together and approximating the truth. Also, everyone has informal contacts elsewhere in the community. This is why outright lying can't work. There will always be someone, sooner or later, who might call your bluff.

Still, had others checked, KC probably wouldn't have cared. In his case it didn't matter whether his peers—other senior NCOs—doubted whatever the men on 309 and other teams chose to think. By never really saying anything, he wasn't exaggerating. In fact, he wasn't doing anything beyond using ambiguity to his advantage.

Still, mystique did set KC apart. Most senior NCOs used some sort of hook to distance themselves. Given the intimacy of team rooms, they had to.

In 1991, 3rd Group moved from World War II–vintage, two-storied wooden buildings on one side of Ft. Bragg to a new brick cluster across post. Drafty but spacious, the old buildings had afforded each team its own warren of rooms, where Schwarzenegger posters competed with pinups, lockers easily accommodated all of a team's rucksacks and field equipment, desks offered ample surface space, and there were plenty of windows—allowing teammates numerous ways to escape one another. But no longer.

Teams now were squeezed into windowless, single-occupant rooms which, while more secure, were also exceedingly cramped and depressingly bare. Each battalion—eighteen teams' worth—occupied its own single-storied building, where three separate doors led to three separate companies, but where every company area was exactly alike.

Walk through a set of double glass doors and you were in B-team territory. This was the space allotted the company commander and his staff: the major, sergeant major, warrant officer, operations sergeant, and company supply sergeant, as well as soldiers pulled from ODAs to assist them. Traditionally, the B-team acts as the company nerve center, although working here was an assignment most team members tried to avoid because paperwork

was the everyday routine, and administrative coordination of training schedules, jump schedules, school assignments, and personnel
records proved a constant headache. In fact, there were few benefits at all to serving on the B-team. Z Company's major, sergeant
major, and supply sergeant each had his own small office, but often
the rest of the staff had to play musical desks. Also, the B-team area
was continually accessible. ODA members were always stopping
by, asking questions, seeking favors, straightening out mistakes.
The one compensation? The B-team area did have an executive toilet. The rest of the company—six teams of twelve men each—were
stuck sharing a grand total of two stalls.

As if two toilets was not problematic enough, the company's
new quarters had only three showers. The lack of showers was just
one of a series of design flaws that suggest ODA members had had
too little to do with designing the new buildings. Ridiculous as it
was that bathroom facilities were so limited, worse still was the
dearth of parking spaces. At 0600 every morning the entire company performed physical training (PT). Without being able to
shower at the company after their four-to-six-mile run or hour-
long ruck march, most men had no alternative but to drive home to
change out of their gray PT shirts and shorts before returning to
begin the real workday in camouflage fatigues at 0900, which also
meant having to compete for parking all over again. And there were
other complaints. For instance, during weapons cleaning—in team
rooms with poor ventilation—everyone quickly choked on strong
chemical fumes. During isolations it was even worse, when the entire team might be confined to its own space for as long as forty-
eight or seventy-two hours straight.

Enter one of these rooms and you found yourself in a linoleum-
floored, cinderblock cell. The only saving grace was a high ceiling.
In fact, before dragging in its gear each team had briefly turned its
new home into a carpentry shop. Following 7th Group's lead, every
Z Company ODA constructed a loft. Some teams used the additional space strictly for storage; others perched desks on their new
second floors. But even so, only five or six desks reasonably fit,
given all the teams' equipment, which meant that not even every

twosome (of medics, engineers, weapons, and communications sergeants) could claim their own corner. The team sergeant and his assistant had to have desks and shelves. So did the captain and/or the chief. And though every team configured its furniture slightly differently, still only so many arrangements were possible. Worse yet, no one could hide from anyone else's view. And no conversation could go unheard.

The decor was an uncomfortable mix of government-issue furniture, wooden desks, desks in cold gunmetal gray, swivel chairs, old wooden chairs, folding chairs, metal wall lockers, team-built wooden wall lockers, military footlockers, shelves full of military manuals—a hodgepodge. No team room felt particularly homey. At least for the first year of occupancy nothing heavy was allowed to be attached to the walls (the building contract forbade it), which meant few teams could display plaques received for joint training missions or anything else important enough to the team to be framed. All that set 305's team room apart were a press bench, a couch, and a skimpy rectangle of shag carpeting. The center of 308 was taken up by an elaborate display table with a captured Iraqi flag under glass; 309's concession to making something more of its room was a coffeemaker, while 304's door split open an oversized poster of a woman's scantily clad rear.

With not enough differences among team rooms, the most significant contrast remained that between these new quarters and those only recently vacated. Despite the teams' best efforts to personalize cinderblock and linoleum, there was no way these new institutional surfaces would absorb the same kind of roughhouse history. Not only were they too smooth and sterile, but their tightness just reinforced the sense that SF itself was being squeezed, constrained, and made more uniform. Was this just cost cutting, or did it reflect some grander design? If the latter, it was hardly in keeping with SF's charter. It couldn't be.

THE CREATION OF SF SHOULD RANK AS ONE OF THIS CENTURY'S most significant military developments, even if it rarely receives the attention it deserves, overshadowed by the never-ending development of ever-more sophisticated hardware. Whole shelves full of books have been devoted to how both world wars changed the face of battle, and how nuclear weapons have changed the essence of warfare and the ways in which wars must be fought technologically. This is all true, but these same changes have also required the invention of something like SF.

The development of SF shortly after World War II signaled two things: certain elements within the U.S. government recognized the significance of unconventional warfare, and the United States should be capable of waging it.

Official mythologies, counterhistories, and popular versions make contradictory claims about SF's origins. Either U.S. military involvement in unconventional warfare can be traced all the way back to the American Revolution or it can be pinpointed to the Office of Strategic Services (OSS) during World War II. Certainly, those who lobbied the hardest for the creation of something like Special Forces were World War II veterans. They were convinced that the U.S. military should continue to build on the successes achieved during the war by small groups of American, British, and French soldiers who helped local resisters coordinate behind-the-lines activities, both in Europe and Asia. Such coordination came in two forms: units like the Jedburgh teams, which were dropped behind Nazi lines in France, and Detachment 101, which operated in Burma. These helped supply and organize resistance forces, but they also helped ensure that resistance forces directly contributed to larger war aims. By parachuting in to help organize bands of brave but beleaguered European or Asian locals establish intelligence and escape and evasion nets, engage in sabotage, and attack from the rear, special operators helped achieve a quicker Allied victory.

Proponents of preserving such Special Operations capabilities argued that the United States had every reason to remain equally determined and self-interested after the war. The world remained an unstable place. Strategically, guerrilla warfare was something the Communist powers—both Soviet and Chinese—seemed poised to foment in Latin America, Asia, and Africa. And adeptness at guerrilla warfare could well prove critical if the United States had to confront the Soviets in their European backyard, where the Soviets would always have the conventional upper hand. Allied Special Operations capabilities would at least help even the Cold War playing field. This is why, advocates argued, it only made sense to build on the unconventional strengths the OSS and the army had developed in Europe during World War II.

Such strengths were more than organizational; they also had to do with how the OSS recruited. To join OSS's operational groups in Europe during the war (and the famed Jedburgh teams), soldiers had to display some degree of familiarity with a European country, including fluency in its language. Since their primary task was to help organize and train resisters behind enemy lines, it wasn't enough for volunteers just to look like the Europeans they would be helping. One point emphasized early was to recruit individuals who could go native because they practically were native. From the outset—less than a decade after D-Day—SF was still attracting significant numbers of East European refugees who had fought in their country's army and then fled communism.

This strong initial bias toward soldiers being able to go native has suffused SF ever since, though an attendant catch quickly developed. SF's second set of World War II and postwar (and Korean War) roots were Asian, where going native for U.S. soldiers was far more difficult. Not only would the vast majority of SF recruits never look Asian, but it was unlikely enough could be found with competence in languages like Kachin (spoken in Burma) or Tagalog (one of dozens of languages used in the Philippines). Rather than knowledge of a language per se, requirements had to be shifted to linguistic ability. Likewise, being able to adapt to any location was substituted for coming to SF already possessing deep local knowledge.

Still, just like special operators during World War II, Special Forces soldiers were meant to have skills in four different but interconnected areas. First, there was unconventional warfare (UW), which is defined today to include guerrilla warfare, the training of indigenous personnel in subversion and sabotage, intelligence gathering, and construction of escape and evasion nets. Second, there is foreign internal defense (FID): assistance to another government that seeks to protect its citizens from subversion, lawlessness, and insurgency. Third, direct action (DA): short-duration strikes and small-scale offensive actions, such as raids, ambushes, and sabotage. Fourth, special reconnaissance (SR) entails learning the capabilities, intentions, and activities of an actual or potential enemy or the disposition of a site.

Hand-in-hand with these four types of missions goes civic action and the careful wooing of hearts and minds. Unconventional warfare and foreign internal defense both imply lengthy stays on foreign soil. Just to secure their own safety and comfort, soldiers must build local rapport. This is achieved by medics and engineers especially, who can heal and treat the halt and the lame, dig for and purify water, build outhouses and other structures, and engage in goodwill activities that are more than mere gestures.

Over the years SF soldiers have assisted villagers throughout the world: in Laos as early as 1954; in Bolivia, Panama, Colombia, Venezuela, El Salvador, Honduras, Ecuador, Iran, Nepal, Thailand, Brazil, Nigeria, Liberia, Jordan (to list just some countries) in the 1960s. Yet it is still Vietnam most people think about whenever they think SF.

For better *and* worse, Vietnam gave SF its most enduring public face. Deeply enamored of unconventional warfare and fascinated by counterinsurgency capabilities, President John F. Kennedy as commander-in-chief ratcheted up the deployment of Special Forces advisers to South Vietnam in the early 1960s. Without question he also proved to be SF's most generous patron. It was he who gave dispensation to Special Forces soldiers who insisted on setting themselves apart by donning green berets. That two Special Forces soldiers, wearing green berets, then marched alongside the caisson bearing his body to Arlington Cemetery bespeaks the significance he accorded them.

Vietnam as the setting for SF's greatest exploits, both heroic and villainous, has easily received more ink and attention than any other period in SF history. In Vietnam SF soldiers' activities ran the gamut, from UW through FID and the training of Vietnamese Special Forces soldiers, to DA employing South Vietnamese troops as well as Montagnards, and SR with or without accompanying locals. In virtually all instances SF soldiers served as force multipliers. One team of twelve men would fully train an entire battalion of Vietnamese soldiers in one sector, while a few SF soldiers might serve as advisers to an entire company of Cambodians elsewhere.

Other teams sat in lone but heavily fortified positions, serving as probes, tripwire, and deterrent all rolled into one, with hundreds of local soldiers and villagers dependent on them. In such cases, SF soldiers' responsibility was not just strategic but also humanitarian, and demanded civic attention and diplomacy, as well as military daring. SF teams were designed to be self-sufficient, both in the manner in which they were deployed (attached to foreign forces or on their own) and in their mode (sometimes penetrating deep into enemy territory, sometimes sitting in the same location for weeks at a time). However, in some instances self-sufficiency backfired. Some SF soldiers engaged in illegal enterprises, while others took the law into their own hands.

Without question SF attracted rogues. The usual explanation for unconscionable SF behavior during Vietnam is that too many soldiers were inappropriately passed through the Q Course in the frenzy to ship more and more U.S. bodies to the war. Many of these individuals never should have been allowed to enter the Q Course in the first place. But then, too, many individuals were drawn to SF because they viewed the entire organization as renegade. For officers in particular, SF was considered to be the place to serve if you didn't want to conform and liked rough living. SF represented an end (and if you stayed in too long, a dead end), not a means to higher rank.

But it wasn't just bad soldiers running wild or good soldiers gone bad that plagued SF and tarnished its image. SF soldiers were also assigned to dirty jobs by people outside the SF chain of command. At times SF soldiers *were* ordered to use extreme force in targeting civilians. Or, worse, the rules for what they should and shouldn't do to accomplish a particular mission might be left purposely vague, allowing civilian operatives then to hang them out to dry. Much of the rationale for this is rooted in SF's history. The CIA and SF both grew out of the OSS, but the CIA was first-born (in 1947).

When 10th Group was officially created in 1952, the CIA should have relinquished its oversight of unconventional warfare, but it never did completely disconnect. Thanks to government hierarchies, the CIA continued to exert itself, by either directly or indirectly involving soldiers on the small scale of intelligence gathering or the larger scale of projecting lethal force—something it continues to do today.

Essentially, all the same pressures that existed for infantrymen, Marines, and other combat soldiers in Vietnam existed in SF, but amplified. Thus, when SF soldiers did good by treating diseases, organizing schools, and defending villages, they often worked what amounted to miracles, while when they did bad they perpetrated true horror. Still, for many SF veterans today, the Vietnam War represents an anomalous period despite its being regarded as SF's heyday. As one 3rd Group major reflectively put it, Vietnam represents a spike in SF's EKG. The war didn't go according to an unconventional design, even though it offered American soldiers their longest unconventional moment. At the same time, on countless missions in Vietnam (and Laos and Cambodia), SF ODA members did prove themselves just as effective at guerrilla warfare as the North Vietnamese and the Viet Cong. And this in the enemy's backyard, which was about as alien and different from the training areas of Ft. Bragg (where Vietnam-bound 5th Group was based) as rice paddies are from pine forests and steamy mountains from sand hills.

Today, many Americans seem to assume that one reason the war was lost was because the North Vietnamese and Vietcong proved to be better guerrilla fighters. But in fact, SF soldiers performing direct-action and reconnaissance missions did as well, and, many times, better than their enemy counterparts. Thus, in a strange sense Vietnam did vindicate the vision of SF's founders: elite U.S. soldiers can excel at unconventional warfare.

In the immediate aftermath of the Vietnam War, however, SF's eliteness and its record drew withering fire. Excoriated for being baby killers by the public, SF soldiers were regarded as little better than this by conventional military commanders. Conventional officers regarded SF as being too close to out of control. Thus, it was almost cathartic for the military to begin purging itself of its unconventional, unorthodox capabilities. Organizationally SF was gutted. Whole groups were deactivated. Whatever successes teams had achieved didn't matter; the view was that SF soldiers couldn't be trusted.

In the face of such an onslaught, SF had to improve. The demise of groups and the severe reduction of forces post-Vietnam was more than just a wake-up call; it was a warning, signaling that SF could no longer afford such an objectionable image. Negligible budgets only underscored this. The Q Course didn't have the wherewithall just to accept bodies. Also, with limited funds, teams had little choice but to train themselves.

Thanks to team structure—revolving around two medics, two engineers, two weapons sergeants, two communications sergeants, and two experts in operations and intelligence (the team sergeant and operations sergeant)—teams could at least cross-train. And committed NCOs worked lessons learned in the jungles and hamlets of Vietnam into strikingly realistic training scenarios. Veterans had a lot to teach young recruits, and the recruits whom SF selected automatically deferred to their combat-hardened teammates. In this way, the ODA design not only proved durable post-Vietnam but became critical to SF's survival.

Still, no one inside the organization during the 1970s could be sure SF would survive. It took the 1980s to reverse SF's decline and the 1990s to realize that SF's resurgence hid a number of serious shifts. Despite what numerous NCOs might currently think, conventionalization didn't suddenly creep into the team rooms, and the push to standardize didn't just happen to silently steal up in the 1990s. These changes, like most others, still trace back to reactions to Vietnam, the premier example of which was the very thing NCOs complained about most bitterly as they endlessly filled in paperwork in their shiny new team rooms: in 1987 Special Forces was made its own separate branch of the army.

Never mind the impact of real-world events, Hollywood imagery, politics, or the end of the Cold War; SF veterans blame the crush of uniformity squarely on this: a realignment of, by, and for officers.

LOGICALLY, EVEN STRUCTURALLY, CASTING SPECIAL FORCES AS its own branch made sense. Historically, it stood to reason even more. Hijackings, uprisings, terrorist activities, Soviet moves, and Third World stirrings throughout the 1970s all reminded the United States that, despite whatever excesses might have occurred in Vietnam, it still needed special operations capabilities. This was underscored every time a daring counterterrorist mission by the Israelis, British, or Germans succeeded. However, the real proof of special operations' worth to Americans came in the wake of America's own failure at just such a mission. Not only did the aborted 1980 effort to free American hostages held in Iran prove devastating to President Jimmy Carter's reelection bid and embarrassing for Special Operations (and Delta Force specifically), but Desert One's failure publicized just how hollow the U.S. military was. The hostage crisis itself then became a major factor in the election of Ronald Reagan as president.

If John F. Kennedy should be regarded as SF's first patron saint, Ronald Reagan inherited his mantle. Reagan reinvigorated Special Forces through a revival of funding and, thanks to his foreign policy interests, whole groups (including 3rd Group) were reactivated. This automatically boosted morale. Of course, so too did certain deployments, as Special Forces soldiers once again engaged in unconventional warfare and quite active foreign internal defense, this time on the edges of Afghanistan and in Central America. In fact, the boom Ronald Reagan initiated held all sorts of promises—promises that Hollywood especially liked.

Hollywood first cast actors as Green Berets in 1968, when John Wayne starred in the movie *The Green Berets,* based on the book of the same title, by Robin Moore. This Vietnam-era portrayal is one most older SF soldiers continue to prefer. As they point out, at least in John Wayne's world Green Berets were trainers, defenders, humanitarians, *and* warriors. Ever since, identifying someone as a "Green Beret" or "former Green Beret" has generally meant, "watch out, he's a cold-blooded hair-trigger killer."

For two decades Hollywood has sold the public on SF soldiers as sociopaths whose mission is either to defy or to defend some secret wing of the U.S. government. Consequently, many new recruits who've grown up watching these movies join SF expecting to wage secret wars in exotic climes, while the sheer number of films boasting killers with SF credentials has provided members of the public who distrust the military with all the proof they need that the military does engage in nefarious activities—and maintains SF expressly for this purpose. Even many conventional soldiers presume they know what SF is about from watching these on-screen bad actors. Ergo it's now a virtually universal expectation that SF soldiers will engage in atrocities if they are not properly controlled—a fear that making Special Forces its own branch also neatly addresses.

Not only has granting Special Forces its own hierarchy begun to tame it, but awarding Special Forces the structural equivalence of the infantry or artillery has made SF's leaders respond more like commanders of conventional units, too.

For instance, SF is no longer the dumping ground for individuals who can't succeed elsewhere in the army. SF officers have to act like other army officers and progress according to standard military criteria. Because SF now provides the full range of officer slots to shoot for, including general officer positions, officers can take a real, long-term interest in the unit. For officers, this is good, but for NCOs?

For NCOs this spells closer monitoring and more officer control, and not just by SF officers. SF's "autonomy" has actually guaranteed the army significant new leverage. This is because, to prove that Special Forces is as worthy as any other branch, SF commanders have no choice but to make sure SF stays in step with wider army standards, which are invariably officer-driven, nonelite, and conventional. At the same time, it's not just SF that has been recalibrated.

The military in general has hardly been standing still. Since Vietnam the trend has been toward increasing integration among services, as well as within them. Which in turn demands greater organizational control. Not surprisingly this has inspired the army to adopt more and more business school–speak and increasingly businesslike methods of management. Combine this with computers, the paperwork (and red tape) to justify and prove results, and corporate demands to streamline, and it's easy to see how so much weight might confound hierarchy. The rhetoric claims better management, tighter control, and more efficiency. From the top down, SF officers themselves talk about the need to enhance accountability. But in the team rooms this is viewed as micromanagement and provokes older soldiers to view SF as increasingly officer-driven, which also makes them worry: SF *as* SF might not survive.

3 Missions and Tours

IF ROGER HARMON COULDN'T HANDLE 307, YOU HAD TO WONDER. AS laid back as he looked, he had a reputation in the company for being difficult and arrogant. But his team had an even worse reputation. A critical core on the team regarded 307 as the "baddest" ODA in the company. Harmon, who was their team sergeant, didn't disagree.

Sporting glasses under short brown hair, and in his late thirties, Harmon comes from German homesteading stock and grew up in the heartland, though you wouldn't know that to listen to him. He speaks pure GI—slang, acronyms, profanity, and all. Also, every other sentence drips with sarcasm, and most of what he says is straight and to the point, with a twist. Irony could be his middle name. Certainly it has filled his career, which is actually so generically GI that it's at least worth outlining, particularly since so many members of his generation entered and stayed in the army for the same reason: their options after high school were limited—what else was there to do?

Raised on the South Dakota–Nebraska border, Harmon went through the eighth grade in a one-room schoolhouse where twelve schoolmates was the largest student body he knew until high school. His graduating class held fifty seven. Although his father had planned to carry on the family's farming tradition, he hurt his back while serving in an antiaircraft unit during World War II, and instead found himself having to drive a 478-mile-long rural mail route every day to support the family. Even so, he still insisted on raising the family's traditional mainstay: cattle. But since he couldn't milk them, this meant Roger had to. Every morning before the school bus swung by at 6:45, Roger had to have milked all seventeen head.

School, meanwhile, was boring, high school particularly. The only instructor Roger remembers at all liking was an English teacher, largely because she'd show up and drink beer at parties during the summer. Plus she smoked a cigar. That was exciting. Between cows and classes not much else was. As Roger put it, there were more people in an SF battalion than in his entire hometown, and a lot more different kinds of people. For instance, Roger didn't have a clue that the palms of black people's hands were anything but jet black before he joined the army.

As for the army, Roger was lower-lower middle class with no political pull. His lottery number was eleven and the Vietnam War was on. He came out of a high school with an eight-man football team. There was no hope for any kind of scholarship. And he had his father working against him.

Reading between the lines, Roger's father was a taskmaster. Roger moved out of the house before he graduated from high school. In the meantime, he worked breaking horses, bought a pickup truck, moved up to a Chevy Impala, worked in a gas station, ferried kegs of beer across state lines, hired on as a construction worker, worked on grain silos, asphalted roads, and built houses. He was making good money, but with high school behind him he was also running wilder than his father would have preferred.

In retrospect, Roger's pretty sure that his father suggested to the local draft board to call Roger up. Hence, his first plane ride was gratis, courtesy of the U.S. government, which relocated him to Ft. Lewis, Washington, for basic training. Roger remembers this as a cinch, the payoff to having milked cows all winter, every winter, for most of his adolescence.

After basic training Roger was assigned to an artillery unit, even though he wanted to go infantry. He hated Ft. Sill, where he was next stationed. This made it all the easier when a model soldier showed up one day seeking volunteers for airborne school. Roger had just received a letter from his sister, who needed money. He could almost double his pay if he made it through jump school. Roger volunteered.

The second plane Roger flew in became the first plane he jumped out of. Then, with airborne training behind him, it was off to Vietnam, which is not anywhere he wanted to go. Indeed, he was among the last draftees to have to serve in Vietnam; not even everyone in his battalion got sent. Perhaps this explains why, within a week of landing, he wound up in big trouble for being drunk and disorderly. This cost him a stripe and also got him shipped off to a fire direction center (FDC), which Roger really objected to. Too much noise, confusion, and yelling went into the effort of directing artillery fire. Thus, when a forward observer team needed a radio telephone operator (RTO), he leaped at the chance. Anything to get away from the fire direction center.

As far as his tour in Vietnam went, all Roger wants to say about it when questioned is that it was scary. In fact, few soldiers in Z Company seemed to realize that 307's team sergeant had even served there. It's not something he brought up.

Back home after the war, Roger had every intention of jettisoning the army. He didn't have a steady girlfriend, and nothing was tying him down. His first sergeant gave him a thirty-day leave so he could go back to South Dakota and see if he could find a job; he needed at least to make enough money to keep himself in tires and car insurance for the old Corvette coupe he bought. But the best job he could find was as a gas station attendant in Sioux City. The first sergeant had been smart; Roger reenlisted.

Then came the rest of the 1970s, not a fun decade. Roger describes the army as being a mess at the time. His worst forty-eight months came in Germany, where he was assigned to an eight-inch howitzer unit, a historically black outfit. Race riots and drugs meant that there needed to be an armed officer stationed on every floor of the barracks. Soldiers were perpetually stoned and couldn't be trusted. Roger ended up being the only sergeant (E-5) who could pass a common skills test, which meant he could handle a compass, read a map, and navigate a five-kilometer drive. Consequently he was assigned to duty every third night, which eventually got him promoted. Then, as an enlisted hand-receipt controller for a nuclear weapon–equipped NATO site, he was on duty every other night. His marriage, which had been a shotgun affair in the United States, rapidly deteriorated.

In 1977 Roger finally maneuvered his way out of Germany. At first it looked as though he would be reassigned to Ft. Sill, but at the last minute he managed to have his orders changed to Ft. Bragg and the 82nd Airborne. In quick succession he became a gunnery sergeant, acting first sergeant, and then fire-support sergeant for his brigade. In 1979 he was gone 267 out of 365 days—to Panama, Alaska, Turkey, and Germany. This doomed his first marriage.

What sealed its fate was an episode in the same string of events that funneled Roger into SF. Roger was just on the verge of going to Ranger School—he had a slot—when his 82nd Airborne brigade was called out for a rapid deployment exercise. During the parachute jump Roger broke his leg. So much for attending Ranger School. But sitting outside his house later that night he did get to see his wife's boyfriend drop her off. Then he learned that his father had cancer. With his marriage dead and his Ranger School slot gone, Roger requested a compassionate assignment, which would move him closer to home and his father. This is how he briefly became an army recruiter in Omaha. His supervisor, a sergeant major, had served as both a Ranger and a Special Forces soldier. He encouraged Roger to put in an SF packet.

It was late 1981, early 1982, when Roger, by then a sergeant first-class (E-7), went through the Special Forces Q Course. To a certain extent this was bittersweet. He remains convinced he never lived up to his father's standards, because he was still "just" a paratrooper when his father died.

Given Roger's rank when he entered the Q Course, he became within fairly short order the senior-ranking NCO on the first team he was assigned to. On completing Operations and Intelligence (O

& I) School in 1985, a prerequisite for running a team, he became the team's sergeant. From 1985 to 1990 this remained his team. There was one eighteen-month stretch when the ODA suffered under a bad captain, but otherwise how could Roger complain? At least seven of the team's NCOs stayed with the team the full five years he was its team sergeant, until he was selected for the Sergeant Major's Academy and then shunted to 3rd Group.

On the personal front Roger also couldn't complain. He met his second wife at Bennigan's (a popular Special Operations hangout in Fayetteville). She had shiny long hair and big brown eyes, and he couldn't believe no one else was around her at the bar. She, as much as anything, helped bring about his domestication. Then came children and Roger really became rooted, staying home after work while his wife waited tables; during the day she pursued her paralegal degree. While at home, Roger puttered. He also liked to read history, or tune in to the Discovery Channel.

In these two regards Roger had plenty of company. The Discovery Channel has lots of fans in SF, and by the time most soldiers reached Roger's rank, they are far more mature than they probably imagined they could be. Which is also why it was ironic that, having finally straightened his life out, Roger wound up as team sergeant of 307, the one ODA in the company that was full of anything but mature soldiers. According to other soldiers in Z Company, Roger would have been better off if he'd been assigned to bash his head against a wall. There was no way he was going to be able to teach this team any of the lessons he himself had had to learn the hard way.

In 307 there were too many newbies all on one team, too many hotheads, too many soldiers who bought into all the Green Beret hype. While Roger had grown up watching *Combat* and *Rat Patrol*, this team he inherited hadn't grown up at all on Chuck Norris, Sylvester Stallone, and Arnold Schwarzenegger. The critical mass on 307 belonged to action seekers. Roger's charges didn't seem to understand that SF's primary mission was unconventional warfare, of which foreign internal defense is an integral component. Their great love was direct action; second-best was special reconnaissance.

Technically, SF soldiers have to be capable of performing all four types of missions. Significantly, direct action—the dramatic fa-vorite—is the least common. In fact, countless SF soldiers spend their entire six- or twelve- or fourteen-year SF careers without ever seeing any sort of knockdown, drag-out, techno-thriller action. Some SF soldiers retire without participating in a single firefight. On the other hand, none retire without having completed at least one foreign internal defense mission.

Foreign internal defense is SF's real bread and butter. Plain and simple, it is what SF soldiers do when they teach armies elsewhere in the world how to defend against internal insurgencies. Nonetheless, no one on 307 was particularly interested in foreign internal defense. Outsiders' impressions of 307 were that its team members felt they had plenty to prove and little to learn, and would outperform every-one else so long as they just kept practicing hard-charging tactics.

It only entrenched this bias when 307 was chosen to perform a reconnaissance mission in the Gulf War, although the main reason 307 was dropped behind enemy lines had less to do with the NCOs' overinflated sense of themselves than with their salesman—the captain—and whom he appealed to. If it had just been left up to the Z Company commander, 307 would probably not have been sent into Iraq. But the battalion commander, one level up, was mightily impressed; 307 was just his type of team: hard-charging, physically fit super-Rangers.

Coming from a Ranger background himself, the battalion com-mander at the time overtly favored direct action. And 307's team captain saw eye-to-eye with him, or at least made it appear this way. He also did what he thought a good captain should do: he strove to outshoot his men, kept them competitive by always attempting to best them, got them going, and at every turn encouraged their pas-sion for action.

On almost every score this captain and Captain Tucker (of 309) were utter opposites. I never heard other teams use any sort of nick-name for Captain Tucker. But 307's captain was often referred to with "Brain Dead" prefixed to his first name. Not that this would have swayed his NCOs; little did. For instance, members on other teams in the company occasionally commented on 307's fanciful tales of der-ring-do in the Gulf. Apparently 307 came back from one patrol through Kuwait City claiming to have been caught in a hairy firefight, presumably with Palestinians. Members of other ODAs found it funny that, given the descriptions of the battle 307 only narrowly escaped, its vehicle remained unscathed—no bullet holes or scratches.

At any rate, this is the team Roger inherited. It's also the team that, despite his best efforts, he couldn't really change. Nor did it help that by the time he came along there was only a hard core of four of the Gulf War veterans left. That this is all there was to represent stability—just four of ten sergeants who had been on 307 more than two years—and that it then had to be these four meant the team could not cohere. Putting it most generously, these four had simply learned to compete too well; none of them would subordinate himself to another.

They weren't bad soldiers. In fact, one of this foursome, the team's sole black, was regarded as outstanding by virtually everyone in the company. Luther was conscientiousness personified and superb as a communications sergeant. Any team would have happily accepted him, though it is telling that he probably wouldn't have been as happy on any other team. Hints of this surfaced even on 307. For instance, there was his reaction to two other blacks' joining the team. The first represented no threat. As someone on the team later said, this individual all but drooled on himself after two beers; he was a dud. However, the second new black team member did pose a challenge. He not only had more infantry time than Luther but was also Ranger-tabbed. Potentially his joining the team meant Luther would no longer be 307's black favorite son. For Luther, happening to be black had presented him with a perfect role. He hadn't had to play up his blackness but could behave just like everyone else and still be noticeably different and unique. What such an attitude in turn suggested, though, was that in Luther's mind 307 wasn't so much about blending in as standing out, hardly an acceptable attitude on a team that wanted to cohere.

Luther himself was one of 307's biggest boosters. In his mind he and 307 actually represented the new cutting edge of SF. As far as he was concerned, the wave of the future was direct action and

special reconnaissance. Everyone who didn't agree was a di-
nosaur: "You have to adapt or die." In Luther's view, the battalion's
previous commander (who sent 307 into Iraq) was all but clairvoy-
ant. He had trained the battalion for direct action, and then along
came Desert Storm. Obviously his was the correct philosophy, for
look how it paid off.

Talking about this future one hot and humid evening, Luther
became impassioned about his willingness to die at the age of
twenty-nine so long as he could do so in a blaze of glory. Forget that
this was not quite the measured and mature attitude the founders
of SF would have sought in someone so talented, or the sentiment
that SF training should have induced. Luther was dead serious
when he said this. Nor was there any reason to doubt his sincerity
as he gave voice to an unbridled lust for action, although listening
to him did make me wonder how he would ever cope on a six-
month or yearlong foreign internal defense deployment, which
provides the only real-world peacetime training SF soldiers get for
unconventional warfare.

THE SF SOLDIERS I MET IN SOMALIA WERE ASSIGNED TO THE U.S.
Embassy for a year and worked out of the Office of Military Cooperation. During most of 1988–89 southern and central Somalia were
still relatively peaceful. The team's primary mission was to supervise Somali officers training their own soldiers one hundred kilometers from the capital. Over the past half-dozen years small split
teams of three NCOs and an officer had laid the groundwork for
Somalis to train themselves. Initially SF soldiers traveled biannually
to Somalia to train Somali officers, but now the whole program was
bearing fruit, at least theoretically.

The problem was that as their year progressed in Somalia, all
four members of this particular team became increasingly disillusioned. The Somali officers they had to deal with were corrupt.
Even worse, Somali officers didn't care one whit about their soldiers. This made it particularly hard for these three NCOs and their
captain to want to have anything to do with them. But they still had
to show the Somalis respect.

Fortunately, the low point came relatively early. According to the Americans' ethic, their Somali hosts deserved to be trusted as soldiers who would live up to universal military standards. But not long after the Americans settled into the routine of helping supervise training, three Goretex jackets were stolen from them. It was bad enough that the Somali officers stole and even worse that they lied about it. The team considered itself betrayed by professionals.

And there were other frustrations connected with this tour, one of which lay in the very nature of the assignment. Six-month-long mobile training team (MTT) and yearlong technical assistance field team (TAFT) deployments essentially serve as U.S. government–sponsored goodwill gestures toward foreign governments. While their purpose is relatively straightforward—to provide military training to foreign troops at the invitation of a foreign government—arranging these missions turns out to be anything but simple. When they take place, it is generally only after complex negotiations at more levels than most soldiers realize exist. Ambassadors, government ministers, defense attachés, the State Department, and all sorts of personnel from the Department of Defense participate. In some cases the invitation originates with the host government. In others it is the result of careful lobbying, usually undertaken by Special Forces group and battalion commanders who travel to their area of operation at least once during their commands and simultaneously try to sell American diplomats and their foreign counterparts on the worth of SF soldiers as a nonlethal humanitarian asset. The group commander's operations and training officer (S-3) assists in this lobbying effort. His job is to cultivate congressional staffers and Foreign Service officers in the United States with a dual purpose: every advocate helps, and these junior people will be senior one day.

Extremely persuasive arguments can be made for why U.S. taxpayers should want to fund more mobile training and technical assistance field teams. Most obviously, SF teams help to establish military-to-military contacts in countries where the military often rules. Building rapport is a skill SF emphasizes and expects its soldiers to be good at. In the same way that the group's operations and training officer lobbies civilians in the United States to further SF's aims, Americans in uniform establishing personal ties with their foreign counterparts in uniform helps personalize American goals, which, at least at the level of rhetoric, are decency, democracy, and development.

More to the point, though, SF soldiers can help professionalize Third World armies. Despite how this may sound, professionalization is not about teaching foreign soldiers to kill more effectively but how to behave according to ethical standards. SF training is largely SF soldiers teaching by example. The model that mobile training and technical assistance field teams try to develop is of soldiers putting others' interests before their own, pitching in, and not taking advantage of civilians.

SF has extensive expertise in assisting civilians. Whether exercises include engineers digging wells or setting up Quonset huts, or medics treating long lines of villagers who otherwise never see a medical practitioner, SF soldiers rarely conduct a mission without doing a large-scale civic action. SF can even attach veterinarians to units deployed on joint training exercises, so that in places like Somalia, where livestock is integral to the local economy, cows can be tended right alongside their owners. In many regards these capabilities render SF one of America's most important but underrecognized development agencies. Certainly it is the most innovative and probably the most cost-effective. In 1992, for example, a fifteen- to thirty-day trip to Africa for fifteen soldiers could cost as little as $50,000, but triple this if 3rd Group had to pay for the soldiers' flights.

Transportation was invariably the big expense, principally because Special Forces does not have access to its own aircraft, which helps explain why so few mobile training teams were sent to Africa the first few years of 3rd Group's reemergence. Once in-country, though, teams often proved dirt cheap. SF soldiers were used to operating at ground level and did not expect to be put up in hotels or expensive housing in the capital city. In fact, being stuck in the capital city was exactly what most members of teams did not want.

For diplomatic reasons, teams didn't always get to stay out in the field or among the people, as they would prefer. In Somalia during 1988–89 two problems developed. Somalia was falling apart and increasing violence in the countryside, midway through the team's stay, confined the team to the capital. Yet because the U.S. government wobbled in its response to an increasingly repressive Somali government, the soldiers weren't withdrawn to the United States, though they were ordered to curtail their training. At the same time, the team received conflicting messages in Mogadishu. While the U.S. ambassador officially restricted the team to stay within a well-defined area around the capital, the colonel heading the Office of Military Cooperation encouraged team members to carry on as if nothing had happened, even though their training site was well outside the ambassador's designated perimeter.

In a number of ways this team perpetually found itself caught between a rock and a hard place. At its training site team members lived in the same kind of housing as Somali junior officers, on the same grounds. But in Mogadishu they had their own spacious house in a two-house compound shared with other American soldiers. The U.S. government rented the compound from a Somali general for an exorbitant fee. Electricity alone cost more than $1000 per month, even though the team ran its own generator and never tapped into the fickle municipal supply.

Corruption reared its head everywhere. And in the team's view, why they were even in Somalia was less a matter of being needed or used wisely than the U.S. government's offering them as a benny to the Somali powers-that-be.

The three sergeants and captain the team comprised nonetheless strove to keep up professional appearances. Their ethic demanded that they take seriously the training they were offering, despite the fact that the Somalis they were working for didn't seem to. They also tried to take under their wing the one Somali NCO they regarded as most like themselves, a scrupulously honest young sergeant whom they treated as a friend. Otherwise, the work was hard and stressful. No matter how much they seethed privately, the smiling mask still had to go on in the name of fostering strong bilateral ties.

One thing that made life easier was that the jacket incident occurred relatively early in the team's tour, enabling the soldiers to quickly develop a rule of thumb: not to trust the Somalis they had been assigned to work with. The timing of this theft also helped them figure out that not just their expectations had to be scaled back. The previous team, occupying the same house the year before, had been corrupt. Somalis and expatriates alike had frequented the house and its infamous rooftop bar for cheap liquor, black market money, and prostitutes.

The only time I saw the previous team's ringleader was from a distance, which is about as close as it seemed possible to get. He was ringed by Somali women dressed in sleazy Western garb, holding court among an even sleazier-looking group of drunk expatriate men. There was nothing friendly or helpful-looking about him. Indeed, his whole demeanor seemed to advertise that he would ruthlessly take advantage of anything that came his way.

It took only two weeks after he and the house's previous occupants were finally out of the country before the rooftop bar was dismantled. It took somewhat longer before Somali women stopped dropping by every weekend night. Eventually, too, the Somali officers who used to frequent the house moved on. Initially the new team had no problem with officers visiting to play pool in their dining room, though this wasn't a partying team and relations were bound to cool. Once the jackets were stolen, the front door stayed more or less permanently shut. Somali women who ventured by risked being evicted, though this was sometimes tricky because the team's sole unmarried sergeant grew so attached to one that at the end of the yearlong stay, Mike had to fill out reams of paperwork before he could procure her a visa so they could marry in the States. His intent was both romantic and realistic. He professed to really love her, which is also why he felt good about what he was doing; even if the marriage didn't work out (most people warned him it would not), he would know that he had helped at least one Somali escape her country's impending collapse.

As for Hawa, his intended, she couldn't believe her good fortune. Skeptics were sure she had been angling for this all along; a visa is exactly what the Somali women who hung around with expatriate men sought. Money was fine, but consorting with Westerners made it virtually impossible for these women ever to reclaim their virtue as good Somalis. Leaving the country was their only real avenue to a better life, an opportunity that rarely arose. Hawa was unusually lucky; she found the one soldier who was completely unbothered by her past and only wanted to guarantee her a future.

For Mike this was a first, but not in the annals of SF. SF soldiers typically make the best of difficult situations, for themselves as well as for others. Doubtless the previous team sergeant would argue that this kept him busy, too. And in a certain sense, it did. Even in breaking the law, he had been quietly professional, inciting no international incidents. Tellingly, though, the team that replaced his found his conduct reprehensible and regarded him and Somalia both as exceptions that proved the rule: foreign internal defense should benefit *all* involved.

FOREIGN INTERNAL DEFENSE, AND COPING WITH ADVERSITY IN places like Somalia, is as close to unconventional warfare as noncombatant soldiers can come. It makes many of the same demands as UW: on their diplomacy, ingenuity, and stamina. In at least one significant regard, however, foreign internal defense can't simulate what unconventional warfare requires. Foreign internal defense missions are top-down. Just as with the team in Somalia, teams engaging in foreign internal defense work through the embassy, out of the capital, and with organized forces. By definition the emphasis is on teaching, not organizing. Soldiers can practice direct action and special reconnaissance as they teach patrolling, ambushes, and other components of internal defense, but while conducting foreign internal defense at the invitation of a foreign government they may not organize a military structure from the ground up. They don't organize a resistance movement or help an opposition group become a guerrilla organization. The only practice many soldiers have to organize for unconventional warfare is in the Q Course, not thereafter.

Nevertheless, to the extent that practicing foreign internal defense during peacetime might not keep soldiers adept at everything unconventional warfare requires (e.g., building organization from the ground up), practicing direct action is more removed still. For a whole slew of reasons, emphasis on direct action may actually diminish foreign internal defense and unconventional warfare skills.

While direct action is quick, strengthening internal defenses (for foreign internal defense) is slow. Direct action is clean (provided the mission is successful), while foreign internal defense is fuzzy. Direct action is military, while foreign internal defense is largely political. Direct action also happens to call for youth or at least physical vigor, while foreign internal defense requires maturity. Before undertaking direct action missions, soldiers are wound tight as corkscrews. In contrast, foreign internal defense demands tremendous patience. Finally, direct action missions have to go like clockwork, which means practice, practice, practice until responses are automatic. For foreign internal defense to work, soldiers must be able to stay flexible and think on their feet; they cannot afford rote responses.

In short, the two kinds of missions make completely different demands, which holds all sorts of implications. For some soldiers, like Luther and his teammates, the lure of SF lies strictly in DA. Direct action tends to appeal to many of the younger NCOs, while older NCOs and SF veterans are increasingly appalled to think that this has become SF's chief attraction. Accordingly, there is real potential in this divide for tension, for teams to feel split, or for veterans to simply accede and retire.

Of course, 307 didn't face this problem, because there weren't enough old-timers to threaten to split the team. Instead, 307 members were as one, preferring action. Luther, for instance, craved it, and everyone else on the team seemed to want to be a hero. This is why it defied the imagination to picture Luther in a flyblown village somewhere, where the business of the day would be to line up children for vaccination, let alone Luther in Mogadishu.

For a tense forty-eight hours, in July 1989, Mogadishu came unhinged halfway through the technical field assistance team's stay. But even with one long day and night of serious street fighting, as bullets zinged over their rooftop, there was absolutely nothing these highly trained American military men could do. This wasn't their fight, even had they known whom to support. There was no question about staying out of it for this particular team, though as tension mounted in the days to follow, an air of anticipation did build in the house. While one team member was left inside at all times to guard the team's property, other team members began to make preparations in case the violence threatened them.

In the event of an overland evacuation, the team rethought its escape and evasion route, an essential component of all missions. They recalculated how much fuel they would need to make the long drive to the Kenyan border, pored over maps to choose which towns and villages to avoid, and debated which weapons to take and how much ammunition to carry. There was no question that such plotting got adrenalin pumping. Consequently, as Mogadishu calmed down, there was also palpable disappointment, though this came more in the form of wistful sighs than explicitly expressed regrets. As quickly as team members anticipated risk and challenge, they settled down to redefining the daily training routine under newly strained conditions. It is hard to imagine how 307 might have stayed so reserved under the same circumstances. That should be one worry about an addiction to direct action.

A second concern is that foreign internal defense requires real finesse. The local constraints NCOs must respect don't quite square with the secret squirrel activities a lot of the younger, newer SF NCOs think SF soldiers should engage in. Consequently, the double-barreled realization that most SF missions are peacetime foreign internal defense assignments and that the drama in foreign internal defense is far more mundane than exciting is especially disillusioning to young soldiers straight out of the Q Course.

But it's not only new recruits who see things differently from experienced SF soldiers. No matter how much NCOs might like to think that group and battalion commanders, who are here today and gone in two years, don't make a difference, such commanders *can* set the tone in the team rooms. If the team captains under them either agree with their philosophy or think they had better act as though they do, then the teams wind up being pressed into the commander's mold. Or to bring this back to Z Company, when the battalion commander wanted direct action—because he viewed this as the key to ensuring SF a future—then captains like 307's had their team sergeants put direct action on the training schedule. New arrivals to 307 never got disabused; for them direct action defined SF.

On other teams, if the captain and team sergeant disagreed with the command philosophy, there were ways to make it look as though the team enthusiastically supported the battalion commander's dictates, while still sticking to what the team leaders regarded as doctrinal principles: unconventional warfare, foreign internal defense, *then* direct action and special reconnaissance. Clearly this was not the case on 307, where the captain, along with the NCOs, lived for firefights. Only Roger's predecessor strenuously objected to the direction in which he saw the team headed. And he got no backup. The members of 307 were so used to mainlining the idea of direct action that he had no hope of getting them to tone down or check their individual egos. It took all his energy just to keep the captain reigned in so as not to commit the team to something truly dangerous *before* Desert Storm.

Nor did Roger have much better luck once 307's infamous team captain was gone. The team's reputation in the rest of the company remained unshakeable; 307 was regarded as being full of self-centered crybabies and personalities who couldn't get along. In the company sergeant major's view, the only solution to the team's problems was to break it up. Otherwise, team members' inabilities to curb their individualism would doom them on any foreign internal defense mission. What 307 members didn't seem to realize was that not being able to coalesce could also get them killed doing their beloved direct action.

As it turns out, Roger himself may not have been completely immune to 307's incessant one-upmanship. Perhaps the company he was keeping was just too insidiously infectious. Or perhaps his charges' lack of self-discipline eroded his own without his realizing it. Alternatively, it's possible he never entirely lost the streak that landed him in trouble as a young soldier in Vietnam. At any rate, he momentarily did what anyone on 307 might have done. On a non-SF exercise away from Ft. Bragg, he picked up a female soldier's camera and, without her being present or knowing, photographed his penis. His team thought this was great. She didn't, once she had the film developed. And in this new, post-Tailhook climate, his admission, when elicited, got him written up.

Actually, this incident would have been considered tame as recently as a decade ago, when there were still barracks queens and Green Beret groupies, or when soldiers knew that a woman who was touted as being "three-hole qualified" had given in to oral, anal, and vaginal sex. One warrant officer even remembers a period when one of the company medics used to invite his teammates over to help him sate his wife, though not all such stories were true. For instance, nobody I knew had ever attended a "key party," although numerous people were sure that these had taken place, when team members and their wives or girlfriends would put their keys in a common bowl, only to have to go home with whoever fished out their key. At the time, such events, even when wildly exaggerated, only enhanced reputations rather than ruining them. Nor was partying—no matter how outrageous—likely to torpedo anyone's career. The punishment for rowdy behavior "then" was losing stripes, not job security; this was before careers required the kind of careful management they do today.

Ironically, considering the new climate in SF, Roger himself might not have lasted very long had he joined a team as recently as Luther did. It is likely he would not have made it even into Special Forces Assessment and Selection (SFAS), the selection stage just prior to the Q Course. Certainly he didn't have the clean record that soldiers like Luther currently have to have. But perhaps this is better for SF. Perhaps it signals a higher standard of selectivity, *if* the soldiering traits being selected for in the new, more prudish, careful army are also the traits that best serve SF.

4 The Q Course

SPECIAL FORCES ASSESSMENT AND SELECTION TAKES PLACE JUST down the road from Ft. Bragg, in the same kind of pines, swamps, and heat and humidity. Thus, in June "flushed" is probably too mild a word to describe the faces of the candidates. They're red, gleaming, and drawn all at the same time. Most of the SF wannabes keep the clear plastic tubes leading from water bags in their rucksacks clenched between their lips the entire hike. They suck and breathe, suck and breathe, determined to keep going.

Rob should probably be pleased. The candidates seem to want in badly enough. But Rob's having a hard time being an evaluator. After years of foreign internal defense assignments, in which his job was to instruct and help other soldiers, his current task is simply to pass judgment. He's not supposed to do anything but monitor these young SF candidates and, if he has to, prod them on. He can't correct, advise, or befriend them. From the candidates' point of view, he must seem like more of an automaton than they feel. In the choking heat Rob is cold, steely, unforgiving, and flawless.

Like so much else about SF, SFAS fulfills unintended as well as intended functions. Its main goal is to screen potential SF candidates for the Q Course. But at the same time it sends failed students away even more impressed with SF soldiers: the SF sergeants running the course appear virtually untouchable. This preserves and enhances SF's mystique. Only the candidates who make it through the Q Course come to know better, though by the time they receive their SF tabs, they're convinced they, too, deserve them.

This is exactly how an initiation should work.

SFAS is twenty-one days long and divided into three sections. The first section is devoted to psychological and mental testing. Soldiers are subjected to a battery of different tests measuring basic reading and mathematical skills, intelligence, foreign language ability, and state of mind. State of mind is particularly important. Does a candidate have character quirks that make him potentially unstable? Special Operations psychologists admit they are looking for a potentially volatile mix. They want soldiers who will take on dangerous assignments. At the same time, SF can't afford individuals who voluntarily engage in risky behaviors. This presents a very fine line, with an incredibly costly margin of error. Because of the training they receive, SF soldiers who do go bad have a tendency to go very bad. As one psychologist put it, they've got the skills to do some very crazy stuff. It rarely happens that an SF soldier turns into a serious criminal. But when one does, his organizational skills make him a formidable opponent. To preclude this, psychologists probe.

The entire SFAS process is one of elimination. In large part this is because there is no ideal SF type. Nor is there a profile the army can use to select *for* SF candidates. Not even the most powerful army computers can process all the data and spit out names, ranks, and serial numbers of worthy candidates. So far no one has come up with a paper way to find creative people who can tolerate high levels of stress, cope with frustration, but also act. Action, meanwhile, may be in the woods or a foreign capital, with high-ranking foreign officers, or illiterate peasants.

Army psychologists recognize that the best they can do is filter out the people who their methods indicate won't fit. It is up to SFAS and the Q Course to sort through the rest.

This is fortunate. The Q Course is staffed chiefly by NCOs. Like Rob, most are right off of ODAs. Most also will be going back to teams after they complete their four-year tour at the Special Warfare Center and School (SWCS). Thus, it is more than just conceivable that an evaluator can wind up serving with candidates he has helped pass through the Q Course. This is one incentive to be tough and demanding. His life and the lives of his teammates depend on how well he screens these wannabe ODA members. At the same time, no one understands how teams operate or what they need better than NCOs whose lives have revolved around them. The psychologists—not all of whom have been through the Q Course, never mind out in the field with an actual ODA—will probably never be able to devise a series of tests to match the judgment of actual ODA members. And, given the frequency with which commanders and command philosophies (and manpower needs) change, the NCO corps offers bottom-line continuity. The bottom line never changes: would I trust my buddies' lives to this candidate?

Of course, this doesn't mean all evaluators are fair or always correct in their judgments. Given their individual experiences, it is likely that few share exactly the same standards. But with enough evaluators in place and enough segments to the Q Course, it is likely that most mistakes will be caught. Again, this is where the overall Q Course philosophy, of selecting people out rather than in, proves advantageous.

Along with psychological tests come physical training (PT) exams. The combat swim test alone, requiring candidates to swim fifty meters fully clothed, knocks out sixty of the close to four hundred candidates in the course I visit. This, evaluators say, is ridiculous. There is nothing secret about SFAS's physical training requirements. In fact, candidates know what is expected of them before arriving at Camp Mackall. Evaluators believe that most candidates who train hard for the six or eight weeks prior to SFAS should have no problem meeting its physical requirements.

During this initial stage failure to meet the standard is enough to eliminate candidates. By contrast, the second segment of SFAS requires that both candidates and evaluators begin to demonstrate more judgment. This is when the rudiments of soldiering—land navigation, for instance—are both taught and tested. Here, too, the basis for success is physical endurance—can the candidates keep at it?—but with an added kicker. Can they also learn, apply what they have been taught, and perform on little food and sleep?

The first review board meets after completion of this second segment. Evaluators discuss whom they would cut and why. At this point, most of the candidates dropped are found physically wanting; this amounts to seventy more men. The remainder pass into their final week. Presumably all 200-plus are physically fit enough to make it through the two following phases of the Q Course. This is one fundamental way in which the Q Course differs from Ranger School, which is so physically punishing that soldiers often lose twenty pounds before they reach the end of the grueling sixty-day patrol and leadership program. Also, SFAS is nothing like Hell Week, the infamously brutal segment of Navy SEALS selection during which candidates are pushed beyond most humans' tolerance for pain and suffering. After two weeks of physical challenge, designed to measure endurance more than tolerance, SFAS turns to testing soldiers' ability to work together in teams.

The instructors split up candidates into mock ODAs. A series of different tasks is then assigned each ODA, requiring soldiers to work cooperatively while still proving themselves individually. In this trickiest part of SFAS, the stresses all begin to converge: physical, mental, interpersonal, although perhaps toughest of all, candidates receive no feedback. Yet they know they are being watched all the time.

Evaluators rotate daily from group to group to stay inhuman. The idea is to prevent them from growing attached to any one ODA and also to give them a chance to evaluate every candidate. On occasion the evaluators speak to the candidates to assign leadership roles or bark admonishments: "Team leader, let's pick it up" to a team that's dragging. Otherwise, it is as if the candidates are being shepherded by Big Brother, not by anyone made of flesh and blood. One result of so much objectivity is that the candidates can't glean any sense of their standing. This in and of itself makes room for real assessment: *Can* the candidates work without guidance? Will they perform appropriately under duress?

Already they've been kept hot and tired for two weeks. They still aren't getting to eat or sleep enough. Four hours of rest a night is all they're allowed. It could be worse; Australian SAS candidates, for instance, have it much tougher—no barracks, less sleep, less food, more punishing tasks. Portions of SFAS were modeled after the Australian program. However, the Australian course is designed to select only 10 or 12 men out of a class of 120. Special Forces is selective in a different way.

Demonstrating endurance is one thing, but surviving masochism reveals nothing about maturity. For SF soldiers, being able to withstand prolonged cultural isolation and mental stress is critical. Therefore, inherent in SFAS's design is the notion that randomly dispensed comfort—showers (cold), three meals a day (never hot), unbroken sleep (even if just for four hours)—winds up being more discombobulating than a steady ration of discomfort. Since some soldiers can easily adjust to continual misery, better to mix up relief and suffering.

Being adaptable is key. Candidates have to be able to switch gears without effort: from sleep to wakefulness, from a water break to more slogging, from leading to being led. And they have to remain unflappable throughout. No matter how tense they might feel, they can't allow their anxiety to show. Putting on a face is important, and while expending effort is a good thing, displaying disgust is not. Control is being tested: maintaining control when nothing at all is within your control.

Evaluators acknowledge that a lot of candidates come to SFAS armed with plenty of G2, or prior intelligence. Accordingly, evaluators try to switch around the schedule of exercises from one course to the next. A lot of candidates are warned about what they'll have to do by friends who have been through the course or by candidates being recycled. These are individuals who, having failed to make it past the first review board for some physical reason, receive a second chance. Nevertheless, evaluators believe that even if candidates know exactly what the exercises involve, this doesn't necessarily help them. They still have to function as a team to move three hundred pounds of sandbags from point A to point B by stretcher. And this is while each one is still carrying his seventy-pound-plus rucksack and six-and-a-half-pound M-16. And evaluators have their own intelligence.

Candidates are never addressed by name. Instead, each wears a number, either on his shirt when he is in gray (PT) shorts and shirt, or on his pants legs when in camouflage fatigues. Evaluators address candidates only by these numbers, though each evaluator has a roster matching numbers with individuals' unit and rank. This way evaluators can single out officers for the harder leadership tasks, and determine whether No. 32 is dragging because he is a genuine laggard or because he happens to be a former cook thrown in with a bunch of hard-charging Rangers. Although the playing field should be level, evaluators recognize that serving in some units indisputably gives some candidates a leg up. Two-monthlong Ranger School itself is a physically daunting gut check. On the other hand, Rangers have a reputation for bulling, not finessing, their way through problems. Thus, evaluators find themselves screening different candidates differently, taking into account what they know about individuals' backgrounds and what they also know candidates will learn later on. What they are really looking for in SFAS isn't know-how anyway but mettle. The Q Course will supply know-how. Meanwhile, what's mettle?

Soldiers refer to any exercise designed to test stamina as a "gut check," and getting through all military gut checks requires focus. Often, sheer willpower and persistence prove enough. Just wanting something so badly helps. So does simply refusing to give up. Not quitting can either come from within (high personal standards) or it might depend on not wanting to feel humiliated. In SFAS the drive behind focus hardly matters. What counts is the end result: the ability to outlast the weight, distance, heat, sweat, blisters, aches, without succumbing to the mindlessness of the ordeal. Candidates cannot just tough out the assignments as they might on any old interminable road march. SFAS requires that soldiers deal with one another too, which means being able to go into cruise control for the marathon trudge and then snap out of it when faced with hurdles. If candidates get too lost in the recesses of their own daydreams, they won't be able to anticipate, and although they have to be switched on, they can't be so hyped up that they burn out. All of this demands a balance that not everyone can either achieve or sustain. Yet this is precisely the state the evaluators themselves are in: attuned, antennae out, but also detached and able to keep going.

METTLE IS ALSO ABOUT BEING ABLE TO DEAL CONFIDENTLY WITH the unknown. Soldiers have the necessary drive or they don't, but uncertainty—over what comes next, how they're doing, what they should be doing—never makes for a pretty sight. For one thing, it's grossly hot and humid. Second, there's Rob, the evaluator. Without knowing exactly what Rob's looking for, or even whom he's looking at, the candidates need to be doing their best all the time. For instance, they know they can't go anywhere without clutching their M-16, not even to the latrine. If they forget their weapon this lapse will be noted. They've been told this, but they've been given only the briefest of guidelines. They're not so sure what else might count as a lapse, nor are they sure what their evaluator is paying attention to, whom he's looking at, whether he's even paying attention, and what he's likely to remember. It's all agonizingly unclear. Candidates can't even be sure how it's best to act—cooperatively or competitively. Uncertainty only adds to the tension.

The juxtaposition is brilliant. Rob leaks no indications. Nor does he sweat. He, too, is carrying a rucksack. All evaluators haul a pack that holds minimally thirty-six pounds of radio equipment and looks at least bulky enough to sustain the impression that the cadre members are in phenomenal shape. As it happens, Rob is in great shape, which means thirty-six pounds count for nothing on his back, but the radio is hardly deadweight. Rob is on it continually, using it to stay in touch with other cadre members and with the staff at Camp Mackall. Cryptic communication ricochets back and forth, about who's where, when they expect to be at which water point, whether the candidates are too hot, too blistered, whether someone has twisted an ankle—though the candidates are not the only subject of discussion over the net.

SFAS fields eight courses a year, often with four hundred-plus candidates per course. For the evaluators this amounts to an endless parade of close-shaven, identically clothed soldiers, and relentless repetition. Prior to becoming an evaluator, each has to have gone through these exercises. This means they know the candidates' tasks intimately. Thus, despite whatever they may encourage the candidates to think, there is no reason to watch them every marching minute. With ample time on their hands, why not tease one another over the radio net?

Banter—full of acronyms, abbreviations, and incomprehensible cadre slang—in turn achieves a number of things. It further distinguishes candidates from SF soldiers. At the same time, it allows cadre members to form their own bonds. Evaluators need to get along; this makes the course, and the review boards, run smoother. Also, evaluators are used to operating in teams; they're used to camaraderie. Being sent to SFAS is a wrench in and of itself—out of team rooms, out of familiar surroundings, away from friends. Part of what being assigned to the Special Warfare School means is that evaluators have to prove themselves all over again to one another, never mind to candidates. Often they have to do so from scratch. Occasionally members of the same battalion—or if they're really lucky, the same company—wind up in the same teaching cohort. More often a new evaluator finds himself thrown together with members of 10th Group, 7th Group, 1st Group—people he's never seen, and whom he might not be able to find out about easily.

SF is a small organization but not that small. Being assigned to the Special Warfare School is one way it shrinks. Soldiers become friends across groups; in turn, this breaks down differences between groups and helps homogenize SF culture. In a sense, this parallels what the Q Course did for these same SF soldiers once upon a time. No wonder, then, that Rob spends most of his day trying to one-up his fellow evaluators over the radio. He's trying to assert himself in that pecking order, while making sure the candidates remember he sits atop theirs.

This isn't hard for Rob to manage. He's assertive and not shy about dominating others. Usually he gets away with this because he's good enough at everything SF requires. Even if he isn't, he drills you with eyes that refuse to flinch. They take in more than they give away, but just barely. Usually they indicate that you're not making much of an impression. In many regards this is typical SF confidence, edging on arrogance. One truism in SF is that brown eyes don't have to be warm.

The poor candidates. When Rob sizes them up it's not with a great deal of sympathy. When he went through the Q Course in 1987, there was no SFAS. Instead, candidates went straight from a brutal physical training (PT) prephase into what was then called Phase 1. This was also back in the days when instructors had far more leeway in abusing candidates. They yelled, screamed, harassed, intimidated. Evaluators didn't have to be objective. Some took quite seriously the challenge of breaking people. If sadism wasn't sanctioned, it wasn't disallowed. This is in direct contrast to the current approach, which is to simply apply the same tests to everyone, then watch and wait. There's no spraying someone's face with spittle; evaluators don't yell. Nor are particular candidates singled out for extra needling. Instead, there's simply assessment. Consequently, Rob and the other evaluators consider the current system infinitely easier than what they went through.

Still, the new emphasis on distance may be far more effective than the cadre members who have to implement it realize. With no feedback, candidates are left to twist in the wind. Because every real-world mission (and even every training exercise) charts unknown territory, SFAS's built-in uncertainties approximate what actual ODA members face. Even in routine exercises something is bound to screw up, so soldiers' ability not only to act but to react can spell the difference between success or failure. At any point an ODA can find itself in a situation in which the only outcome of whether team members are making the right decision is life or death. On a real-world mission a monitor won't scream at you until you get it right, or intercede to straighten things out for you. Meanwhile, there is never only one right solution to a problem. Team members must be able to persuade one another—and be persuaded—that the method they choose is the one to go with under the circumstances. Nor is persuasion just a fine art. It is what makes needing to be confident but also competent so tricky, because, on the one hand, SF soldiers need to know their own limits—so they don't lead one another down the wrong path—yet, on the other, be willing to push themselves beyond the familiar to get down that path at all.

WHILE SOME OF THE TEAM EXERCISES REQUIRE CANDIDATES TO WORK together in a straightforward manner, others require them to think through what they need to coordinate before coordinating it. How else are they going to move three hundred pounds of sandbags several miles by stretcher? Such a task, in and of itself, might not sound too Herculean, but on straight roads the destination might as well be days away; the distance seems interminable, the weight ever heavier. Worse, the stretcher isn't long enough for the full team to handle. Thus, candidates should devise a relief system, but this isn't always as easy to organize as it sounds. How often should soldiers spell one another? Who enforces this? Then, too, the stretcher carries much better if soldiers of about the same height are positioned across from one another. How does the relief system accommodate this?

One of the things evaluators pay particular attention to is who isn't pulling his own weight. Then there is the leadership issue. Does the designated leader allow himself to be taken advantage of? Does he let the soldiers call too many breaks? Does he notice and reprimand individuals who aren't doing their fair share? Is he in control?

The leadership role is particularly tricky, and this is where officers especially have to excel. Each ODA receives two tasks a day. And yet another thing evaluators watch for is whether the tall, gangly or short, stocky officer who was the designated leader in the morning forgets he is still an officer in the afternoon. Again, part of what the evaluators are after is whether these candidates could perform as they should with no one evaluating them. An officer has to demonstrate that he realizes he is always a leader. In general, self-confidence and competence are not quite enough. Candidates had better display consistency as well, and a healthy attitude.

IT'S AFTERNOON AND THE THREE TEAMS WHO NERVOUSLY SHUFFLE within sight of one another are each pointed to their pile. All three jumbles contain identical items: one telephone pole, six heavy steel pipes, four well-worn automobile tires, and a tangle of lashings.

The mission: transport the telephone pole from one spot to another, as the teams are shown their destinations on the map. Then the frenzy begins.

Each team must build a contraption to make the ostensible mission—conveying the telephone pole—as easy and effortless as possible. Ideally, the quicker the candidates agree to a design, the faster they can get moving, and the sooner they will be done. Candidates are sure that in the evaluators' eyes speed counts. But orderliness quickly turns to fumbling as pressure builds. Also, while teams aren't so close to one another that members of different ODAs can spy, they are close enough so that they are well aware of just how much better the team on the left or the right seems to be doing. This, of course, adds to the tension.

There is variation after variation on the get-from-here-to-there-lugging-this theme. In one twist on the telephone pole exercise, candidates are presented with a fifty-five-gallon drum of allegedly hazardous materials. This means they can't drop, roll, or otherwise jeapordize their cargo. In Round Three they must deliver six extremely heavy ammunition crates packed with high-security, sensitive items. But this time they get no tires. Instead they have to do the job using six pipes and twelve lashings.

The catch to all of these tests is that while some methods of putting pipes and tires, or pipes and lashings, together may yield an easier trudge than others, a number of different configurations will work.

Often teams don't come up with a workable device. Sometimes as soon as the team begins to roll away what it thinks is a viable contraption of pipes and tires, the wheels fall off, or the telephone pole collapses through the middle. Sometimes a contraption wobbles a short distance before its wheels turn so far inward that there is no pushing, pulling, or tugging the thing any farther. Team responses to such "disasters" are telling. Some ODAs continually try to readjust a bad design. They lash and relash the tires, change the knots, rearrange the pipes. Others redesign the entire configuration. I watched one team reassemble their pipes and tires four times. According to the evaluator, any one of their four designs would have worked if only they had done their lashings differently.

Whenever these assemblages work, the task is relatively easy. In two, three, or four hours the team is at its destination and has time to rest before its next assignment. For teams that can't manage an efficient construction, the allotted time slips away and they can run three or four hours behind schedule. Still, from the evaluators' point of view team failure doesn't necessarily mean everyone on the team is a failure. Of course, the candidates can't know this. But it's *how* candidates confront failure and frustration that evaluators pay special attention to. How they cope with one another in such a situation is critical.

Invariably some candidates realize on their own they're not coping very well. Others come to the realization that this type of high-pressure teamwork—and SF—is not for them. Candidates can quit at any time. This is one of the reasons there are always cadre members (and medics) patrolling the course in large four-wheel-drive vehicles: in case someone needs extraction. As soon as a candidate indicates he is giving up, he's separated from the rest of the ODA. The cadre member radios those on patrol that he has a VW (voluntary withdrawal). He notes the team's location as it plods on, and the VW is sidelined, to await pickup. The object is to effectively sequester VWs from the rest of the group as quickly as possible. They're not demeaned, but they're not coddled either. No one tries to convince a VW that he might be making a mistake or that he should perhaps rethink his decision. SFAS is all about elimination. It makes the evaluators' jobs much easier if candidates eliminate themselves.

CURRENTLY A SOLDIER MUST PASS THROUGH THREE SEPARATE phases of testing and instruction before he can wear the SF tab. SFAS is only the first portion. Soldiers who pass SFAS's final review board receive military occupational specialization (MOS) training in what is referred to as Phase 2 of the Q Course. This is when candidates are taught to be SF engineers, SF medics, SF communications, or SF weapons sergeants. Phase 2 amounts to months of grindingly difficult classroom work. If candidates can pass this phase, they move on to put it all together—specialty training, fieldcraft, teamwork—in Phase 13, the final section of the Q Course, which teaches and then tests SF soldiering skills and guerrilla and counterguerrilla techniques. The culmination of Phase 13 and the Q Course is an elaborate field exercise: Robin Sage.

Ironically, none of the instructors I met had been through this exact sequence of phases: SFAS, Phase 2, and Phase 13. Instead, most had entered SF when the series more logically ran from Phase 1 through Phase 2 to Phase 3. Both SFAS and Phase 13 were relatively new in 1992, although SFAS included some elements from the old Phase 1, while Phase 13 combined portions of the old Phases 1 and 3 (hence its nomenclature). None of the instructors seemed to think this new combination was much of an improvement. In fact, those who taught Phase 13 worried that it was too short and didn't teach enough. For instance, survival training had all but been cut out. Intensive survival training was taught in a completely different school (SERE school), which not all SF soldiers were likely to attend.

NO MATTER WHAT THE POPULAR STEREOTYPES, THE MILITARY IS full of change. Officers have to make changes to distinguish themselves. At the same time, officers who hope to succeed can't rock the boat too much. The system is not at all conservative; it's cyclical. As officers cycle through command positions, the same old ideas gradually become recycled. Inevitably a lot of what immediate predecessors did is undone. This is the easiest way to affect change. However, there is a valid reason—beyond the demand of career advancement—why so much back-and-forth restructuring also takes place. The system is complex; as a result, there is ample opportunity for imperfection and inefficiency to crop up. Smoothing out a set of problems in one area generally creates new problems elsewhere. As soon as these are addressed, problems in old areas resurface. Change this and you have to change that. Change that and you have to rechange this. . . .

"If it ain't broke don't fix it" is a line many officers use but can't afford to live by. It is almost as if the officer code of conduct demands that things always be fixed so that they will break so that they can be fixed again. Not only does this keep everyone gainfully employed but it also provides one way for just enough people to move ahead. And problem solving is continually being tested, which can be good. Problems are ultimately what the military must stay alert to face. Having problems to solve also ensures that no one can afford to grow complacent.

Because few officers stay in command positions for as long as many SF soldiers stay on teams, NCOs are often able to offset and negate superficial changes. They simply outlast them. Still, as obstinate and wily as NCOs can be, they can't counteract everything. Some changes are made at such high levels they suffuse the entire system. Alternatively, lots of little shifts can accumulate. For instance, even if it was only coincidental that Q Course phases were rearranged around the same time that a new policy concerning review boards came on line, and manpower needs called for a ramp-up (or increase) in the numbers of SF soldiers, NCOs still viewed this as a change. To them cumulative discrete events always added up to a coordinated effort to remake the organization. Because they were so far removed from critical decision making, NCOs at the team level had no alternative but to view changes suspiciously. No one usually bothered to fill them in. However, they were rarely alone. Not even the major in charge of the SFAS cadre knew exactly what prompted certain orders to be handed down from on high, which he then had to make sure the cadre implemented. What the cadre, in turn, thought of such decisions rarely if ever traveled back up the chain of command past him.

MAJOR PEREZ WAS ONE HARD-PRESSED INDIVIDUAL WHO HAD strong opinions about SFAS, and he certainly knew the cadre members did. But there was only so much he could vent. He couldn't agree too vociferously with his NCOs, since he needed to maintain some amount of distance from them to command. But he also couldn't always let them know why he disagreed with them (when he did), because some of the information to which he was made privy was privileged. Even if it wasn't, possessing it when the NCOs didn't is one of the things that set him apart. Distance again.

At the same time, Major Perez could never pass enough of his concerns about SFAS back up the chain of command. If he did, this would either suggest he wasn't in complete control of the situation or didn't sufficiently support the program. Thus, he too was caught on a tightrope. He had *the* best possible view. Overseeing SFAS positioned him to understand how realistic or unrealistic the demands on cadre members were, in light of what the chain of command expected. This meant helping get the NCOs to see that SFAS represented the front lines, and that they were in the trenches. Whoever slipped past them could screw up SF. Whatever screwed up SF hurt their ODAs. The challenge came in reinforcing this while he met quotas. He (and cadre members) knew that a certain number of candidates would always have to be passed through, regardless of the consequences.

IN MANY SENSES THE Q COURSE HAS TO BE A NUMBERS GAME. THIS was most obvious whenever there was a demand for more SF soldiers, either because of wartime needs, a drop-off in reenlistments, or a surfeit of retirements, or because a new group was being brought on-line. Such a ramp-up was underway as 3rd Group was being formed, with whole battalions needing to be filled. Yet the rhetoric promised that Q Course standards still remained consistent. This was largely rhetoric. Something had to give: either tinkering had to be done during SFAS or the Q Course had to be made easier. Given the structure of the Q Course, it was unlikely NCO instructors would agree to ease up just so SF could accept inferior soldiers. It made far more sense to allow more soldiers who would be likely to make it through the Q Course into SFAS in the first place. An obvious solution, but how was it implemented?

One method was to lower rank requirements. As 3rd Group was being brought on-line, this is exactly what SFAS did: there was a continual demand for more bodies, so bodies were selected for. Instead of accepting no one below the rank of E-5, SFAS was newly reopened to E-4s (at various points in SF's past, rank requirements had been dismissed altogether). This, of course, created its own set of problems. Most of the E-4 promotables suddenly allowed into SFAS had not attended a leadership school. Scads of them had not served as squad leaders. Consequently, while they were physically fit, proficient in soldiering skills, and smart enough in the class-room, they remained woefully immature. ODA members through-out SF agreed. Too many of the newly tabbed soldiers being sent to join their teams were too young.

But was this SFAS's fault? After all, cadre members were busy screening for motivation and team spirit. Phase 2 and Phase 13 would have to plumb for maturity, although, as it turns out, these other phases had their own unintended (but institutional) blind spots, too.

After SFAS, the candidates' status subtly changed. Not only did advancement to Phase 2 (the phase during which candidates learned SF specialties) mean that soldiers could be called by name again, but Phase 2 signaled that instructors were about to invest considerable time and energy in them. Through the months of teaching to come, instructors would aim to enhance and no longer just evaluate candidates' worth. Meanwhile, the army was also mak-ing an investment. Economically this one was harder to discount.

SFAS candidates came to Ft. Bragg on their own, without their families. But while SFAS lasted only twenty one days, the remainder of the Q Course could take well over a year. The army therefore transferred soldiers and their families to Ft. Bragg for the dura-tion—which cost money. Some instructors believed that the cost of permanently changing soldiers' duty stations explained why so few soldiers were being dropped during Phase 2. Even if they were flunked by their instructors, review boards could demand that can-didates be recycled. A lot of instructors saw students being recycled. Some even saw the same students being passed through portions of the course more than twice. One NCO reading of this rise in recy-cles was that the army needed a return on its investment, at what-ever cost to SF. Otherwise, by partially training but then dismissing these men from serving in SF, the army stood to lose too much money. Of course, there were other reasons to explain how so many soldiers were being recycled. The review process itself had been al-tered as SF strove to make its selection process less arbitrary. In a sense this could be traced to a general restructuring of SF, as SF was brought more into line with the rest of the army, which was busy re-working itself into a more humane institution.

While previously evaluators may have had too much leeway in determining why someone didn't make the grade, with personal likes and dislikes often being *the* determinant, the pendulum had since swung to a system full of seemingly endless checks and balances—assessments were written down, evaluations noted, everything had to be documented and verifiable. In general, the decision-making process had become much more accessible to candidates. The downside to accessibility, though, was that it created all sorts of room for dispute. Questioning and complaining often got a candidate recycled.

There had long been some recycling in SF, but now the perception was that recycling was out of control. More particularly, it was growing out of NCO control; it wasn't those running the courses but invisible individuals overseeing them who were helping to pass soldiers through. Review boards were partially to blame. But worse, what multiple recycles were recycled through—generally weapons training, sometimes engineering training—was altering the meanings attached to SF specialties themselves.

Originally, all four specialty (MOS) courses comprised a true division of labor and the ideal was to start off in one specialty and then become cross-trained in the others. However, needing to keep up-to-date on ever more technical knowledge has made this increasingly difficult. Also some people are clearly more gifted at one particular specialty, and part of what Phase 2 has always been good for is sorting this out. Not everyone is cut out to be a medic, for instance. Consequently, there has never been a stigma attached to dropping out of the medic course into one of the other three—engineering, communications, or weapons. Nor is it just having to undergo the longest Phase 2 schooling, which causes people to fall out of medic training. Even if a candidate passes through the thirty-one weeks of medical coursework (as opposed to the eighteen in the other specialties), he might still not be able to perform when it comes to hands-on training, which is necessarily bloody.

The Medical Lab at Ft. Bragg is infamous. Animal rights advocates have long objected to this school, but that is not what makes it so well known throughout SF. What SF soldiers see in the school is not students inflicting harm on goats—who become their patients—but rather just what extraordinary lengths future medics will go to save their patients' lives. It is through simulations here that medics learn to treat combat trauma and practice military emergency medicine, including certain surgical procedures. Just being able to handle this lab is a test in itself. No one thinks any less of an individual for not making it through such harrowing coursework, especially because the vast majority of SF candidates don't try.

Likewise, the communications course isn't for everyone since it, too, tends to appeal to soldiers with a particular technical bent. Before they are permitted into the course, soldiers have to prove themselves adept at learning and transmitting Morse code. Then it is hands-on training with countless varieties of radio, antennae, and communications equipment. Not only do commo sergeants have to feel comfortable working with electronics, but, with the added weight of radios and battery packs, they typically shoulder more weight in the field.

There are advantages and drawbacks to each of the four specialties. The engineering course is no less mathematical than communications training. But with radios there is no chance of making a mistake and blowing yourself up. While engineers are usually second only to medics in building local rapport in a foreign setting because they know how to construct all sorts of useful structures for the civilian population—latrines, bridges, weatherproof shelters—demolitions does represent a major component of their course. Besides having to know how to build bunkers and fortifications, engineers should be able to destroy anything civilian or military engineers can design: dams, generators, multistory buildings.

Weapons sergeants, while also highly trained, have the least civilizable skills. They learn to identify, break down, repair, and fire literally dozens of different classes of weapons from throughout the world. They are also expected to be excellent marksmen, and most teams boast at least one weapons sergeant who has been to sniper school (which is among the army's most selective and demanding). In many regards, weapons sergeants epitomize soldiering. But at the same time, the best weapons sergeants tend to be the most stoic and the least likely to brag. Perhaps for this reason weapons training tends to be considered the least demanding. Also, everyone is just familiar enough with weapons to presume his own expertise. The result: candidates who aren't doing well in other specialty training inevitably drop into, or recycle through, the weapons course. This further hurts weapons sergeants' image. Nor can the prejudicial thinking this fosters be good for SF. By design, SF's division of labor is meant to be complementary, not unequal.

WHILE STREAMING SOLDIERS INTO SPECIALTY TRAINING IS UN-avoidable, Phase 2 has other impacts. It creates networks among all the engineers, all the medics, all the commo, and all the weapons sergeants passing through the Q Course at the same time. It bonds them and provides them with a common base of knowledge, as well as long-lasting ties that will cross-cut the insularity of team room and even company life. Phase 2 also dissolves the teams and cliques SFAS created. Candidates aren't mixed up and reconfig-ured into ODAs again until Phase 13, which exactly foreshadows how SF works.

Phase 2 specialty training is a good preview, too, because not all of a soldier's career is spent in either the team room or the woods. A large proportion is spent sitting behind tables or at desks being lectured to, with long hours of homework to follow. SF soldiers probably spend as much time being taught as they do teaching oth-ers. How well they've learned what they've been taught is what going into the woods then tests throughout a soldier's Special Forces career. Beginning with Robin Sage.

5 Initiation: Robin Sage

THE GUERRILLAS (Gs) ARE BICKERING WITH ONE ANOTHER. NOT everyone finds it funny when two of them begin to pry skinks out of the logs they're sitting on, only to toss them into the fire. Obviously they're bored. They've been out in the woods a couple of days already and are antsy to get on with the show. Where are the Q Course candidates?

The wannabe SF soldiers are doubtless wondering that themselves. At the moment they're tramping through the woods, smashing through spider webs. Not having had enough sleep, they are easily misoriented (their current euphemism for being lost). Meanwhile, they're uptight for a second reason: they can't help but be concerned about how they are doing.

What they should really be most concerned about is who yet awaits them. Robin Sage, the final field exercise of the Q Course, is designed to test candidates' ability to train a band of guerrillas. The Gs are actually a hodgepodge of soldiers drawn from a range of different army units. Some are soldiers who never spend time in the woods. Some don't want to be in the woods. Others regard this break in their own routine as a relief, while for a number it's already beginning to resemble a chore. A few have steeled themselves not to be impressed. But at least two admit to having thought about joining SF themselves; they regard this as a sneak preview.

Meanwhile, from the point of view of the guerrilla chief (who is a senior SF NCO), this moody conglomerate is perfect. Some of the Gs will be motivated; others won't be. This will approximate what ODAs often face: foreign soldiers not all of whom want to be trained, while those who do often have their own notions about how and what they should be taught. Something else implicit in Robin Sage's design is that the guerrillas won't be feigning ignorance. Many have never been taught what the SF students will try to teach them, while those who have practiced patroling and ambushes will now be required to relearn these skills the SF way. Thus, how well the guerrillas perform should directly reflect how successful the candidates are at wooing and training them. On the one hand, nothing will be possible without gaining the Gs' confidence (and interest). On the other hand, not even this is likely if the ODA members themselves don't know what to do or can't cohere.

Physically, just getting to the Gs' camp proves a trial for the team the Gs anxiously await. Not only are the twelve candidates discombobulated from having wandered around all night trying to reach the linkup, but they're now worried they may be too late. Consequently, four of them peel away from the rest of the group in an attempt to rendezvous within the four-hour window they've been given. They leave their rucksacks behind to get to the meeting place faster, although as it turns out they reach the designated spot well within their allotted time. Two Gs, along with two course instructors, are casually waiting for them in the honeysuckle that frames the linkup point, an abandoned farmhouse.

At contact, the two Gs and the four students exchange passwords, and the students look hugely relieved. Maybe everything is going fine after all. Neither of the two course instructors lurking on the sidelines seems to indicate otherwise, not even as the two Gs promptly lead the four students away.

The G chief's directive to his guerrillas was to spend some time marching the SF candidates in circles, to confuse, frustrate, and, it is hoped, annoy them. And it's a goad: will the team leader eventually assert himself and demand to be taken to the Gs' camp? How long will he allow himself to be led around by the nose? And then, how calm will he be when he finally does meet the G chief? Also, are the team members keeping track of where they are? If they pay attention to their maps and compasses, then it should be a relatively short time before they realize they are chasing their tails. If not, they're trusting the Gs too much. Putting themselves in the Gs' hands isn't exactly what their advisory role demands.

But being led hither and yon actually turns out to be the least of the candidates' problems. After making sure the four ODA members do indeed have every intention of obediently following the two Gs up a red dirt road, away from the rest of the team, the two course instructors have to intervene. Just what are the four candidates doing? Where's the rest of the team? What happens if the Gs are taking them up the road just to put them on a truck, then drive them off? What happens if they wind up on one truck, only to be transferred to another? How are they planning to communicate with the rest of the team? If they're away too long, what's the rest of the team supposed to do? What are their contingency plans?

The questions come thick and fast, although they're not questions so much as pointed criticisms. The message is the team shouldn't have split up, but given that they did split up, they now shouldn't remain separated. In a real-life situation the team would potentially already be in grave danger. Of course, in this simulated situation lurks an even greater danger—the students have to assume they're already failing. Pressure builds. For the team's sake, this is not a good way to begin. It only adds doubt to the tension: why did they agree to such a stupid plan anyway? Maybe their leadership *is* no good.

In reality, of course, the two course instructors are far more pleased than annoyed. None of this is scripted. The team really has made a major mistake. And now there's the opportunity to see whether they learn from it and can handle the added pressure of being told they've messed up. Plus, such criticism from Sergeant Baker, the easygoing course instructor who's been with them throughout Phase 13, should set off loud alarm bells. He's no longer there just to help; he's now evaluating them. So, too, is the second SF NCO, whom they don't know and who doesn't know them. Any room for slack vanished at the old farmhouse linkup.

As part of the current Robin Sage design, as many as three instructor/evaluators hover around the students at any one time: Sergeant Baker, who stays with the ODA throughout Phase 13, a second instructor from the Special Warfare School whose job is to rotate from ODA to ODA every three days, and a guest evaluator who's been temporarily brought in from one of the active-duty SF groups as a further guarantor of objectivity. This assures the students of at least one evaluator who has no prior knowledge of them. Not that this is necessarily such a good thing from the candidates' point of view. After all, the guest evaluator's gauge is that of someone coming right off a team looking at men who might wind up on his. If anything, this means he will probably be more rather than less unforgiving. He's yet another person the students will have to try to impress.

While ideally such a mix of evaluators makes for a good final screen of the students, it also lifts some of the burden of making final choices from the school instructors alone. It ensures that at least some ODA members are also responsible for who gets sent to the teams. And bringing actual ODA members to the Special Warfare School is just one further insurance that SF stays homogenized. Instructors, whose tour is four years at the school, operate in a different world from ODA members. They are surrounded by students, few of whom are really up to the standards of most ODA members—they couldn't possibly be, given their lack of experience. It's easy for instructors to lose perspective, with six courses a year and hundreds of candidates to judge. Bringing in guest evaluators helps shake up everyone's tunnel vision. Guests return to their groups with more appreciation for what their counterparts assigned to Phase 13 are up against. And they also get a firsthand look at the recruit pool. Of course, actual ODA members are probably not used for any of these reasons. Rather, "inviting" guests solves a manpower problem; the Special Warfare School just doesn't have the bodies to manage everything itself.

Still, Chief Stouffer isn't about to complain. He's a wiry, ginger-haired warrant officer drawn from 1st Group to be the G chief. He also has a lot of opinions about what's good and bad about SF these days. Thus, it's easy for him to take seriously the role he's about to play in helping decide who will get tabbed. He's also out to have fun. He's been given the general scenario. Robin Sage compresses into one day what real-world teams would expect to accomplish in thirty. The ODA's linkup with the Gs is not supposed to be easy, nor are students supposed to be able to build rapport quickly. The first two days at the G camp should be touchy. But then the ODA has to be allowed to get down to its real business: teaching. With this as the broad outline, Chief Stouffer is free to fill in the details. It's up to him to keep the candidates on edge.

As INSTRUCTED, THE TWO Gs LEAD THE TEAM IN CIRCLES BEFORE the ODA winds up below the Gs' camp. Once there the Gs halt the candidates while one bounds up the trail to report to Chief Stouffer. Chief Stouffer asks that the ODA captain and his senior-ranking NCO be brought into the Gs' camp first.

Up the hill they come, faces still streaked with camouflage paint, one hundred-pound packs on their backs, looking drained already. Nor is Chief Stouffer's reception designed to put them at ease. He projects moody instability. Hostile, hesitant, self-interested, he begins by addressing these two leaders separately, although it's obvious, as soon as he starts in on the captain, that the captain isn't thinking on his feet. His responses to Chief Stouffer's barrage of questions—why are you here? what weapons have you brought? how much money do you have?—are too flat and uninspired. Besides, they are too rote—"we are here to help you," "we have machine guns," "there is money in a bank account." The captain exudes no character or confidence.

The E-7, however, does worse; he's a smart-ass. When Chief Stouffer asks him what time the team made the linkup at the farmhouse, he responds, "Don't *you* know?" What an invitation. Chief Stouffer digs right in.

"So you don't know. What does this mean, 'don't *you* know?' *You* don't know! How is it possible *you* don't know. . . ?"

The E-7 doesn't respond well to needling. He's too tightly wound, and though he tries to talk his way out of the G chief's bad graces, he only angers Chief Stouffer more. Chief Stouffer can't resist. He doesn't have to tolerate defiance; he's the G chief. To prove it, he orders the Gs closest to him to surround the E-7 with their weapons ready. As the Gs close in the E-7 automatically clicks his own M-16 off safety. This is dumb. The Gs begin to react without Chief Stouffer having to tell them to. Several of them actually have their rifle butts drawn against their cheeks and begin to take aim. It is a few tense moments before it dawns on the E-7 that he's in over his head. He winds up lowering his muzzle.

Now Chief Stouffer really lets him have it. He no longer has to role-play. He can't get over the E-7's behavior. He's still worked up about it as he calls for a second pair of advisers to be marched up the hill to the encampment. His rant begins, "Do you have any idea how your soldier has just insulted me? Do you know he insulted me and my men? Is this what you do? I should send all of you packing off this mountain. Why shouldn't I? It would be easy. What use could we possibly have for you. . . ?"

After beginning his tirade with an attack on the E-7, suggesting the E-7 has single-handedly sealed the team's fate, Chief Stouffer suddenly switches tack. Earlier in the morning, when the candidates were on one of their many circumambulations below the camp, the Gs and Chief Stouffer heard one of them scream out. Obviously someone had twisted an ankle or done something else to hurt himself.

"Don't you so-called advisers know how to be tactical? You're too noisy. You're too sloppy. What can we possibly learn from such sloppy advisers?"

Chief Stouffer briefly hammers away.

Then it's on to a third topic. He had previously asked the captain and E-7 where the ODA gets its money, what its sources are, and where it has an account. One of his plaints is that the Gs need more. But he especially pursues this line of questioning with the one soldier in this new twosome who seems the least capable of being able to explain how the ODA is funded. All the soldier will say is that the funding comes from somewhere "higher."

Chief Stouffer takes this "higher" and runs it into the ground: "What is this mystical higher? Why won't you tell me? Obviously you don't trust us. That's too bad. If you don't trust us, why should we trust you? If you won't even tell us about your funding sources then how can you expect us to ever trust you? Clearly we won't be able to work together. Now, let me look through your rucksack."

He makes a move toward the soldier's pack, but the soldier refuses to let him open it. This gives Chief Stouffer a new reason to savage and belittle the ODA. From this point on, every response from this soldier simply provides Chief Stouffer with more leverage. Nor does he let up as he has a third pair brought from below.

Meanwhile, the rest of the team at the bottom of the hill is in turmoil. Their number reduced by half, they have no idea what is happening in the G camp (or whether their fellow team members are even in the G camp), and are justifiably worried, especially because they have now been effectively split up and only a few hours earlier it was made painfully clear to them that they should never allow themselves to be separated. Worse, they're being led away two by two. They're not just worried—they're scared.

So far so good.

Nor is Chief Stouffer particularly anxious to release the six candidates he's already got in his camp. He wants the concern at the bottom of the hill to build. He also wants these six to stew. When he finally does dismiss them, it's with two ultimatums. He's giving the team two hours to get their purpose straight so that they can present him with a coherent plan. He also wants an apology from the E-7. Meanwhile, as the six students head down the hill, Sergeant Baker tells the ODA captain they're not allowed to escape and evade (E & E) at this point. In other words, though the normal ODA response might be to withdraw, given such an initial encounter, this option is not open to the candidates.

Chief Stouffer's six victims shuffle back down the trail, their hair slick with sweat and their packs bowing them down. As they disappear Chief Stouffer reclines, obviously pleased to contemplate what he has wrought before comparing notes with the course instructors.

Although the chair he eases into hardly looks comfortable, it's definitely imposing—a sort of throne fashioned out of branches, built by a previous G chief. Even better, there's a dollar sign bent out of twigs at its center, whether because dollars are what previous bands of Gs worshipped or because someone simply decided to be humorous—the original intent hardly matters. Chief Stouffer has appropriated money as his theme, too. He's been obsessed with it. Part of his refrain with the candidates is that he has run out. The Gs haven't been paid in four months, he owes a lot of money to the locals, and the Gs are low on ammunition. Not only is this realistic—he continually refers to his own experiences working in Southeast Asia and Africa—but harping on money sets up all sorts of additional scenarios. In a few days the Gs can start talking about desertion. He can also have them begin to act unruly.

Or they might simply revolt. Chief Stouffer has made it quite clear that he doesn't like "Canteth," who is the supposed leader of "Pineland," the country the candidate-advisers are visiting. SF teams are supposed to be adept at dealing on all levels, able to keep goodwill flowing between guerrilla factions. Thus, Chief Stouffer's criticism of Canteth means the ODA may well find itself dealing with a breakaway movement, or at least trouble between guerrilla camps.

Other traps get baited with the indefinable but critical issue of trust. For instance, when one of the six candidates earlier referred to Chief Stouffer's own area as Sector Sword, the chief went ballistic. "What? You mean you Americans have already carved up the area and given it names? Why? What's the purpose behind all of this? Whose side are you on? Everyone knows you Americans can't be trusted. Look how you let the Kurds down. Look how you let the Contras down." Chief Stouffer even weaves in the savings and loan scandal as evidence for why Americans shouldn't be trusted and why the U.S. military's establishment of a trust fund for his guerrillas couldn't possibly impress him; it's meaningless.

One reason Chief Stouffer keeps pounding away at trust from as many angles as possible is because trust is key to establishing rapport. But also, all the instructors have picked up on the candidates' wariness; they're acting far too skittish. Chief Stouffer intends to jolt them out of this by getting them to realize that their own mistrust is provoking his. Thus, the candidates' most important mission at 1530—when they're scheduled to return and present their plan to him—will be to convince Chief Stouffer and his Gs that the ODA really is there to help. Time constraints alone demand that Chief Stouffer manipulate the issue of trust to teach the students a lesson, while also allowing them to move on.

AT 1530 THE ENTIRE ODA MATERIALIZES AT THE EDGE OF THE Gs' camp. The Gs assemble and closely examine these great American soldiers, who don't—in reality—look the least bit impressive. How could they? They're dirty, hangdog, fearful, especially the E-7, who is the first to speak. He apologizes. Chief Stouffer accepts his apology. Then it is the captain's turn to speak. He is still not very animated as he outlines the advisers' role. But, surprisingly, Chief Stouffer doesn't interrupt him either. Instead he simply nods, and when the captain finishes, directs two of the Gs to show the candidates to a spot just below the Gs' camp where they can sleep. Then, after demanding that medics take a look at one of his men (who has a persistent cough), he leaves the ODA alone.

Other than the ODA's two communications sergeants moving off to send a radio transmission, with two Gs right beside them, there's not much activity once rucksacks have been dumped. The less the candidates do, the more troubled the two course instructors become, especially as late afternoon begins to blur into early evening. As far as they're concerned the candidates are hanging themselves with all the rope Chief Stouffer has provided. They shouldn't be off on their own like this, concerned only about their own camp. For one, the team leader should be on the G chief like glue, pumping him for information, doing everything within his power to secure rapport. And the rest of the team should be busy with a million and one other tasks.

First and foremost the candidates should be checking security and making sure the area *is* secure. Both instructors wind up having to tell the candidates that they're being remiss. This sends them scurrying. For the next three hours the team captain and another team member are at the G chief's side. They've got their maps out and Chief Stouffer is busy giving them all sorts of information about the Gs, the area, and so on. Before the candidates arrived, the Gs themselves muttered about just how much Chief Stouffer could talk. He's perfect in this role, especially since much of what he tells the two candidates isn't the least bit useful. Yet he's got them so cowed they're not about to cut him short.

The Gs likewise begin to play to their audience. They've got a roaring fire. The candidates, meanwhile, know they are supposed to stay tactical, which means no fire and no warmth. For awhile some of them manage to huddle with the Gs, as they attempt to make friends. Most of the Gs maintain their stance as Gs, although occasionally one will break and forget that he's a guerrilla as he answers a candidate who wonders what army unit he's really from. By morning, though, two of the Gs are completely in character. They purposely ask dumb questions or try to trip up their "advisers" with impossibly difficult hypotheticals.

Just after dawn Chief Stouffer also is back to rattling the candidates. Before training begins at 0800, the ODA conducts a stand-to, which is standard SF practice whenever a team is tactical. Once all the ODA members are awake there is a half hour of complete silence. This allows the soldiers to adjust to the light, the noise, the woods around them. One obvious goal is to determine whether enemy forces are anywhere around, especially since first light and last light are when most surprise attacks occur. A second purpose is simply to allow the soldiers to "situate" themselves during a period of utterly still awareness.

This morning's stand-to goes off without a hitch. But then, once everyone is up and moving around—the advisers in their camp and the Gs just above them on the flat top of the ridge—there's a sudden crescendo of gunfire. With Chief Stouffer's blessing the Gs are busily test-firing their weapons. Three or four rounds burst from every gun. So much for quiet, although remarkably this shooting brings none of the advisers running to chastise the Gs, which is what they should be doing, just as the night before they should have insisted that the Gs douse their fire. When the ODA captain asked the Gs to put out the fire and they didn't, he just let it drop. Clearly the ODA hasn't yet figured out how much assertiveness their adviser role requires.

One thing positive the candidates do is at least incorporate what being tactical requires in their first lessons. They tell the Gs there should be no more test-firing of weapons and explain why: the Gs can't afford to give their camp away. Correcting the Gs this way indicates that the candidates are able to improvise somewhat. But Sergeant Baker still has to prod them—"have you thought about teaching aids?"—right before the first scheduled class is due to begin, which produces momentary panic. The candidates quickly brainstorm. Then, they remember: poncho liners are supposed to work well as blackboards. Chalk even works OK on Ensolite sleeping pads. They scramble around the camp as they round up items they can use, though the first lesson—camouflage—is relatively easy and requires little beyond what the candidate-instructor and his assistant have already collected: their teammates' camouflage kits.

Each kit contains green and loam-colored grease sticks or little pats of green and loam face paint. With the Gs arrayed in front of him and one G volunteer beside him, the candidate-instructor proceeds to describe and then demonstrate how to "cammy up" by applying green to the hollows and loam to the ridges of his volunteer's face. Meanwhile, Sergeant Baker mutters to himself that while this is all well and good, the adviser could be doing much more. For instance, once the G's face has been painted, the candidate-instructor could send him to lie down in the woods alongside an uncamouflaged G, facing the rest of the Gs so they can see how effective camouflage is. Gradually, the candidate-instructor does begin to get more creative. When it comes to showing the Gs how, by inserting leafy branches into their web gear, they can break up their human outlines, he does send volunteers to pose in the woods beside his uncamouflaged assistant.

In fact, as the lessons progress—from applying camouflage to fast-crawling across the forest floor—the four candidates responsible for presenting this block of instruction visibly relax *and* become more animated. They increasingly put more of themselves into the teaching, so that Sergeant Baker finds himself needing to intercede only once, at the outset.

Sergeant Baker wants the candidates to reorganize the Gs. The ODA initially divided the Gs into three groups. While one group was in class, a second group would pull security, and the third would attend to operations and support—fetching water, making improvements to the camp, and the like. The plan was to rotate each group of guerrillas through the lessons separately, but as Sergeant Baker and the other two evaluators point out, this is hardly an effective use of time. Instead, the candidates should be instructing all the Gs together. After all, only two ODA members—an instructor and an assistant—are needed to teach at any one time. The rest of the team can divvy up the Gs' chores.

Once implemented, this reconfiguration works. And it doesn't take long before candidate-instructors realize they can not only answer all the questions the Gs pose but also they know more than the Gs, and do have something to teach. Plus they discover that their audience is more or less captive; the Gs aren't about to bolt. All of this builds confidence. The candidates improve by the hour, as if the simulated condensation of Robin Sage time really does intensify ability.

THE SPECIAL WARFARE SCHOOL DOES HAVE MUCH OF THIS DOWN to a science. Just as Chief Stouffer has been following the broad outlines of what every G chief is supposed to do—discombobulate students—there is a method to the madness he tries to inflict. At this stage just getting the hang of teaching is stressful enough for the candidates. The next wrench won't come until nightfall, when the ODA captain and a team member of his choosing are scheduled to attend an area command meeting.

In terms of the anxiety this nighttime meeting builds, school instructors consider it second only to the team's initial encounter with the G chief. Not only do they have to establish rapport all over again with a new guerrilla but, worse, with Chief Stouffer as their escort. Chief Stouffer isn't exactly an ally yet. The advisers can't be at all sure he will support them.

This meeting is also at night, which means the two candidates won't have gotten any sleep. They won't know where they are, which makes them doubly vulnerable. Moreover, the area commander—a local civilian—is a real pro, far more practiced than Chief Stouffer. The meeting is not supposed to go smoothly, and course after course, role-playing local residents ensure that it doesn't.

As for the rest of the team, back at the G camp, they will have their own reasons to be anxious. Everyone's still being evaluated. Will they all be evaluated on the performance of just these two team members? What if the captain and his second completely screw up?

Robin Sage is an unsettling mix of being made to cope with surprise and on-the-job-training. Potential confrontations loom even when there are no scheduled meetings. For instance, Chief Stouffer will have the Gs try to snatch the ODA's M-60 machine gun (the team's heaviest and most powerful weapon) one night while the ODA's guards are sleeping. Once the Gs have it, they will then claim it is theirs. Periodically the chief will also agitate for money and encourage his Gs to threaten to desert. In addition, he's planned for one of the Gs to be told by a phantom ex-policeman he meets from time to time at the stream (where the Gs and the ODA draw water) that his wife is sick. This should pose a number of problems for the ODA: Is the ex-policeman a security risk? Can they allow the G with the sick wife to go home? How can they convince him he shouldn't go home? But for the most part, after the area command meeting, the exercise should go well, provided solid rapport building is well underway.

ROBIN SAGE IS NOT MEANT TO BE A PHYSICAL TEST. THE INSTRUC-tors realize that the students have already passed numerous physical tests during SFAS. The point of Robin Sage is to see whether candidates can cope with head games and whether they can work with "foreigners" and at the same time in teams, and in an unconventional warfare setting.

Of course, instructors all wish they could make Robin Sage still more realistic. For one thing, they remember Robin Sage as they went through it, when it marked the finale of Phase 3. Not only were time constraints looser then but instructors also had more leeway. Candidates were often made to smoke unfamiliar herbs and grasses and drink vomitus brews. G chiefs routinely made candidates bow down before altars and memorize gibberish chants. This was initiation in the literal sense. Strange invented rites were common, as if all candidates who made it into SF would one day find themselves training a Stone Age group to be guerrilla fighters. The implied equation was that somewhere, in some remote jungle, American soldiers would be made to do such things to gain acceptance; therefore, Robin Sage had better test their preparedness and adaptability now, in North Carolina's Uwharrie Forest.

While some of these rituals may have been exaggeratedly drawn from real experiences—either of SF soldiers with Montagnards or British commandos in their jungle wars—the real initiation candidates were made to undergo as they were "forced" to declare allegiance to ersatz relics and sacks of bones was simply *into* SF. Just how far were they willing to go? Could they readily submit to a different culture and, more specifically, to SF's?

Robin Sage has always been as much a performance by the instructors as a test of candidates' abilities. The instructors are the ones, after all, who come up with the scenarios and the sketches, while what they must ultimately decide is who among the candidates will make good team players. Play is the operative word, with the SF play on conventional thinking as significant to teams' performance as any specialized training.

In this regard Robin Sage remains unchanged. It is the final phase of a complex initiation. Most initiations are about the devolution of responsibility. At the same time, initiations often double as a long and confused moment of shared truths. Essentially, what the adults, elders, or senior members of the group share with the initiates is the knowledge they possess, and then they admit to a terrible secret, the secret of the "tribe"—that beyond the knowledge the initiates have just been given there is no special knowledge. Experience may grant the group elders wisdom, but their innate ability to problem-solve is no better than it was before they themselves underwent initiation. Initiation didn't reassemble them, or even really improve them. But it did guarantee them an edge: noninitiates don't know what is or isn't known, and they can't be told.

During Robin Sage candidates learn where their own individual limitations lie and are made to acknowledge that they have them. What makes Robin Sage so tricky, and that much more significant, is that this self-knowledge has to be acquired while the individual remains a member of the group.

This is why it may not matter so much that the bizarre has been sanitized. Also, sensibilities in developing countries have changed, as have sensibilities in the army. Guerrilla leaders can be very sophisticated, no matter how rudimentary their material culture. Nor are their demands those of isolated or naive bumpkins—especially not when automatic weapons are the weapon of choice everywhere in the world today, and affording them, not finding them, is what is most difficult. Hence, Chief Stouffer's preoccupation with money isn't something he just concocted as a frustrating substitute for noxious soups and phallic altars. It is something he knows, from experience, is a major preoccupation of the "indig." Similarly, the U.S. government does have a credibility problem when it comes to lasting commitments. Ergo his reference to the Kurds and the Contras—two commonly heard gripes among many SF soldiers. In Chief Stouffer's view, candidates who make it into SF today are most likely to have to convince future clients of funding and staying power.

Again the Q Course both mirrors and prefigures reality. Just as the shuffle between classroom instruction and field exercises is career-long, theory always gets altered in practice. The chief lesson that Robin Sage teaches is that students have to adjust what they learned in the classroom to what local conditions in the Uwharrie Forest demand. Likewise, SF soldiers, who canonize the lessons learned in Robin Sage, have to be prepared to alter these, when and if they experience unconventional warfare for real.

Experience is the ultimate teacher in Robin Sage. While course instructors might lecture on and even preach the importance of building rapport in a thousand different ways, just repeating this is never enough. What ultimately drives the significance of trust home is the Gs. Their attitude is everything. Attitude determines how well the Gs learn the lessons the candidates teach, and then how well they act on what they've learned. At a certain point the candidates wake up and realize they are no longer role-playing. Never mind that they're *supposed* to be instructors, they *are* instructing. They *can* get the Gs to do what they need them to. More significantly, if everything works, trust flows both ways.

Trust also develops within the team. The candidates learn about this, too, from having to present a united front, with some give. Lesson 1 they learn as they neutralize the G chief. Lesson 2 they learn as they draw the Gs in. The rest of the mission depends on how well they can continue to apply both these lessons simultaneously. The longer they can manage to stay a step ahead while avoiding being tripped up, the more confidence they will gain. The more confidence they gain, the less easy it will be for Chief Stouffer to throw them. The less often Chief Stouffer humiliates them, the more the Gs will look up to them. Which, dissecting Robin Sage from afar—and without having to be made mincemeat of by Chief Stouffer—seems obvious enough.

But on the ground, in the midst of unpredictable events, what could be harder than determining what to do next when what you've already decided you should do isn't working? And when it does work? What would then be easy about being full of specialized knowledge—possessing more deadly knowledge than most people realize exists—without this going to your head?

6 Fitting In and Standing Out

ALTHOUGH SHAWN IS NEW TO 305 AND STRAIGHT OUT OF THE Q Course by way of language school, team members don't expect him to be with them for very long. From their perspective this is too bad. They need bodies and Shawn is clearly strong. But he's not a particularly good swimmer, and 305 is Z Company's scuba team. Affinity for the water is what defines them. Working in water is how they bond.

Shawn just doesn't look very comfortable in the water. Surface swimming appears to be an effort for him, never mind having to swim underwater. Nonetheless, Shawn's obviously a good sport.

When Shawn presented himself to the company sergeant major, fresh from the Q Course, the sergeant major asked him if he wanted to join the scuba team, knowing the team was desperate for new members. Shawn, who felt he would be off to a bad start in the company if he said no, said yes. Without doubt, scuba wouldn't have been his first choice; swimming wasn't his forte. Still, he felt he had to prove something.

Every company in the battalion had a combat diving, or scuba, team. Yet of all the men on those three teams, only two were black. On learning this Shawn decided he had to be the third.

SCUBA SCHOOL IS INDISPUTABLY DIFFICULT. EVEN PRESCUBA school is hard. That there is a prescuba school indicates how unforgiving combat dive school can be. Yet the irony is that combat diving is only a small fraction of what a scuba team is about.

Scuba amounts to a specialized means of insertion, period. While 305 might swim underwater to a designated mission site, once out of the water its members still have to move on land as skillfully as anyone else. Thus, scuba represents only a small portion of what scuba team members have to know, but it is a definitional portion. It is what sets scuba team members apart from members of other teams. And it can even set apart scuba team members from one another, since anyone assigned to a scuba team who isn't yet scuba-trained must be regarded as temporary at best. Only those who can successfully complete scuba training really belong. And not everyone passes the training.

Even before prescuba school there is training. For instance, 305 has six soldiers currently interested in joining it, and two are already assigned to the team. Yet the team makes the effort to help all six work on their strokes, their endurance, and their comfort in the water. Most evenings after duty hours, at least one 305 team member shows up at one of Ft. Bragg's recreational pools to work with any of the six wannabes who seeks guidance. The idea is to give the soldiers who want to join 305 every possible advantage—305 desperately needs more men.

Only six out of eleven soldiers currently assigned to the team are scuba-certified. Thus five of the men on the team don't do it much good unless they can be persuaded to try out for the school or, if they have no intention of trying, can be replaced with soldiers who have made it through.

And 305 knows the bind it is in. Although it can't afford for scuba to be the pivot of its training, scuba is still critical to why the team should train. So long as some team members are only temporary, there seems to be little point in trying to get the team to gel or even perfect something so basic as ground patrolling. Therefore, scuba-qualified 305 members are making more than just a good faith effort toward these six potential teammates. They want a full team, and they know there's no need to be too particular at this stage. Scuba school will make the ultimate selection. With scuba their lodestone and the school unbelievably difficult, their task is simply getting enough people used to the water to have a shot at making it through the school. Starting with prescuba school, the water will do the selecting for them.

In prescuba school candidates are required to swim endless laps in all sorts of configurations. Soldiers have to prove they are equally comfortable under and above water, with and without weighted belts, for lung-bursting periods as well as for short sprints, before SF will even begin to train them on bottled air. That comes in scuba school. But beyond the obvious divide—scuba school teaching scuba diving, prescuba school testing endurance and ease in the water—there is a second difference between the two schools. Much of prescuba training takes place in a pool, where bodies can be pushed to their limits in a controlled setting. Scuba school then takes soldiers from controlled waters and challenges their endurance in real waters. Although the school itself is located in Key West and sounds appealing, the weeks candidates spend there hardly amount to a vacation.

By all accounts scuba school is punishing. Of course, as with so much else in the army, it's been made significantly less masochistic recently. Which also means that the myths about how hard it was have grown. Still, it remains one of the most taxing schools SF soldiers can attend. And, as always, physical rigor is the least of it.

At the best of times, the ocean scares a lot of people. But what about a dark night when you are swimming essentially blind, on your back, towing a one hundred-pound pack, miles from shore. Far out there is nothingness, patrolled by jellyfish and sharks. Closer to shore there are waves, powerful currents, and undertows that pose only slightly more predictable dangers, since charts, weather forecasts, and good intelligence can offer at least some warning about these. What's unknown—what might go bump in the night—is harder to steel oneself for. Nor do mangrove swamps or blackwater rivers necessarily offer any improvement.

Even longtime scuba team members well experienced in the art of nighttime swims have a hard time predicting who will make it through scuba school. Water puts invisible pressure on minds as well as bodies. It's impossible to gauge exactly how well a person is able to drown his fears—of water, the dark, dark water in the dark.

Scuba-qualified 305 members readily admit they are often scared. They acknowledge there is nothing to like about being waterlogged, blind, connected to one another by a single strand of rope, having to swim endlessly. But they also believe that being able to do this, having to do it, makes their team tighter. That not everyone makes it onto the team only adds to the tightness and the sense that each member is special. Because of this, members of other teams sometimes refer to scuba team members as prima donnas. And in fact an added conceit may come from being on a specialty team, especially since there are only two types—scuba and freefall parachuting—and generally only one of each per company.

Along with scuba teams most SF companies have HALO teams. Like scuba, HALO—high-altitude, low-opening military freefall parachuting—is a specialized means of infiltration. HALO jumpers use different parachutes than SF and other airborne soldiers. Essentially, military freefall parachutists are skydivers. They decide when to pull their own ripcords and, because of the rectangular design of their "wings," have much more maneuverability in the air than paratroopers who are spit out of planes en masse and clunk down under round parachutes. Also, HALO jumpers can float for longer distances and land with pinpoint accuracy under their much more controllable chutes. Basically the whole point of jumping high and opening low is stealth and delivering an entire team as close to the mission site as possible without detection. However, as with scuba teams, once on solid ground HALO-qualified soldiers still have to be able to accomplish everything that members of regular, or ruck, teams can.

Of course, as far as members of ruck teams are concerned, specialty teams rarely operate on the ground as well as they do. In the ruck teams' view, this is because specialty team members spend too much time practicing infiltration. Nor do they know how to suck it up; they complain too much. For instance, HALO team members rarely make a secret of how much time they would spend practicing HALO jumps if they could. Thus, when they don't get to train as often as they'd like, they tend to whine and mope. Or, at least, this is how members of other teams interpret their behavior. From the HALO team's perspective, everyone else is just jealous.

Especially Shawn. Shawn would probably have done fine in HALO school. Not only does freefalling through no more than several minutes' worth of cold, dry darkness appeal to him much more than having to spend long hours in cold water on a cold, dark night, but, with far fewer slots than applicants, the hardest thing about HALO school for most students is getting in. Not so with scuba school. No matter how hard getting through prescuba school might be, it's nothing compared with making it through scuba training. Nor—had Shawn been sent to the HALO team— would his teammates have predicted, on sight, that the odds were so against him.

MEMBERS OF 305 BELIEVE THEY ARE JUST BEING REALISTIC WHEN they predict Shawn won't make it through prescuba, let alone into scuba school. Conventional scuba team wisdom says blacks don't like swimming and they don't have enough body fat. Consequently, going out to Mott Lake for a day of team training right on Ft. Bragg is meant to kill two birds with one stone. Scuba-qualified members can dive with tanks on, while the six wannabes can practice swimming. Of course, turning them loose in the lake will also put the lie to the swimming pool.

Stained the color and almost the temperature of lukewarm tea, Mott Lake has no concrete sides to grab onto or push off from. Once out in the middle there's nothing to do but tread water. And swimming across affords no escape from the slap of small waves, nor does the treeline seem to grow any closer; the middle is too far from shore to gauge movement forward against receding trees. It's perfect.

Significantly, none of Mott Lake's attributes seems to impede Shawn. He's already doomed. It's obvious he's uncomfortable long before he's told it's time to strike out for the far shore.

Just watching Shawn swim around the black rubber Zodiac

boat makes it clear that he's unhappy. The three team members who monitor him from the boat aren't optimistic. His kick isn't smooth enough, so strapping fins to his feet for the swim across only adds to his struggle. All of this just serves to confirm what the team already suspected. Nothing racist is meant when 305 blames Shawn's difficulties on his blackness. After all, his bad swimming, not his race, is going to keep him off the team.

BACKGROUND IS ALWAYS A DOUBLE-EDGED SWORD IN SF. If Shawn could swim better, his color would mean nothing to 305. Doubtless his teammates would occasionally rib Shawn about being black, but that's because everyone winds up being kidded about something. Nothing is sacred in a team room, except perhaps team members' wives, and then only when their husbands are actually present.

In team rooms individuals have to be soldiers first and members of other groups second. By definition, belonging to the team should render all other allegiances insignificant. Only when someone doesn't fit the criterion of being a good SF soldier is he likely to be castigated as something else. Then, rhetorically, he might well be deemed an idiot, a slackard, a beaner, a nigger, or a redneck. Members of some teams freely used all sorts of derogatory terms to describe other individuals in the company. But I never heard anyone on a team refer to one of his own teammates by serious epithet, despite whole conversations comprised of them. The business of categorization was actually quite elegant.

The same team members who generically referred to all blacks as "niggers" would never use "nigger" to describe a black soldier they liked. Of course, they would also never use the word in front of officers, or blacks they didn't like. But this was more because the military considered ethnic slurs censurable than because team members worried about offending anyone. From their perspective, anyone who was SF had to know that speaking in stereotype said nothing about whom teams were willing to fight next to, or for. Rules for judging other soldiers were sophisticatedly simple: prove to us you are like us as a soldier and we won't care about anything else; prove to us you aren't and we'll write you off. Writing people off is when epithets flow.

In the military four-letter words tend to be common coinage, and stereotypes fit along with this currency. For instance, Z Company could seem microcosmically Southern. Not only did accents tend to sound more Southern than generically Midwestern, but in some team rooms country music was all that team members could agree to listen to. Jesse Helms tended to be popular, and there were also common pastimes: four-wheeling, hunting, fishing, flipping through back issues of *Guns & Ammo*. In reality, many of these seeming commonalities were merely least common denominators, as much a result of being in North Carolina and the army, and being adept at survivalist soldiering, as they were a reflection of any individual's personal interests or views.

Also, talk came cheap—it was filler. Days and nights could be long, and too often togetherness was boring. In other workplaces how individuals use language might be productively studied for all sorts of subtexts. But on teams, actual behavior always counted for more. Nor did words used in team rooms mean what those same words might mean elsewhere. They couldn't. Language was used as a probe more often than as a weapon. Twisted into humor, it could be unbelievably acute. It could shame people into conformity or crudely but effectively defuse otherwise tense, ego-driven situations. Crude as it sometimes was, humor could also be quite clever. Invariably it sought any opening it could find, often settling on the most convenient of hooks, like race or size. But it also loved to glorify personal failure. And once it found a chink, it returned again and again, digging deeper.

No doubt at stake in most of the jibes that flew back and forth within and sometimes between team rooms was SFness, as well as one-upmanship. Identity was continually being tested: you're SF, right? So you can handle this, right? These slurs don't apply to you, do they? Because you belong to "us," you're not a "them," correct?

Such testing was hardly conscious. At the same time it was perpetual. In a sense it was also all of a piece with what SF requires: individuals who can roll with the punches, who are flexible, even tolerant of what they can't control—like skin color—but who are hypercritical and exacting about what can be controlled: behavior, attitude, and comportment.

THE MEN IN Z COMPANY TENDED TO HAVE PLENTY OF PROOF TO back up the stereotypes they adhered to. In large part this is because all SF soldiers have spent years in what they regard as the equal-opportunity army, where all segments of American society are represented. In this sense their opinions are not based on hearsay or ignorance but emerge from firsthand experience. If someone lumped together all blacks—or Asians, Southerners, West Pointers, or Pennsylvanians—he did so because they'd proven themselves to have more in common with one another than with him. Sometimes this grouping would be based on little more than how soldiers sort themselves out in terms of who seems to be attracted to which military occupational specialties (or MOSs). At other times it would be based on who partied with whom and what kind of music they listened to. Often it was personal, based on finding that, for whatever reason, you've never gotten along with anyone from Michigan. Regardless, the bases for stereotyping were never illogical. If anything, they made perfect sense, given the givens. Nor were the givens ever quite so simplistic as outsiders might assume.

In fact, in the broader scheme of things snap judgments wound up being made about everyone based on categories far more unforgiving than just class, color, or education. Appearance, period, speaks volumes. Demeanor, posture, attitude, all of these hold military meanings. All are self-generated. Thus, only soldiers themselves can prove or disprove the logic of the pigeonholes they get stuffed into, although some do get stuck with harder holes to climb out of than others. If a soldier reminds others too much of a type that tends not to be well represented in SF, the hole is deeper. In this sense, SF selects for soldiers most like others already in the fold. This makes for a definite circularity to acceptance and might well reinforce certain prejudices. Nevertheless, the way out for everyone is always the same: prove yourself SF and everyone will disregard whatever else he thought you were. Conform.

The catch for many soldiers was that it took time to demonstrate how well they defied a mistaken stereotype but fit SF. Soldiers new to teams were often desperate to prove themselves, wanting nothing more than to be accepted. They were convinced that until they were accepted, they were missing the experience they joined SF for. Without doubt, being part of a team is what graduating the Q Course promised them they were on the brink of. At the same time, trying too hard to belong invariably annoyed the very team members who were busy passing judgment and whom new soldiers knew they had better impress. Worse, how to belong invariably depended on the mix of personalities already on the team, which no one could prepare for.

Indeed, contrary to civilian-held stereotypes, soldiers do have personalities. In Z Company there were self-effacing extroverts, generous introverts, soldiers who had no idea what they would do when they retired, and others who had the future entirely mapped out. The trick on teams, then, was for everyone to fit in so that all the personalities could coexist as a whole, which could be tricky. Fitting required flexibility for sure. But even more than the ability to alternately subordinate or project their own egos, individuals had to be able to compartmentalize. Also, they couldn't lie.

STEVE DIDN'T LIE BUT HE COULDN'T COMPARTMENTALIZE. AS A RESULT, he was having real problems on 309, and was, along with Shawn, one of the six soldiers trying to make it onto 305. Tired of always being treated as the smallest fish in the pond, he needed some sort of success. Moving to a new team, even if only across the company hall, would at least let him think he was starting over again. Maybe he would even be able to recoup his reputation; 305 had a different sort of makeup than 309.

After all, there was Dave. Dave, who still turned women's heads at the ripe old age of twenty-eight, had entered SF at an unusual time, when even privates were accepted into the Q Course. Consequently, SF reared him. His entire army experience was in SF. Coming in as a lowly private, he had no illusions about his starting place on the totem pole. He knew he belonged at the bottom—ten years ago. Now, still not very senior, he at least rated high in unofficial pecking orders, especially since he had more team time than any number of sergeants, who formally outranked him.

Even so, Dave retained his finely tuned sense of place. He always knew how far he could push familiarity, and where familiarity stopped and hierarchy began. Dave probably understood the system too well. Young enough so that he didn't have to work too hard at staying fit, he could get away with being a team room couch potato. And raised in SF, he knew how to have fun. Good-looking, self-assured, with nothing left to prove to his teammates, he *could* party. Which meant he also had demonstrable fun. This, meanwhile, attracted Steve, who was almost ten years younger than anyone else on 309, but—unlike Dave—was still a cherry.

One of Steve's problems was that he refused to accept what being a cherry (or newby) meant. Instead, he tended to regard 309's treatment of him as hazing, though it wasn't. Having excelled as a soldier in the conventional army, Steve assumed there should have been some carryover. When there wasn't, he tried to make the transition himself, through talking. He talked incessantly, which is also how he hurt himself—he exposed too much, while the more he talked, the more everyone else withdrew. The more they withdrew the more desperately he tried to win them over. In essence Steve dug his own hole.

On paper, Steve had everything going for him. He was doughwhite, solidly built, born and bred on the Great Plains. His background was fairly typical: broken home, uncles who had been in the army, siblings who did better than he in school. In fact, among the handful of background commonalities SF soldiers seem to share is boredom in high school. Like so many others, Steve managed to slide through without ever really applying himself.

Staring high school graduation in the face, he had two options: the army or college football. Being too small for the latter, he enlisted. Airborne.

After basic training there was advanced individual training (AIT), then jump school. Steve's career path prior to SF was as straightforward as it possibly could have been. After two years with an Airborne unit in Panama he submitted his packet for SFAS, and while still just an E-4 was admitted to the Q Course. The most unusual thing about Steve was that he made it into SF so quickly. As a result, he was the youngest man in the company, if not the battalion and group, for a time.

Despite his youthfulness Steve lived up to SF's sketchy profile in at least one other regard; he was married. He met his wife at a local club in Fayetteville, while she was visiting a relative married to someone in the 82nd. Like so many other marriages, Steve's was thus thanks to a military connection. Again, this made him more rather than less ordinary. And there was nothing unique about the fact that Steve's wife was older. Steve did become an instant father by marrying her, though gaining a stepson was a bonus as far as he was concerned. Unfortunately, there were no bonuses to being an army spouse, as far as his wife was concerned.

Whether Steve's marriage was rockier than most is almost impossible to say, but it was rocky. The catch is that no one else on 309 talked about his domestic life to the extent Steve did. No one else aired so many of his problems. Nor did anyone else's wife call KC to try to have her husband straightened out.

This is one way in which Steve proved incapable of compartmentalization: he didn't keep his marital problems out of the team room, or off his mind. Worse, he was too impassioned and indiscriminate in discussing them, portraying himself alternately as dominator and dominated at home. This did nothing for his image in the team room. Nor did he display much sense about how others might interpret his invasion of their privacy. He never seemed to recognize that no one was very interested in this area of his life. After a while all that Steve's perpetual airing of his troubles left his teammates to assume was that fights sustained his marriage. Unfortunately, this only tended to confirm their overall impressions—he was too immature, which then bled into doubts about his dependability.

The unspoken judgment was that Steve should have known better. Certainly he should have maintained more control over his wife. That he couldn't was troubling on a number of counts. For SF soldiers security is a serious issue. A wife who doesn't understand the bounds of appropriate behavior poses a potential threat to the whole team. If a wife doesn't respect her husband's privacy his teammates have to wonder, is she likely to respect theirs? If she tends to overdramatize, this, too, can have serious consequences. If she doesn't understand that there are some things better left unsaid, the team worries whether she can be trusted with anything of a sensitive nature. Compounding this in Steve's case was an incident that took place among team wives during the Gulf War. Steve's wife apparently discussed something about the team over the telephone that she shouldn't have. Without necessarily realizing she was passing along privileged information, she signaled to team members that if Steve couldn't effectively convey the importance of security to her, that suggested certain inadequacies in him.

If Steve and his wife hadn't brought their marital problems to the team's attention, no one would have bothered factoring these into their overall assessment of him. For the team the real problem was that too often Steve appeared not to listen. That infuriated some team members. That he wasn't listened *to*, in turn, frustrated Steve. And there was more. Not getting into the field enough meant Steve couldn't prove his competence by doing the kinds of jobs the Q Course had convinced him he was good at. Instead, as low man on the totem pole in a unit where there are no clerks or privates to do sergeants' bidding, Steve found himself performing tasks that he never would have had to do at his rank in the conventional army. Clearly, in his view, 309 was taking advantage of him and treating him as a peon. But clearly, too, he was confused by the informality of the team room. Being able to call even KC by his first name, coupled with what seemed to be the intimacy of close quarters, had to make it easy for Steve to forget that he *was* outranked by everyone else on the team. It didn't help that SF wasn't supposed to be like the conventional army. There wasn't supposed to be so much bureaucracy or paperwork. And there were supposed to be more missions, more opportunities for new members like him to strut their stuff and gain approval. The real catch came in what occurred when the team was in the team room, though: reminiscing about their experiences in the field.

Shared experiences are critical to bonding. At the same time, shared experiences automatically exclude new members, and new team members realize this. Steve certainly did. But the problem with his response was that his talking about similar experiences— of being cold or wet or on target—never added up to his having shared these with 309. It was the sharing—not so much the experiences—that was pivotal for the team. Steve didn't seem to realize this, or if he did, he must have thought that the more the rest of the team knew about him, the faster they would accept him as someone they wanted to share new experiences with.

But there is knowing and knowing. The intimacy of the team room is not what it appears. Just because teammates spend hour upon hour cooped up together does not mean they know everything about one another or that they want to. They tend to know a lot but are far less interested in learning as much as outsiders, including Steve, might presume.

Compartmentalization is critical to bonding, and applies not just to the details of people's private lives but also extends to their pasts. For instance, some individuals on 309 had committed felonious crimes for which they'd never been caught. Teammates had no idea. Equally invisible was the divide between those who had done drugs and those who had not. It was unlikely anyone was able to indulge anymore because everyone was subject to drug testing at any time, but soldiers with a drug-laced past still tended not to talk about it. Implied was the recognition that everyone didn't feel similarly about breaking the law.

Across the board, teams were far from monolithic in terms of individuals' practices and beliefs. Still, certain common assumptions did hold sway, and challenging these made little sense. If the moral tenor was broadly conservative, this didn't mean select individuals didn't have stray liberal thoughts. It just wouldn't have done them much good to broadcast themselves as more liberal than their peers. Comfort lay in conformity—not in being true to beliefs or opinions that clearly had nothing to do with the purpose of the team.

The bottom line was actually quite simple: teammates had to be able to trust one another. They had to be able to trust that what someone presented himself as knowing or being capable of was indeed what he could do. To a certain extent, all that was required was no bluffing. The mere suggestion of dishonesty cast too much doubt. Bluffing could get everyone killed. Better to remain silent than pretend.

Thus, soul baring is not at all what teams required. To do their jobs team members didn't need to be familiar with one another's deepest thoughts. At the same time, not being forthright did not amount to dishonesty so long as the team's assumptions couldn't be disproved. And there were certain broad assumptions that revolved around being male and heterosexual, a soldier, and in SF. Recognizing these assumptions was itself a mark of belonging. Fitting into them—and not faking the fit—was all that being on a team really demanded; this came easily to some individuals and required only slightly more work of others.

This also explains why the kind of bonding Steve thought he was achieving by talking about his home life—since almost everyone on 309 was married—was superfluous. He had a wife, he had a kid, he was healthily heterosexual. That's all the information anyone needed. More only gave people more to be critical of. Better to be someone no one bothered to form extraneous opinions about. Astute SF NCOs strove *not* to stand out, *not* to draw attention to themselves, *not* to be the subject of conversation. Clearly Steve hadn't quite made these connections, or those between compartmentalizing and conforming—yet. Instead, he mistakenly assumed conformity could be advertised, while the point is that it can't be.

COMPARTMENTALIZATION NOT ONLY KEEPS HEARTFELT OPINIONS and hot-button issues out of team rooms, locked away, but it can make SF soldiers seem more rather than less alike. This, in turn, might make it seem as though the army *should* be able to develop a fuller SF profile, eventually rendering the need for the Q Course obsolete. But how do you test for compartmentalization?

Steve himself had appeared the perfect candidate. He was a model soldier in the conventional army who outstripped his peers. He was quick, strong, intelligent, and sure of himself. He had just the kind of background that seemed to predispose him for team life. Yet he also happened to still be young and showed signs of never being able to develop the right sensibilities. He was actually much more a model product of SFAS and the Q Course during a ramp-up: promising, but of what? His own teammates couldn't predict. Either a deployment would settle Steve down and wise him up, or it might make him still more intolerably know-it-all.

Ironically, Steve did demonstrate his ability to learn in at least one regard. *If* he could make it onto 305, then trying out for scuba school would have been an exceptionally smart move. But not because he would finally be proving his worth to 309, or because 305 was any less demanding a team. Rather, 305 just happened to be predicated on a shortcut to conformity.

Scuba rendered 305 both different from, but also a more condensed version of, all the other teams in the company. This is because scuba school tended to do the team's culling for it. Because of the self-reverential nature of scuba, not many scuba-qualified members failed to fit. Just passing through scuba school would get Steve nearer to acceptance on 305 than he had managed after a year of working so hard at it on 309.

At the same time, the scuba team could also act much more quickly than other teams when it came to closing ranks. For instance, after the day at Mott Lake everyone realized Shawn was unlikely to make it through prescuba school. The consequence: he would never be part of the team. Hence, without needing even to agree, team members noticeably cooled toward Shawn.

From the team's point of view such a change in attitude was nothing if not practical. Team 305 had to cut its—and Shawn's— losses, a severing that was not racially motivated, though it was race-based. And uncomfortable though the chill may have felt to Shawn, it was still fair; the rules had always been obvious. Trying so hard proved Shawn was SF, just not scuba material. For someone like Steve, on the other hand, the reason for his not fitting on 309 was much less well defined; 309 didn't have as clear-cut a denominator as 305. There was no single test. Unfortunately, this meant that there was also no single thing Steve could do to redeem himself. Whatever initial impression he made remained permanently etched. This much he did understand about team room dynamics. And once he felt he wasn't fitting in—and wouldn't be allowed to— he decided he didn't want to fit. Better to just cut his losses. Consequently, his desire to switch.

But was the problem only with Steve? Greg, too, was having a rocky time on 309.

7 Standing Out and Fitting In

IT IS DAWN ON THE SECOND-TO-LAST DAY OF OCTOBER, EASILY THE coldest day of the year so far. While it is still dark, the entire company piles into two-and-a-half-ton army transport trucks for a bitter ride to the back of Ft. Bragg's beyond.

The purpose of this trip is to requalify in land navigation skills. The entire company is in Green Cycle, a four-month period of intensive training and testing. Every day the soldiers are either out on the ranges or in the woods, being put through their soldierly paces, practicing and being tested on basic infantry skills at the most demanding levels. Thus, there will be two land navigation courses: one to be run during daylight hours and the second after dark.

Like so much else in the army, land navigation serves myriad purposes. It is essential to any patrol, reconnaissance, raid, ambush—to any foot movement across any type of terrain. Simple as it may seem, it is not particularly easy. To successfully complete a land-nav course, a soldier has to grid-plot, map-and-compass read, and even stride correctly. He has to translate three sets of grid coordinates on a slip of paper into three corresponding points on the map. Then, with these locations plotted on the map he must reach each of them in the woods, where thin metal stakes mark the coordinates.

On this particular course homemade ticket punchers dangle

from more than two dozen stakes. Each makes a different pinhole pattern. A piece of paper bearing these pinholes is the grail soldiers have to return to camp with, proving that they've translated numbers into dots on the map, and those dots into precise locations on the ground. Also, their rucksacks must still weigh fifty-five pounds. The points can be visited in any order, but roads can't be walked on for more than one hundred meters at a time. These are the parameters for recertification. Even I can figure out how to cheat.

Greg, however, is not a cheater. His nickname is Sensei, which should be a giveaway. He is good enough at everything he does so he never has to cheat, which allows him to believe that only the weak and incapable succumb to shortcuts. He runs faster, ruck-marches harder, even types better, and is right more often than most of the other members of 309. But at least one of them believes Greg is too competitive, and others aren't sure Greg's attitude works on a team. Greg, whose dog tags list his religion as shamanism, may be too much of an individualist. He may also be too enamored of pain. It is almost as if his standards are those of immortal youth; without doubt, his expectations are.

Still, diligence as much as karma may explain why we reach his points so effectively. It's certainly not his size or his build, neither of which makes him stand out. Rather, the two things that most distinguish him are a vivid tattoo dedicated to his wife, and his face, which is open and friendly. And his smile—Greg definitely likes to smile. And why not? He *is* good at everything he does. It's also easy to see why he thought his wife had better join him at Ft. Sam Houston, where medics receive their Phase 2 training. All SF medics comment about just how friendly the women in San Antonio seem to be toward anyone they think is SF. But Greg has the kind of looks that would allow him to attract women anywhere—so clean-cut, all-American, fresh-faced, innocent.

ONE THING THAT MAKES THIS LANDNAV COURSE SUCH A CHALLENGE is that countless dirt roads and tracks bisect Ft. Bragg and its hinterlands. All of them look identical, but not all of them appear on even the most up-to-date maps. Regardless, each still qualifies as an automatic landmark as soon as you're astride it. The critical issue then is to determine exactly which one you are on, and whether it does indeed appear on your map.

Unless you have stuck to a set trajectory and know the distance you have hiked since the last landmark you and the map agreed on, the most benign dirt track can waylay you. Essentially, a map can help tell you where you are only if you've accurately kept track of where you've been. Distance is key.

Beads keep distance. In fact, a string of what look like worry beads suspended from web gear is just one of a lot of clues that can point to a soldier's occupation: whether he is in the medical corps, support, infantry, or Special Operations. All SF soldiers (along with Rangers, many members of the infantry, and anyone for whom landnav is routine) wear beads. And any beads will do so long as they are large and distinguishable by feel. Generally they are suspended from the left shoulder and are threaded on doubled-over 550 cord. If the cord is thick enough, they won't slide freely. The point is to have to manually move the beads up or down the cord to mark distance in 100- and 1,000-meter lengths.

Every soldier walks at a different pace. The number of steps he takes to traverse one hundred meters becomes his pace. So long as he knows how many footfalls it takes him to traverse one hundred meters, he can then use his pace to measure distance. For instance, if Greg's pace is eighty strides in one hundred meters and he needs to reach a stake three hundred meters north of where he is standing, all he has to do is keep count for three sets of eighty strides heading due north and we should wind up at his point.

It's a lot to do at one time: keep count, maintain a direction, know where you are on the map, and still be alert for enemy movement, tripwires, ambushes, anything. This explains why when a team is on patrol one man is always "on" point, another is on compass, and the rest of the team or squad patrols. It also helps explain why patrols move so slowly. Not only is caution key but continual cross-checking is critical—and boring. So much double-checking is tedious and, to those convinced of the rightness of their own instincts, a seemingly redundant exercise.

Greg's instinct, though, is to always check. He's exceedingly careful and I can begin to see why one of his regrets is that he never became a rock climber. He thinks he would have liked clinging to rock faces and attempting seemingly impossible moves, knowing that if he fell that could be it. He certainly wouldn't climb to make a fatal error, but the adrenalin that comes with always knowing that you might . . . what a rush. Though I actually think that control—and his love for a certain type of control—might explain even more.

Greg joined the army only days after high school graduation. As for many SF soldiers, entering the service seemed the path of least resistance. Already, Greg had plans to marry his high school sweet-heart, who still had a year before graduating herself. Given the depressed, rural area in which they grew up, he had to find some way to support her. His track record in school wasn't likely to land him a decent job.

While Greg sometimes did extremely well in the subjects he liked—English, math, and creative writing—school was never really the focus of his attention. It certainly wasn't the center of his social universe. That tended to be his best friend, Bill, whom he'd known since third grade. The two of them did everything together. They ran wild and did a lot of bad things—criminal, vicious things—that Greg still doesn't like to describe. For a long time Greg just assumed he'd become a professional criminal. He and Bill clearly had a knack for not getting caught.

But instead they enlisted. Unfortunately—or perhaps fortunately for Greg—they were separated almost immediately. And though Greg thrived in the army, Bill was kicked out. Greg was surprised. He didn't consider any of the training particularly onerous; jumping out of planes was definitely a thrill. Greg also realized that he could do all kinds of things better than legions of his peers. Add to this his marriage, and the birth of his first daughter, and suddenly responsibility was OK; he wanted to do well. He credits the army with instilling in him both newfound pride *and* remorse. The army also helped him develop a strong sense of discipline.

For Greg self-control became key: being in shape, staying in shape, and remaining impervious to pain. Greg always tries to outdistance, out-endure, and out-gut everyone else by shrugging off discomfort, fatigue, and miserable conditions. Competitiveness and assertiveness don't drive him to such lengths so much as does his own insatiable need to keep pushing and testing himself.

Consequently it doesn't take us long to finish our eight-kilometer course. Other members of 309 trail in after us as they complete theirs. A few soldiers from another unit don't finish at all, or at least not within the designated time, while others have checked with one another out in the field, maybe even swapping pinhole patterns if they find themselves heading to or from the same points. But beyond doing this, or walking on roads for more than one hundred meters, or emptying weight out of a pack and then recovering it just before reentering camp, cheating doesn't take all that much skill this first time around. What going through the day course does do, though, is allow people to begin to cheat for the points they'll have to make come darkness.

By midday, with most people back, the entire company sacks out. A number of soldiers strip off their camouflage outerwear so that they're down to the olive drab essence of T-shirts and jockey shorts. Everyone else blends into the ground cover. After the ambitious, who have brought stoves to heat their Meals-Ready-to-Eat (MREs), finish cooking, the woods are utterly silent. It's nap time. The only interruption comes when course assessors take orders for junk food before making a run to the small store at nearby Camp Mackall. This briefly leads to in-my-day-there-was-no-store-at-Camp-Mackall stories. A number of older SF veterans remember when just being able to take temporary shelter in tarpaper shacks was a luxury during Phase 1 of the Q Course. They also recall how much physical abuse there was "back then." Otherwise, between reminiscing about the good old days and Chief Morgan from 305 buttonholing everyone to take a look at the unsightly fungus still growing under his thumbnail, it's just a wait until the sun drops.

As soon as light begins to fade, activity resumes. Some of this is anticipation, but most has to do with the temperature. The more the mercury falls, the more people want to get moving, and then home.

Before it's actually dark the second round begins. Men receive their grid coordinates in random fifteen-man iterations. In contrast to how soldiers scattered for the daylight course, eager to get going, teams now reconstitute themselves before individuals fan out. There's a lot of huddling and whispering. Already at midday there were rumors that at least one team had divided the course up into zones during the morning, with each team member responsible for finding each stake in his zone. Clearly deals are still being made. Even Greg gets pulled aside. Mark has drawn the same "lane" we walked this morning and asks Greg for his map, with the points already plotted out. KC, meanwhile, wanders back and forth, while Carl just stands by, shaking his head, smiling, and muttering, "It could get ugly out there."

I wholeheartedly agree, though not necessarily for the reasons he implies. What I'm not looking forward to is branches. I know I'll come through the woods with at least one eye poked out. Nor does it help when a couple of soldiers pull on plastic goggles. No one wants his eyes slashed, which reminds me that Special Forces soldiers don't really have complete immunity from the sorts of things that might give the rest of us longer pause. Also, as Greg assures me, it won't be any less dark for him than me. But this only amazes me all the more. Nighttime is SF's preferred time for infiltration and reconnaissance.

If you've ever walked off-trail through unfamiliar, unlit woods, you know how disturbing this can be. Being alone only heightens the eeriness, which not being able to use a white-lens flashlight intensities. Meanwhile, the moon won't rise until sometime after midnight. The only light soldiers have to walk by is starlight, which, surprisingly, seems almost enough. It illuminates just enough of the woods so we can avoid most tree trunks and large branches. Spider webs, though, are impossible. So are holes and sudden depressions.

With maglights switched to red-lens mode, soldiers can read maps without red light projecting far enough to alert the enemy. This maintains security; more significantly, red light doesn't destroy night vision. Even the briefest flash of white light ruins the ability to half-sightedly feel your way in the dark. White light will also rob you of confidence. For one minute—or five, or however long the world is lit—the illusion of being in control is restored.

Then, with the disappearance of light, impenetrable gauze re-descends. Not a pleasant sensation.

Indeed, night landnav is one of those trials that tends to separate those individuals cut out for this type of soldiering from soldiers who find moving alone through the dark too unsettling. Night land-nav is not just about coping with darkness; there is still navigation to contend with. And much as one might expect, terrain features take on a whole new meaning and a whole new look in ambient starlight.

For instance, distant hills or ridges become meaningless as landmarks. You simply can't see them. And trails and roads are even more alluring than usual, for two reasons: they're identifiable and they beckon. As ribbonlike clearings they're not only easier to see but simple to follow. They require less guesswork to walk on than surrounding mystery ground. Also, they always lead some-where. Psychologically this is of tremendous comfort and tempta-tion, even to Greg, although, of course, I am his perfect excuse.

Actually, Greg begins to succumb to roads and trails once he re-alizes plenty of other people are already walking on them. It is star-tling to suddenly come across looming human figures in the dark. Occasionally one runs past, exactly why we don't know. At other times we can hear people crashing through the underbrush. But most people we run into appear as we cross roads, or near the points. The points themselves are lit by chem lights. Even these, which glow a bright fluorescent green, destroy night vision.

In a number of ways wading through the dark is akin to swim-ming across a murky lake. There are pockets of warmer and cooler air and there's always something to concentrate on beyond just the mechanics of movement. This is not a hike. Even Greg's advantage of having someone to talk to isn't really an advantage. We can't talk for long as he has to maintain a count, which gives us a further ex-cuse to eventually end up on the roads.

As it happens, we are on a side road, heading toward Greg's sec-ond point, when a humvee approaches. The vehicle's lights aren't on so the assessors inside probably can't see us. We duck back into the woods just in case, but not very far. Greg is curious. The humvee is driving slowly enough for us to follow it. And then it stops. We overhear the soldiers inside talking to someone who must be on the road ahead of them. They tell him that the point he's trying to reach is difficult to get to, so they'll give him a break and drive him closer. Greg is stunned. I'm somewhat jealous. Greg claims that if we were offered a ride he would refuse it. I believe him, although he also concedes that we'll now probably continue walking on roads. As far as he's concerned soldiers have to keep honing night landnav skills. But once he's proven to himself that he's still capable, there seems little point in continuing, which is more than fine with me.

I have no idea how Greg is managing so well. I can at least follow him, which means I can hear him hit the branches and limbs I should avoid. Also, he's breaking the spider webs for me. At least one spider scuttles down his neck. Not even he likes that. Spiders were one concern I heard voiced during the afternoon. Branches across the face and in the eyes was the other. Interestingly, no one mentioned what has to be the even greater discomfort: doing this alone. Alone it must seem far more the unpleasant chore than an interesting challenge.

Perhaps that explains why there are so many twosomes on the roads, although we do meet one individual who, having just emerged from the woods, is about to reenter them. As far as he's concerned it's quicker to take a straight course through the trees than go the long way round. Otherwise, few people are very talkative. Greg thinks it's because everyone is wary of who everyone else is. In the dark anyone could be an assessor. Of course, thanks to the dark, most people can also cheat. And walking on the roads is the least of it.

Indeed, the next morning someone from another team tells me that yes, his team divvied up the course the first time around, found all the points, agreed on a rally point for after dark, met up, used pins to duplicate the necessary patterns, then sacked out for a couple of hours. None of them really wanted to hump around at night.

But was this really cheating?

PERHAPS THE MOST BASIC AIM OF COUNTERINSURGENCY AND GUERrilla warfare is to cheat the expectations of the other side. To be devious. To undermine the expected. To get away with murder.

Consequently, some teams and individuals don't differentiate between cheating on a real mission and doing so in training, or even in private life. The perpetual challenge for them is, how much can we get away with? How far can we bend the rules? Even this may oversimplify what really goes on, because the real challenge doesn't just lie in subverting the system but doing so by demonstrating to peers just how cleverly higher command has been suckered.

This is tricky but done all the time. For instance, there are many parts to recertification. Some require that entire nights be spent in the woods, when teams should consider themselves tactical. But with no one likely to find them to check up on whether they are staying tactical or not, there is no particular reason (beyond practice) to comply. Also, few teams are ever fully staffed. As is the case throughout the year, individuals get shunted off to learn new skills whenever school slots open. And many of these schools are located at Ft. Bragg. Some require attendance only during fairly regular daylight hours. Consequently, teammates who are in school become perfect conduits for their teammates in the woods. Either they ferry illicit coolers full of drinks and junk food to boost team morale or, better yet, instead of bringing town to the soldiers they carry teammates into town. This way the ODA manages a night of carousing without anyone needing to be any the wiser (including wives).

Not all teams, of course, are challenged by the need to break rules or fool higher command. There also seems to be a strong correlation between towing the line and having an officer leading the team. However, there may be no rule beyond the rule of dominant personalities, which predicts how strictly teams abide by which rules. It does seem, though, that what is considered field craft exists on a slippery slope.

I am thinking of one team in particular.

ODA 300 HAD FOUND WHAT IT CONTENDED WAS THE PERFECT SITE for practicing patrolling and ambushes. This was on a farm way out in Robin Sage territory, an area several hours' drive from Ft. Bragg. With its combination of creeks, fields, and woods, Mr. Hailey's prosperous-looking farm traditionally hosted Q Course instructors and students. In return for teams of camouflaged men tromping through his pastures and hiding around his barns, Mr. Hailey got to name his civic action. In other words, he had soldiers to do chores. Of course, these were never termed chores. Rather, mowing the lawn, chopping wood, digging fences—whatever the manual labor—such activities were regarded as essential to building rapport. The significance of rapport building is one of the elemental lessons taught during Robin Sage. And Robin Sage is how one of the team members had first come to this farm.

Rapport was also what 300 was now after. Ostensibly, 300 was seeking to build rapport with Mr. Hailey to be able to return to his farm in the future. As it was, only five of the team's members could be there at the moment. Everyone else was in school or temporarily assigned elsewhere. So actually, the rationalizing went, the team really couldn't do much more than build rapport. There wasn't enough of a team to conduct truly rigorous training.

Perhaps this also explained the pillows that 300 members brought with them into the field. But probably not. This was a comfort-driven team. Comfort was probably the main reason the team leader, a warrant officer, wasn't even present. He didn't like the woods. Also, he would rather use duty hours to engage in nonmilitary business back in Fayetteville. Which, as it turns out, seemed to be fine with most of his men. In true NCO fashion they regarded officers as a hindrance, although this particular warrant officer was probably more like them than not; no one doubted that he would have been carrying his pillow too.

Pillows were the least of it, though, and not that uncommon a sight on other teams. In this particular instance the team sergeant had also brought a Coleman lantern and two team members had tents. This meant there was nothing at all tactical, and nothing the least bit hidden or camouflaged, about their camp. Still, these conveniences paled in comparison with what the team also indulged in.

Imbibing beer while the team was on what was supposed to be a serious training mission was the significant breach. Or was it, given that beer was integral for establishing rapport?

Beer came in the afternoon. First, the team trained. This meant surveying the brow of a short hill as a possible drop zone. It also meant conducting a patrol. The training schedule called for ODA 300 to run two patrols, one to be undertaken during daylight hours, the second to come after dark.

The daylight patrol was a short but extremely hot and sticky 1,500 meters. Ticks all but dripped from the trees. Each of the four team members on patrol walked intently, but none too silently. The fifth remained behind in camp. His daughter had accidentally jammed her finger in his eye the night before so he volunteered to serve as "guard." While the four who did patrol didn't speak, dead leaves, branches, and a forest floor covered with debris gave their passage away. This didn't seem to matter, though. In fact, it may have made for a quicker patrol. No one had to check on his rear very often since it was all too obvious that the first man was being followed by the second, the second by the third, and the third by the fourth.

The point of the patrol was to approach a short bridge spanning a small river. Once the bridge was just a stone's throw away (but still around a curve and out of sight), the team stopped to discuss how they would ambush it. There was no walk-through, which there probably should have been. Just a walk back toward camp, along a barbed wire fence and downwind from a pigsty. As far as the team sergeant was concerned, the mission had been completed: training. He was satisfied with the way the team moved together. Given the pressing heat, no one objected.

But neither did anyone object when we didn't return immediately to camp. First, the team detoured and swung by the farmhouse. The aim was to find out from Mr. Hailey what he would like done the next morning. At least, that seemed to be the team sergeant's intent, though the conversation wound up taking a slightly different turn as two of the team members plucked dry grass to suck on while talking "farm."

As the team members chatted up the farmer, exchanging pleasantries about the day, the weather, the crops, it wasn't long before they came to their only real commonality: the Q Course, and who knew whom and had heard which stories. This, then, introduced gossip, and gossip then evolved into an invitation for beer—which meant needing to go buy some. If the farmer drove, the team's two senior members would buy. A deal was struck, and off the three went in the farmer's pickup truck. And what a deal it was.

By suggesting beer the ODA members hadn't just clinched their good-old-boy status (and the likelihood they would be able to return to the farm), but having to go buy the beer in a store also managed to get them an invitation to store the surplus in one of the farmer's barn-bound refrigerators. Talk about clever. The entire beer-buying episode reaffirmed the team's already entrenched sense that to be clever could prove very rewarding, especially since buying beer also got them out of having to perform morning chores.

Time back at camp to celebrate. What a lazy afternoon. What an even lazier evening. Especially because dinner was no more complicated than heating Meals-Ready-to-Eat (MREs), along with boiling water for that other field staple, Ramen noodles. Hors d'oeuvres were Pringles potato chips.

The conversation wobbled between complaints about wives, who could never seem to understand their husbands whenever they said they wanted to go off after work and do "guy" stuff—which for two of the team members was simply a thinly disguised euphemism for going out to clubs—and complaints about SF, which were far more bitter and unrelenting: SF was becoming too conventionalized, officers were ridiculously mistrusting, there weren't enough trips abroad. The litany was obviously well rehearsed. Officers bore the brunt of the blame, though officers' behavior—when it came right down to it—could itself be blamed on SF having been made its own branch; that's what had really ruined SF.

Then came more specific complaining, about particular officers. The two who came in for the heaviest criticism were both former NCOs; 300 wondered how the junior of the two—their current commander—could be so distrusting of them. What cause did he have, they asked quite seriously in lantern light, sipping beer. But it was the more senior whom they really raked over the coals. The team sergeant could remember this particular colonel when he was just a captain and used to go drinking with his team, though even as a major he was still known for downing beers with NCOs and soliciting their opinions. Clearly something had happened to him in his rise up the ladder. Either he liked the sauce too much (which was one rumor) or he had been brainwashed by higher-ups. Now he was simply a dictator, and not a very inspiring one at that.

The more exercised the team got, the more convinced I grew that they'd really prove their commanders right: there *would* be no night patrol. With all this seditious commentary, why would they even bother? Also, no one seemed to be paying any attention to the time—the patrol was down on the training schedule for 2130—nor did anyone mention an impending patrol at any point during, after, or even well after dinner. Thus, I couldn't help but smile—knowingly—when, at 2120, the team's beer-buying ringleader stood up and made as if to gather up his gear. But that's exactly what he did, and what he expectantly looked at everyone else to join him in doing.

What? No complaining now? I stopped smiling. Suddenly no one even joked about not going on a patrol, although the same team member whose daughter had poked him in the eye again volunteered to guard the camp, this time with me. The lantern light convinced me that the night was too moonless to choose more ticks and webs, with branches thrown in, over sitting in such comfort. As far as I was concerned, my succumbing to comfort was all the team's fault anyway.

Regardless, this turned out to be a fine decision. The four team members moved off and were swallowed up by the dark, and though they seemed to be gone at least an hour, that impression was really just the dark confounding everything. The four were actually back in no time, having ventured only four hundred meters from camp. Even they found the night too dark. Also there were too many gullies, and they were patrolling fine for those four hundred meters. Why continue?

"WHY CONTINUE" WOULD NEVER HAVE BEEN BROACHED ON OTHER teams. For instance, on 309 such a question would be regarded as nothing short of heresy. But for 300 (or at least the dominant members on it) outmaneuvering rather than outperforming the standard was typical. It's what they seemed to practice hardest. It's also what they felt SF was all about. A number of older NCOs in the company remember being taught in the Q Course, "If you ain't cheating you ain't trying." As far as 300 was concerned, that was supposed to epitomize SF. If you got caught you were wrong, but the objective was not to get caught.

Only one relatively recent arrival to the team didn't particularly care for 300's attitude. He would have preferred training honestly and hard. He kept hoping that 300 would get an officer or even a new team sergeant to come in and straighten things out. However, until then—Sergeant Ross also realized—he had little choice. This was the team he was on. As a result, he tried to be a good sport and an amiable team player.

Meanwhile, Sergeant Ross was the only member of 300 that 309 would have readily accepted. In no small measure this was because he seemed to share 309's ethic and always made a point of telling 309 members that he wished his team was more like theirs. For 309, his disgruntlement confirmed their own impressions: that hands down they were the better team.

So much for teams' internally consistent logic.

Not only did 300 and 309 exhibit radically different attitudes but excelling by beating the system meant two completely different things to each team. From 300's point of view camaraderie was best achieved through clever play; for 309 camaraderie grew out of hard work. Nor was there anything reconcilable about these two views. Each team strove to make a name for itself in a markedly different fashion, which also meant that the men on each team wound up appearing as though they were of two disparate types—309 was full of ants and 300 was full of grasshoppers—though in reality such typecasting was more situational than carved in stone. Sergeant Ross was proof of this: he would have preferred being on 309 but did fine on 300. As an ideal SF soldier, he had to be able to fit himself to any team.

All SF teams require soldiers who can accelerate from laziness to action, and are clever or devious or serious, depending. Different teams just happen to run with different moods at different times. In a sense they have to. If every team is identically structured, so that on paper all teams are interchangeable, then how else do teams attract commanders' attention except by playing off one another? They have to compete. And blow smoke. Cohesively.

WHILE KC AND STEVE MARKED 309's AXIS OF HIERARCHY—WITH KC both formally and informally the enlisted leader, and Steve low man on the totem pole—the middle was not so settled as the world outside the team room was led to believe. Subtle competition plagued the team, and most of it was provoked by the person who purported to care the least: Greg.

As senior medic on the team, Greg had significant formal status, though he didn't exactly fit the medic stereotype. Medics, who are supposed to be smart, even to the point of being nerdy, can also be laid-back. Some are even said to be spacey. But this was hardly Greg, who was the personification of self-containment in a completely different sense. Greg, in his own mind, lived according to his standards, to hell with what the rest of his teammates thought, though as far as some members of 309 were concerned, this was absurd. Greg wasn't performing in a vacuum; he was always performing against them. Nor did it really matter how much he may have thought he wasn't. If their perception was that he was trying to prove something at their expense, then he should have registered this. That he didn't they regarded as indicative.

The dynamics are complicated, and to get a fix on them requires at least one triangulation: from Chris (309's senior weapons sergeant) to Rob (309's assistant operations sergeant) back to Greg.

AS INTENSE AS GREG WAS, CHRIS WAS ACTUALLY 309's MOST SERIous soldier. Of all the team members he was the least talkative, the least given to horsing around, and yet the most passionate whenever the army did something stupid. He was brawny and blond, young-looking but serious. Chris could easily have been a recruiting standard. It is hard to imagine his having become anything else but a soldier. Not that Chris grew up planning to join the army.

Chris would have preferred to farm. His family moved from a prairie state to the northern Plains when he was ten. By the time he was in the ninth grade the local school population had shrunk so that all twelve grades were housed in the same building. There were twenty-three seniors in his graduating class. Even so he was proud to be president of the local Future Farmers of America. He played football but he also worked for a hog farmer all through school. In fact, that's what he intended to become: a hog farmer. But hog prices fell and instead of being able to farm after graduating, Chris had to work for the local farmers' cooperative, selling feed and fertilizer instead. He also joined the National Guard.

Chris knew he didn't want to go to college. But nothing particularly fired his imagination in vocational school either. He took some classes in refrigeration and heating, but then, after a year in the National Guard, decided he might be better off switching to active duty. Because his National Guard unit was an artillery unit, he slid into active duty through the artillery. He spent his first year in Korea in 1984, with the intention of going airborne at the earliest opportunity. The plan was to join the 82nd, go to Ranger School, then try to join SF, since this seemed to be the natural progression. However, while Chris managed a berth in jump school after Korea and joined the 82nd, where he served a little over a year, a Q Course slot came open before he could get into Ranger School. He thus entered SF before being tabbed as a Ranger. He also wound up in Z Company and on ODA 309 with six of his Q Course classmates.

The thinking at the time (1987) was that building teams by cohorts would strengthen cohesion. Therefore whole clumps of soldiers from the Q Course got sent to teams together. As Chris recollects, this was just short of disastrous. Not only were half of 309's team members suddenly new, but with an incompetent team sergeant, everyone floundered. The new team members were forced to learn almost everything on their own. This was altogether too painful, though in the end, Chris concedes, the team may actually have turned out the better for it. Although also by 1992, only two of those original six teammates were still on 309, so what kind of cohesion had been built?

Quite a bit still existed between Chris and Rob, who by default had become the two longest-lasting members of 309. With everyone else having joined the team since 1988, their seniority lent them considerable weight, separate from rank or position. As opposites, they made a formidable pair; they were so different yet still in agreement about the team.

Rob had dark hair and dark flashing eyes, was gregarious and opinionated, and had grown up a California beach boy. In high school he was a jock. After high school he partied too hard. Ever since he could remember he had always wanted to be a soldier. He distinctly recollects when he was five visiting a family friend who was about to go fight in Vietnam. This made a huge impression on him. He grew up hunting and in the outdoors, and he realized not long after high school that he missed the closeness he had been used to on high school sports teams.

Still, it took a few too many encounters with the law to compel him to enlist. A few too many brawls, a few too many tickets, a mounting record, and he decided to join up. It wasn't the army as opportunity so much as the army as disciplinarian that attracted him. Like Greg, Chris left behind a best friend who never did change. His friend still doesn't have a driver's license and continues to drink and snort away whatever money he earns. Not Rob, who lives in an upscale Fayetteville neighborhood and golfs whenever he can.

Like Chris, Rob didn't initially go Airborne; instead, he was assigned to an engineer unit. It was only when an Airborne recruiter visited the unit that Rob realized he had had options his enlistment recruiter never mentioned. He immediately volunteered for jump school, then wound up in a hard-charging Airborne engineer unit. While he was with this unit, building combat runways along the Honduran-Nicaraguan border, he first encountered SF soldiers. Here was an organization that looked even more hard-charging—and active—than his. As soon as he could he applied.

Thus, 309 wound up with the reserved and determined Chris on the one hand, and the fast-and-loose, self-assured Rob on the other. If they had been husband and wife, the assumption would have been that the marriage was working because the two complemented each other so well. But their accidental pairing probably succeeded because of an even more basic fact: they just didn't compete. Their egos didn't bump, their aptitudes didn't clash, and their goals didn't differ. For both men the goal was always the same: their team had to be the best. No matter how unalike they were in personality, their intent was identical, and their methods for getting what they wanted out of the team more often than not meshed.

They both exuded intensity, but in different ways. As verbally intense as Rob could be, Chris could be just as intensely silent. Whenever he had work to do, Chris would erect a shell around himself; for all intents and purposes, he might as well have been off somewhere, completely incommunicado. He rarely initiated small talk. I never heard him tell a joke. In fact, beyond shop talk the only thing I ever heard Chris gush about was winter in the Dakotas. The cold made a huge impression on him. Otherwise, he was understated, to say the least. Yet he was also incredibly, incomparably dependable. Solid. There.

Rob was much harder to track. Like Chris he was good. But unlike Chris there was nothing tangibly solid about him. Rob was instinctive and volatile. He was also quick, especially at landing on his feet at the spur of the moment. You could rest assured Chris knew what he was doing, yet you also knew that Rob could pull off whatever he was assigned to do.

Part of this ability rested on natural talent—Rob hadn't been a high school athlete for nothing—but part stemmed too from his ability to verbally outmaneuver others. He had a tongue he never hesitated to use. It could be golden, if he needed something, or lashing, when he found someone useless. By sheer dint of personality, Rob was not only more domineering than Chris but more intimidating than anyone else on the team. He actively tried to cow others. The only other individual on the team whom Chris tried to dominate was Steve. It was his responsibility as senior weapons sergeant to groom Steve, the junior weapons sergeant, and Steve needed grooming. However, Chris, like most members of the team, found Steve almost impossible to deal with. Significantly, Rob was not among them. Instead, Rob would have much preferred someone else to disappear: Greg.

Despite being four years Rob's junior and five years younger than Chris, Greg had more time in the army than either of them. With the exception of perhaps KC, Greg also had more experience at squad-sized infantry tactics than any other NCO on 309. However, he was still three years behind Rob and Chris in SF team time. This sometimes led to tension. If you factored in Rob's and Greg's personalities, sparks were bound to fly.

As Rob saw it, Greg's motivation to excel was antagonistic. Greg was always trying to prove he was better than everyone else. What had to irk Rob even more, though, was that often Greg *was* better. Like Rob (and Chris), but in a completely different manner, Greg too was a gifted soldier. He was smart enough to be a medic. But he also excelled at fieldcraft. He was great at land navigation. He was an incredibly accurate shot. He knew how to patrol. He spoke good French. He could think on his feet. And he was an interloper.

Like too-talkative Steve, Greg didn't think twice about voicing his opinion in the team room. The difference between Steve and Greg, though, was that Greg invariably knew what he was talking about and he never talked about himself. Instead, he made cogent comments about tactics, or offered creative suggestions for training. This made it much harder for Rob to ignore him, especially when Greg managed to sway other people. Instead of being able to brush Greg off, Rob found himself having to argue. So did others at times, which was fine with Greg. After all, arguing allowed him to test his verbal skills, just as running hard proved his physical stamina. Arguing invigorated him, which only infuriated Rob, who couldn't stand to be baited. But basically Rob just didn't like Greg.

And Greg knew this. Unlike Steve, Greg was adept at reading people. Because Rob was both the assistant operations sergeant (second to KC) and such a dominant personality, it was easy for him to make Greg's life more difficult than it needed to be. But again unlike Steve, who strove to prove himself through talk, Greg's personality drove him to work harder, which further tested Rob. Rob, in his own mind, was nothing if not a team player. And here was Greg, who played by some but not all of Rob's rules.

SF was personal for Rob. He could get just as worked up about everything bad that was happening to it as Chris could. At the same time, he was brutal whenever anyone who didn't belong dared to criticize the world's greatest military organization. Rob was a true loyalist. And as an SF loyalist there was nothing he was more true to than 309. Indeed, to observe Rob and be around him among men from other teams was to agree Rob *was* 309. The problem was, in the team room so was everyone else. And to Rob's fellow team members, Greg was turning out to be just as indispensable. All of which made for a delicate balance.

Greg worked hard, even if he played differently, and met Rob's standards here. Also, according to the professionalism Rob championed, team integrity was everything. Thus, much as Rob might try to undercut Greg, he could never completely cut him out. He had to tolerate him just as Chris had to tolerate Steve.

Fortunately, this balance was made less delicate and far more stable by all 309 members' acceding to the ethos of hard work. Otherwise, the team could have been shattered if any other commonality had been used as a litmus test. As much as it helped to wear the same uniform and share the same tab, prescribed conformity was hardly enough. Mandated similarities could never achieve for the team what it most needed and what it alone could fashion for itself: cohesion. This would be *the* necessity in combat and what, paradoxically, only survival afterward could probably guarantee. However, in the absence of such potentially costly trial-by-fire testing, the team needed other ways to get all twelve members to feel that what they shared was more significant than what they did not.

Falling into swamps every now and then was one such technique. Being cold and wet and hungry could also work. Temporarily suffering while then succeeding on a practice mission was probably ideal. And yet, simply the practice of practicing could build up enough of a shared stock of experiences to give team members plenty to talk about without having to delve into all their differences.

Clearly, too, the more the team trained together, the more team members grew used to having to accommodate one another. To patrol well didn't mean you had to like whomever you were walking ahead of or behind, only that you felt comfortable trusting one another. In the end this meant knowing when to both put up *and* shut up, something that only Steve didn't (yet) know how to do. For instance, just because Rob and Greg were perpetually at odds didn't mean that Rob wouldn't count on Greg to save his life, or that Greg would think twice before doing so.

In this sense, compartmentalization and cohesion were flip sides of the same coin. And the coin continually got flipped.

8 Exercise on the Coast

EARLY DECEMBER AND ODA 309 FINDS ITSELF ON THE NORTH Carolina coast. Only hours away from Fayetteville, the team has temporarily set up shop in an altogether different setting—a windowless room with thirty-five Marine MPs, none of whom looks particularly thrilled to be present.

The ten-day plan is for 309 to teach these Marine MPs as if the MPs are foreign soldiers, which in a certain sense they are. Not only do Marines speak a different language (full of foreign acronyms), present a different bearing (stiff), and project a different character (sullen yet gung-ho) than army troops, but these particular Marines are not even foot soldiers. Most haven't fired a crew-served weapon since basic training. Certainly they haven't spent a night in the woods recently. Consequently, they are anything but skilled at patrolling or setting up ambushes, the two things 309 is at Marine Corps Air Station (MCAS) New River to teach them. Actually, 309's purpose is fourfold. First, to teach the Marines something new; second, to teach them something useful; third, to practice teaching; fourth, to seek to build rapport with the corps.

There are benefits all around. The more the MPs can be made to think in terms of how to patrol and how to ambush, the better they will understand how to defend their air station (or any other installation they might be assigned to). Essentially, 309 is providing counterinsurgency training. This is exactly what they might teach troops in Niger or Guinea or Sierra Leone, although in Jacksonville, North Carolina, their subjects all speak and understand English, which means it is really style and substance, not cross-cultural communication, that team members will practice.

SF is hoping to build ties not just at the individual or even team level. Given the military drawdown and tight budgets, Stateside training opportunities—never mind overseas missions—are increasingly limited. The Marine stomping grounds of Camp Lejeune and MCAS New River are only two hours from Ft. Bragg. They offer even swampier training conditions. More significantly, they get teams away from Fayetteville-area woods and domestic preoccupations, and out from under the flagpole. The thinking is that with distance put between the teams and all the layers of command at Ft. Bragg, teams can operate more independently, more as if they are conducting real-world missions, and more as if they might.

Usually, such independence is the biggest bonus to being away from Ft. Bragg. However, for this particular exercise elements of battalion command have also decamped to Lejeune. Because the entire battalion is still in Green Cycle—a period of intensive testing and training—officers and staff are also being assessed. This means they continue to breathe down the necks of team members because evaluators are judging them. Then, too, because most of the exercise has SF teams engaged in special reconnaisance and direct action missions against Marines, all sorts of additional pressures and interservice rivalries assert themselves.

Fortunately for 309, it is the only team conducting foreign internal defense and working at MCAS New River. The rest of the battalion, including battalion command, is ensconced at Lejeune, which, while essentially adjacent to MCAS New River, is still just physically distant enough. Battalion staff members are so preoccupied with supervising the missions in their immediate vicinity that 309 might as well be in another country. In this regard, nothing could please Captain Tucker or KC more.

The team has prepared hard for this mission. For a week, team members took turns burning up the two computers in the team room, as each soldier outlined the lessons he would teach the MPs. The lessons themselves are drawn from manuals, which the military produces for everything. For instance, at the battalion assembly prior to departure for Camp Lejeune, the Headquarters Company first sergeant instructed the deploying teams about the appropriate etiquette for the Marine base, and item 'i' on his list was FLUSH.

As for the lessons the team will teach, each is outlined in excruciating detail, with every step carefully spelled out for such things as weapons assembly, disassembly, and remedial action. Nothing is left to improvisation. Although each soldier could doubtless perform the task he'll be lecturing on without looking at a manual, lesson plan, or probably anything at all, lesson plans are vital to teaching standard operating procedures. Standardization is not only formalized but formulaic; there are even procedures for how to proceed.

Once the lesson plans are finally typed and the course binders full, there's the briefback to prepare.

Briefbacks are the sine qua non of all SF missions. And again, there's a procedure. Often a briefback, which is the team's presentation of its plan to commanders, can make or break its reputation. It is not uncommon for commanders to assign the same mission to a number of teams to be able to choose the team they consider the best prepared. The competition this creates—to devise the best plan—especially if teams go into isolation, only ratchets up everyone's levels of anxiety. Nor does it matter whether the competition is real or just simulated for the sake of an exercise. The intensity in the team rooms on such occasions can't be overstated.

If the mission is classified the team has to be isolated. The men are kept incommunicado and confined in close quarters, working around the clock. Contact with anyone from outside the team, other than commanders and two NCOs who act in shifts as a liaison, is forbidden. The team has only itself to consult, only its own members to brainstorm with, and only its own good judgment to rely on. All of which becomes exposed during the briefback. But as if that is not nerve-wracking enough, briefbacks are never about the plan alone.

Commanders have to count on the briefback to gauge a team's

readiness. No colonel or major will be going into the field with the team. Thus, commanders don't just have to be sold on the team's plan. During a briefback the team room, uniforms, haircuts, how soldiers hold themselves, and their level of confidence all receive scrutiny.

As for why 309 is taking its unclassified, "foreign" internal defense mission to MCAS New River so seriously, how everyone comports himself during this briefback can help determine whether 309 will be chosen for a real-world mission. Therefore, it's as if 309 had been told to prepare for a life-and-death, the-nation-depends-on-you, top-secret endeavor. For the team, the immediate mission—convincing superiors—is as-if.

The team conducts run-throughs on top of run-throughs. The order goes like this: as team leader, Captain Tucker will speak first, describing the mission assignment and the course of action chosen, with Steve (junior weapons sergeant) standing by to flip explanatory transparencies on the overhead projector. Chris (the senior weapons sergeant, and acting assistant operations sergeant) will next list the personnel assigned to the mission. KC (the team, or operations, sergeant) will go into greater operational depth. Greg's job (as senior medic) is to outline medical preparedness and to reassure commanders that everyone's "preparation for overseas replacement" (POR, including individual wills, powers-of-attorney for spouses, etc.) and immunizations are up-to-date, and that he knows local procedures for evacuations and where to find medical facilities. Mark (the senior communications sergeant) will discuss how the team will make commo, before turning the lectern back to Captain Tucker, who will finish with issues that have yet to be resolved.

In between practicing the briefback the team room, which is kept clean anyway, is reorganized and scrubbed so that it's *really* clean. Overpowering cleansers are poured on the floor. Glass-covered desks are wiped spotless. Two different maps are pinned on a bank of wooden wall lockers, temporarily turning the team room into a mini operations center, while a more detailed map of the MCAS New River area is placed under glass at the table where the colonel will sit. Lesson plans and the operations order are neatly set out in individual binders for him to flip through. Off to one side another table holds a slide projector as a sample training aid, along with a stack of pocket-sized Ranger guides that the team has managed to procure as gifts for the MPs.

"Bells and whistles" accounts for at least some of what the team must do to impress higher command, while of course bells and whistles is also what higher command wants the team to use to impress the Marines.

Yet no matter how many times the team runs through the briefback, and no matter how spit-and-polished the room, Y Company's major and sergeant major (who have been assigned to oversee 309 during this exercise) can still find fault. In the dress rehearsal they attend, they point to any number of things the colonel might object to. For instance, KC shouldn't describe the transport and transit route in such detail. Better that the training schedule be flashed on the screen in calendar format rather than presented orally. In speaking, team members should substitute the word "soldier" for "guy." The map under glass should also be better highlighted. There are typos in the lesson plans . . .

This critique comes twenty-four hours before the colonel is due to arrive for the final, formal briefback. Clearly, the team's work isn't done.

Already Captain Tucker fears his ulcer is acting up. He blames it on his wrestling days, when he had to lose weight under pressure. But everybody who watches him eat isn't so sure. His diet is fairly consistent: popcorn and Diet Coke, Diet Coke and peanut butter crackers. During this past week there may not have been even this much variety.

Still, despite all the work that seems to remain, the team doesn't deviate from its own training schedule. In the morning it meets at 0630 to perform physical training, then it's straight to the computers. By 1100 most of the editing changes have been made. Then it's time for military cosmetics. Boots have to be buffed. Pressed uniforms will be put on. Captain Tucker will shave a second time. Even Major Geoffries, the company commander, who only just flew in from a site survey three time zones away, will put in an appearance after first going home to change into uniform.

In between all these tasks just enough dead time remains to keep everyone nervous. Chris tries to figure out what a raise will do to his take-home pay, given the latest pay scale in *The Army Times*. Greg unwraps his usual Tuesday sandwich: liverwurst. He also fantasizes: he'd like one day to jump out of an airplane without a parachute and have someone hand him one on the drop down, which, of course, he would then put on and manage to pull open only at the last possible moment. Alternatively, he jokes that maybe it would be just as good to get dropped from an airplane with a hang glider in pieces and have to assemble it while falling. The problem with adrenalin rushes, he points out, is that you only want more.

Except those the colonel generates. The colonel is not well liked.

Still, after all the nervousness, the briefback at 1600, with the colonel in attendance, is the smoothest and least problematic yet. No one misspeaks or stumbles. In fact, the only person who comes in for any critical remarks is the colonel's own logistics officer (S-4), who can't adequately answer one of the team's questions.

It is all somewhat anticlimactic.

Indeed, after the fact, all the preparations that went into this briefback seem a gargantuan waste of time, especially because it is virtually guaranteed that the mission won't go quite as the team wants it to. No matter how carefully things have been presented, reality will railroad the best of 309's intentions. So why go to so much trouble in the first place?

Again, because the briefback serves more purposes than just the most obvious. Clearly the colonel takes measure of the team during 309's presentations. But beyond just the politics of this display, having to prepare for the briefback has energized the team. Like all good rituals, it has also separated the practice of routine from the fact that the team is about to do something else. Everyone has refocused.

Minds have been synchronized, if not to specific tasks then to how individual tasks will need to fit together. In this regard, 309 has acted no less purposefully than a team preparing for a mission abroad. Later in the year, when ODA 308 gears up for a foreign internal defense mission to Africa, it will go through exactly the same procedures. Only two things get done differently. All of 308's lesson plans must be translated into French, because it will be training a French-speaking force. And intelligence briefings the team receives before the mission are classified, because the team is embarking on a real-world assignment. Perhaps, too, 308 does buzz with somewhat more excitement. But the investment of energy by both teams is virtually identical. In part this reflects professionals behaving professionally. In part, though, it stems from 309's vision. The assumption is that the better it handles itself on this MCAS New River assignment, the more likely the colonel will be to pick it for something else. This certainly has proven true to 309 often enough to continue justifying the belief.

There may be no team that thinks otherwise. Every team can read a pattern into its assignments. For instance, that 309 is the only team to be given a foreign internal defense mission away from the main body at Camp Lejeune must signify something. When later 309 is the only team sent to Florida on a direct action mission as part of a larger army exercise, that, too, convinces the team that it is the best in the company.

However, at the same time, those teams conducting special reconnaisance and direct action missions at Camp Lejeune are similarly convinced that they have been chosen for missions against the Marines because *they* are the best prepared, while teams that aren't going to Camp Lejeune but are instead being sent out from under the battalion's control (to other locations) read their assignments as indicative of *their* being the best. It also goes without saying that when teams don't get assignments they can read in a self-fulfilling way, they gripe about the injustice that's been done them. Most often, though, their readings smack of self-reverential credit and only rarely self-critical blame.

Because teams aren't privy to higher command's decisions, the assumption is that all decisions are based on one of only two things: impressions of the team leader and of the team as a whole. Teams often don't realize that far less revolves around them than they would like to think. Often they read too much into decisions. More often they just don't know enough, not having all the information higher command does. Actually, information cuts all ways. Often ODA members have more information about their peers than commanders do, and don't realize that partial information can seem more than sufficient from a battalion commander's point of view. The real problem is that perspectives from within the team room and from on high are rarely the same.

Whether battalion and group staffs realize the extent to which second-guessing takes place in team rooms is unclear. Not a great deal of honest information flows up or down the chain of command. Up the chain flattery seems to color everything. Down the chain "need to know" continually narrows what is disseminated. Because soldiers follow orders, higher command doesn't have to worry about what they think, or completely fill them in. Higher command doesn't need to worry about what teams think either; teams, too, follow orders. From command's point of view, motivating teams thus requires little effort.

Whether or not higher command sees the effects of its manipulation of the information flow, it works to commanders' advantage to have all teams thinking that decisions *are* made as arbitrarily as teams assume, dependent on personality and displays of readiness. Otherwise, how could officers keep everyone marching forward on the same treadmill—and pressing uniforms, polishing boots, and doing other chores that don't reflect how a team can operate in the woods or in a classroom full of conscripts? Explaining little to NCOs encourages them to read into the situation. If their assumption is that there has to be a way to stand out by edging just beyond what is ordered, this means that the best teams perpetually raise the standards of perfection just a little bit higher. Which inflates expectations. Which raises the stakes. Which is good—for command. After all, if teams were left to think that being rewarded were simply a matter of meeting the standard, hierarchy would quickly lose its edge.

The system as it has evolved is remarkably clever.

AT 2130 THE DAY BEFORE ODA 309 IS DUE TO TEACH ITS FIRST classes, team members are on the third deck (floor) of an empty MCAS New River Marine barracks, still busy shining boots and readying uniforms for the morning. Normally no one would wear a starched uniform, and boots are polished only periodically before inspections (or briefbacks). But every effort is being made to impress the Marines. To that end Chris and Steve also take a final run through their lessons. Intentionally or not, the team is bringing out the big guns first.

After a brief flurry of introductions at 0830 in a dimly lit function room, no-nonsense Chris gets right down to business. He is matter-of-fact but clear in explaining how to disassemble and reassemble the squad automatic weapon (SAW). Sam, the junior engineer, is his assistant; as Chris explains, Sam performs the actual functions on a SAW set up on a long table at the front of the room. Once he has finished, the thirty-five or so Marines, who have self-organized into three squads, gather around each of three guns for hands-on training, with pairs of ODA members standing by to assist them. These are the weapons the Marines are scheduled to fire tomorrow. Only two haven't handled a SAW before.

The next class is Steve's—on M-60s—with Dan, the senior engineer, as his assistant. Despite all his self-assuredness in the team room, Steve's clearly nervous in front of the MPs. Also his voice doesn't have Chris's timbre. But team members are encouraging. This is one of his first turns at teaching with the team. Presumably he'll learn. In fact, it is far more important to the team that he learn than that the Marines do.

After lunch Chris introduces the Marines to a still larger crew-served weapon, the M2 .50-caliber machine gun. Again, the MPs get hands-on assembly and disassembly training. Already I'm not sure how they'll keep the machine guns straight, particularly because there is a fourth gun (the Mark-19) to cover before moving on to the final class of the day, which is Mark lecturing about the ANPRC-77 radio.

Fortunately, most of the Marines seem familiar with this radio. While Chris and Steve taught their weapons classes from the front of the room, with a stationary gun as prop, Mark roams around with radio in hand. Also, Chris belted out his delivery. At one point he shouted as someone nodded off in front of him, "If you're going to go to sleep, stand up and move to the side of the class; I'm not going to sleep, I don't expect anyone else to either." In the days to follow this turns out to be one of the team's standard admonishments. But Mark, unlike Chris, never raises his voice. If anything, he speaks too softly and his tone is edged with sarcasm. He is in complete, perhaps too much, control of the material. Also the radio isn't a weapon. He is not explaining assembly or disassembly. Consequently, there seems no particular order to what he says. But his presentation is still compelling; his sarcasm keeps everyone attuned.

As the ten days unfold it becomes more than apparent that no two team members teach anything alike. Each has a different style, some more riveting than others. For instance, KC always begins with a joke. But while KC is a great raconteur in small groups, Dan is the team's most inspired instructor. He's certainly had the most practice, having been a Ranger instructor for fourteen months. But even without so much teaching under his belt, Dan would still be great; he's simply a gifted teacher. A lot of his appeal has to do with his incessant negativity. This makes him sardonic and especially keen at rhetorical flourishes. For instance, "synchronize your watches" is twisted into "circumcise your watches," which keeps the students awake. Of course, the MPs might not learn the most from Dan. He, like Mark, may be too familiar with his own material. But no one dozes.

Beneath such stylistic differences, there is still tremendous uniformity. Much of this emerges from the military method, which is overkill. Walk past any army classroom and invariably there is a slide or overhead projector. Whatever the instructor is saying is usually also simulcast on a screen. Everything is not only spelled out but spelled out as if the students are idiots. It is nothing less than teaching by the book, a perhaps very necessary but still unbelievably boring enterprise that systematizes education.

Three things save the MPs from complete asphyxiation. First, they are getting hands-on training. Second, none of this is theory alone; the MPs know they will be out on the ranges firing the guns and in the woods expected to use what they are being taught within days. Third, some of the team members play the expected SF role during the hands-on training. They banter, talk Gulf War, answer questions about belonging to an elite.

Sam especially warms to this role. For him, SF is about doing those things that other soldiers don't get the opportunity to do. This is what made the Gulf War so exhilarating. It had nothing to do with combat—which Sam didn't see—but with being in Kuwait, getting to know wealthy Saudis and Kuwaitis, being entertained in their homes, firing round upon round of ammunition from captured weapons on Kuwait's beaches. For lots of reasons, Sam would probably be happier in Delta Force than SF, a possibility he's seriously contemplating; he's a consummate urbanite and the woods don't particularly thrill him. He's certainly the only team member who will admit that he likes spending time in Fayetteville's mall, and he's also the only team member who has yet to marry. Perhaps this explains why he drives a black muscle car and why his wallet contains a list of the *Playboy* issues he's missing; he's a serious collector. Or perhaps his still doing these things explains why he's not married.

One irony that surfaces at MCAS New River is that though Sam is not a central figure on the team and doesn't fit any of the SF stereotypes, the MPs take to him over the rest of 309. In part this must be because he unconsciously sells them what they expect to hear from an SF soldier: bending rules in exotic locales and being treated well to boot. Of course, they've never heard Sam in the team room, where he continually complains about how little 3rd Group gets to do. One reason Sam left SF and the army once already was because 10th Group (where he was initially assigned) was never deployed. As he puts it, it was too much "should'a, could'a, would'a." From his perspective, 3rd Group is turning out to be little different. Meanwhile, Sam manages to get away with complaining, despite KC's policy, because the team's assumption is that all New Yorkers complain. This is Sam's right, if not his duty. Funny, then, that at MCAS New River he turns out to be SF's biggest booster. It's interesting how the team works in this wider context.

Another dynamic begins to shift around Greg. But this has less to do with the Marines than with who isn't with the team. Significantly, Rob is absent. He and Peter, the team's junior medic, are in Africa with a mobile training team from another company. Also, this is the first time in months Dan has been back with 309 and not in school. All of which makes for a new mix.

Along with Chris and Rob, Dan represents the veteran core of 309, and significantly, neither Chris nor Dan shares Rob's animus toward Greg. As a result, Greg begins to come into his own. Perhaps, too, because Rob (who is his second in command) is away, and/or because Chris and Dan accept him, or because Greg works hard at working well with Chris and Dan, KC also begins to warm toward Greg. This may be because Greg himself is making a concerted effort toward KC, although I suspect it stems in part from Greg and KC just happening to be in sync. In many regards they probably think more alike than any other two members of the team. At other times this has made for tension, but during this exercise it seems to bring them closer.

Yet a third element in how the team is getting along is Hugh. He's the team's assessor, drawn from a different battalion for this exercise, which means he's an utter unknown. However, he quickly becomes all too well known and is a type that 309 can't countenance. He's an embarrassment. Even haunting. No one on 309 wants to be anything like Hugh when he reaches Hugh's station in life, which isn't very elevated. He's an old sergeant first-class (E-7). Despite the "Killing Is My Profession" tattoos running up and down both his arms, none of his superiors thought well enough of him to promote him to a worthier rank. With more than two decades in the army, he should be a sergeant major (E-9). Also, after eighteen and a half years in SF, he should know better. Fellow SF soldiers are hard to impress and stories alone never cut it.

But Hugh pours out his 201, or personnel, file anyway, detailing where he's been assigned, what he's done, how many schools he's been to, why he's no longer a team sergeant (his knees are shattered). Whenever possible he uses El Salvador as a touchstone. In El Salvador they had no blackboards when they taught in the jungle. In El Salvador the team used parachute silk instead. In El Salvador they taught ambushes with real ambushes. In El Salvador the soldiers they were teaching were engaged in real fighting.

While all this may be true—SF soldiers did see action in El Salvador—no one on 309 is particularly enthralled. At first the team feigns polite interest. After all, Hugh will be evaluating them. But Hugh's storytelling grows tiresome. Indeed, the challenge for 309 becomes avoiding individual sessions with him, especially when he's been drinking.

KC has forbidden drinking, but the very first night at the air station Hugh purchases a personal liquor supply. This creates even more distance. Hugh is sleeping in the bay with the team and is dependent on 309 for transportation; there's no escape. But there's little connection. There's even less when, during the first few days at the station, Hugh, in his garrulous way, finds Marine gunny sergeants to chat with. At one point this creates a problem—he's talked too much—and KC has to forcefully remind him that he's there as an evaluator, not as an intermediary between the team and the Marines. So much for Hugh's acceptance by 309, though Hugh may not be quite so much of an out-of-touch has-been-who-never-was as they imagine.

For one, he's enamored with the team. He claims 309 is one of the most squared away ODAs he's seen. This is apparent to him the very first afternoon of classes, when KC and Captain Tucker are pulled aside and told that the range they had organized on Camp Lejeune for the following day (Thursday) has to be canceled. The plan had been for the Marines to be able to fire the machine guns they were learning about while the lessons were still fresh. But now something else would have to be improvised. After a lot of juggling, Monday's radio classes are shifted to Thursday morning, the Marines get Thursday afternoon off, Friday will be spent on a range at Ft. Bragg as planned, and Saturday the MPs will be out on the Camp Lejeune range to make up for not shooting there tomorrow. Hugh is quite impressed. The team has not only rolled with the punches but come up with something workable in very short order.

Nor does his opinion of 309 change during the training. At least one other mix-up occurs that the team manages to straighten out without cost. Steve forgets to load cradles for the Mark-19s Friday morning. He realizes this during the drive to Ft. Bragg but by the time he does so it's too late to turn back; the cradles are sitting in the arms room at the air station. Fortunately, after a number of frantic phone calls, Steve locates substitutes at Ft. Bragg. The team is actually pleased he's made this mistake. Maybe he will have learned something. Again, no tempers are lost and no one acts as though this glitch will bring about the end of the world.

Still, as much as both of these two unplanned occurrences prove how adept 309 is at improvisation, Hugh may actually be judging the team according to an altogether different standard, namely, his own for what constitutes a real team—clannishness. At the end of the week, when various Marine sergeants herd the MPs and team members together for group photos, Hugh is conspicuously not included. He philosophizes, as though his exclusion were fine: the team is a team and while they are hospitable to outsiders you still know you aren't part of the team. As Hugh puts it, "In five or six years when one of the members of 309 looks at a copy of this photo he'll say 'Yeah, there's Dan and Steve, and who's this guy?' 'Oh just some evaluator we had.'" Hugh knows they won't remember him, which is how he rationalizes his exclusion. As he further explains, team bonds have to be as exclusive as they are inclusive. Perhaps.

But Hugh seems to be engaging in a bit of mythologizing himself, and he is not the only one. On 309, Mark, the communications sergeant, is also consistently sentimental about team unity. Greg and Steve and Sam, on the other hand, aren't, which already says something about what bonds might or might not mean. For instance, there are friendships and then there are relationships. There are also situational bonds, working bonds, and nonnegotiable bonds. The latter come with combat. What 309 develops at MCAS New River are among the former—situational and working bonds.

ON THE FRIDAY MORNING DRIVE TO THE .50 CALIBER RANGE AT FT. Bragg, Greg, Chris, and Dan share the open, unroofed cab of a lumbering army transport truck. It's their job to haul the ammunition for the Marines, who stay warm and cozy in a bus. To call it morning, though, isn't exactly accurate. It is still dark out when we head to Ft. Bragg, and the temperature is well below freezing. That's without a windchill factor. It's impossible to know how cold it is for Greg, Chris, and Dan. They're virtually speechless by the time the convoy arrives at Range 44, two hours after leaving MCAS New River. However, once they have thawed out they begin joking about the ride, and for the remainder of the exercise regard themselves as the Three Compancheros. At least once a day they have to be in enough physical proximity to recall the bond forged that morning, and to mind-meld. Greg even develops a special handshake for them.

By definition such behavior automatically excludes the rest of the team, but this is as much by default as it is intended. Captain Tucker can't be included, owing to his rank. Neither can KC. Mark and Sam would never have voluntarily subjected themselves to riding in the truck, which Greg insisted on doing, so the only person who might feel left out is Steve. But he already knows he's dispensable; he knows Chris wouldn't have wanted him in the cab. In the end, the Three Compancheros may not really signify all that much, though the trio does add humor. And this humor is not exclusive; anyone can laugh at Greg's handshake.

Invariably, humor winds up making bonds far more tolerable that might otherwise be only just workable. It's the leavening in professionalism and one of the unsung talents most good soldiers must have.

EVENINGS ARE THE ONLY TIME THAT TEAM MEMBERS RELAX, BUT not truly even then. The first few nights are devoted largely to preparing for the next day's classes. Afterward whoever has been working in the portion of the bay the team has turned into its storage area cum office usually drifts into conversation, signaling that work is over. But the conversation is almost always shoptalk. It's the most intense the night the team returns from the epic-making (Three Companchero) trip to Ft. Bragg, when everyone is still keyed up enough that storytelling goes on until bedtime. It starts with talk about who reads what; KC likes prisoner-of-war stories. Everyone's read Nick Rowe's *Five Years to Freedom,* about a young SF officer taken prisoner and held for five years in Vietnam before managing to escape. Praise for the book immediately brings up SERE school.

Greg especially wonders about SERE school. He and Steve are slated to attend shortly. Chris, Mark, and KC have already been through it. Sam has no desire to.

SERE stands for survival, evasion, resistance, escape. In nineteen days soldiers learn as much as can be thrown at them about such techniques at a center fittingly named after Nick Rowe, located at Camp Mackall.

Under the Special Warfare School umbrella, SF and Ranger instructors start SERE school students off with survival skills and in short order cover a broad range of topics. They whizz through survival medicine, walk students past field-expedient shelters, demonstrate a whole series of useful rope-and-knot tricks, teach survival fishing, distinguish between edible and deadly plants, rub sticks together to make fire, and discuss how to make field-expedient weapons and tools, how to signal, how to manage water crossings, and how to prepare fish and game. Some of the teaching is classroom lecture, though much is show-and-tell outdoors and, as with all Special Operations schools, there is hands-on learning. Students get to do their own surviving both before and after the course slides into the topic of evasion, which quickly blurs into how to plan resistance and escape.

After nine days of being lectured to and presented with doable tasks, the real test begins. Students are about to experience having to evade and resist. They're turned loose to briefly survive and try to avoid capture in the woods around Camp Mackall. But regardless of how well they've learned what they've been taught, capture is a foregone conclusion. Everyone has to be captured; captivity is the only way the school can teach students the dos and don'ts of being a POW—the real purpose of SERE school. Experientially, of course.

While a lot of what the school teaches in this section is grounded in the Southeast Asian POW experience, it is also classified. SERE school instructors can't describe it, nor should SERE school graduates. Nevertheless, the impact of SERE on most of the soldiers who go through it is such that its effects hardly stay secret. For many participants it's a brutal, miserable experience. Interrogations bring them so close to the edge of hate that years later they talk about how they would like to get their hands on their interrogators. Also, people tend to be ravenous by the time they're released from "prison." Depending on the time of year, students lose up to ten or twelve pounds in just a matter of days.

Considering what does get out about SERE school—it's punishing and unpleasant—it's easy to understand why there are two diametrically opposed schools of thought about it. A lot of soldiers consider SERE school invaluable. Others want no part of it. For the first group SERE school has an amazing demonstration effect. The classified portion—when soldiers are treated as prisoners of war—convinces many that they never want to be captured alive, but on the off-chance that they do wind up in enemy hands, they trust that SERE school will have taught them a few techniques to make captivity somewhat more bearable, like the simple trick of falling from their chair to catch a glimpse of their interrogator's face.

As for the second group of soldiers, their imaginations may already be vivid enough. Their attitude is that no school can simulate real torture. Nor do they feel any great need to play at suffering. Their response to being ribbed about not wanting to go through SERE school is that if one of the lessons is to find out what they are made of, whether they are strong or weak, and under what conditions they might or might not break, why know now? If the time comes, they'll find out. What's the purpose of identifying their breaking point before the fact? And in at least one sense they consider the school bogus. No matter how diabolical school interrogators might be, the school still sticks to a schedule. Every soldier going in knows he will come out—and within a set amount of time. This, for critics of the school, means that the harshest reality of being a captive can't possibly be realized. *The* terror—of not knowing whether you might be released—is the terror SERE just can't duplicate, so any effect on self-confidence has to be hollow.

Listening to Chris, KC, Mark, and Sam debate the usefulness of going through SERE training, Greg and Steve aren't quite sure what to expect. Chris remembers freezing the entire time. Mark describes someone as tall as he (at well over six feet) who was the only person who really scared him, not because of his size but the evil way he used to squint. Greg's biggest worry is that he will lose his patience and hit someone. The school's promise of discomfort and suffering, which is one reason Sam wouldn't go (why volunteer to be miserable?), isn't what concerns Greg. Which makes it all the more apropos to remember that it was Sam who dubbed Greg Sensei. Perhaps Sam already has all the wisdom he needs.

Talk about SERE school leads right into talk about the Q Course, the one experience that all SF soldiers share. This is KC's opportunity to hold court, about his days as an instructor there and what he used to do as G chief in Phase 3 (prior to the development of Phase 13). The team has already heard many of his stories. There's the one about building an altar to a fallen hero who was gored by a giant buck he was trying to kill to feed his ODA. And the one about the squad KC directed to a nearby stream as their latrine; he wanted to see whether or not the ODA's medics would tell him he couldn't allow men to urinate in drinking water. Or the one about getting candidates to sniff stream water at midnight, to see whether they could tell how far the nearest camp was.

KC describes how, routinely, he used to tell officers one thing during Robin Sage and NCOs something different to get them arguing; he did this to teach the candidates how easy it was to turn against one another. Then there was the time . . .

Team members are still running five miles in the morning prior to classes. No one has to go to sleep at 2200, but the stories end so everyone can.

ON OTHER NIGHTS TEAM MEMBERS READ OR WATCH A SMALL portable television. The second-most animated discussion of the trip occurs during a *Star Trek* episode. I comment that *Star Trek* is a male-oriented soap opera. No, they insist, *Star Trek* is just science fiction. As if to prove just how engaging the science is, Steve asks what would happen to headlights if you had them on in a vehicle traveling faster than the speed of light, which brings up relativity, which affords me the perfect opening. I'm curious: when would everyone most like to live if he could project himself back in time? A commercial for the movie *Bugsy* is airing as Mark says he would enjoy the big band era. Sam's choice is the '30s and '40s, when the "family," and he makes himself sound like a mafioso, was "the family." Just days ago Greg and KC had been talking about how they would have wanted to be frontiersmen, pushing the edge of the envelope. KC explained this by saying something I'd heard a number of other SF soldiers express: what a great time it must have been when you could take the law into your own hands. Tonight, though, KC decides he should have fought in the Civil War. Then he could have affected the course of history. This is a thinly veiled comment on race relations, though, more specifically still, it is a reference to the team's relation to race on MCAS New River.

9 Team Dynamics

THERE WAS NOTHING CASUAL ABOUT THE WAY IN WHICH THE TEAM strolled into the enlisted mess hall its first day at MCAS New River. Despite how commonplace green berets are on Ft. Bragg, they're a novelty on most Marine bases. But then, so are soldiers in army uniforms and jump boots. Perhaps that explained why everyone on the team acted more than just a little self-conscious as they filed in. Team members knew they were being sized up. As for how the Marines were processing what they saw, it wasn't hard for me to imagine them thinking: so these are Green Berets, they don't look so tough. And actually, they don't.

No one on the team pumps enough iron to have lost a neck. No one looks like the bodybuilding hulks who play them in the movies. Nor do camouflage fatigues, worn by members of all services, accentuate anything about SF soldiers that might be different, or special, or unique. Indeed, battle dress uniforms achieve just the opposite effect, so that all there is to go on is how SF soldiers hold themselves. Do these guys move like Green Berets (as if anyone knows how Green Berets should move)?

Yet I noticed as 309 joined the food line that everyone *was* moving with attitude. Team members *were* walking as if they knew they were now in a movie, and briefly they confused me.

From time to time I have to remind myself that ODA members really are capable of death and destruction, and that when they talk tough, they are perfectly capable of backing up what they say. On a number of occasions, both on the field and outside work altogether, I've seen Special Forces soldiers angry. Not just peeved or frustrated, but barely controllably angry. They've gone right up to the edge of physical violence, to that point where they can still verbalize a warning though their eyes are actually saying much more. They're cold and completely focused. And they're compartmentalizing whomever they're facing. Dismemberment? Disfigurement? Dislocation? Distance is what their adversary better seek.

It's neither size nor physical strength but the focus and intensity SF soldiers are capable of that is the most frightening. Taking the entire, camouflage-wrapped package into consideration makes the restraint ODA members generally project all the more impressive. If you're trained to be lethal, it must be tempting to allow yourself to be carried over the edge into violence, especially when there is safety in numbers and you know team members will back you up. But this is exactly what the training also disallows. ODAs are not just gaggles of males with something to prove.

From 309's perspective this is in sharp contrast to what they have to sit through on a daily basis in the Marines' enlisted mess hall.

Despite initial stares no one directs a single comment at the team. Nor does anyone say anything about them that team members can overhear. Instead, what the soldiers find offensive is the behavior of certain groups in the mess hall, groups that tend to be almost exclusively comprised of young black males. From the team's perspective they're behaving way too typically: too much posturing, too much in-your-face-talk, too much exaggerated loudness.

All this prompts a tirade from Dan, who has zero tolerance. Such behavior further convinces him that he shouldn't have to occupy the same space as these people, though his jokes question whether he even thinks they are people. Dan's merciless.

Bony and bespectacled, he grew up in blue-collar Pennsylvania, in a working-poor but mixed neighborhood. As far as Dan is concerned, that was fine. His school was integrated and he had numerous black friends until race riots tore everything apart in 1969. He was around twelve at the time. Then Dan watched color separate everyone into groups. Certainly neither he nor his friends were old enough to decide to call it quits because they wanted to, or intellectualized that they should. Instead, color did the justifying; they were blacks while he was white. His family shortly moved out of the neighborhood and Dan hasn't voluntarily mixed with blacks since. He sees no point.

Under different circumstances Dan would have gone on from high school to college. He always liked school and wasn't a troublemaker. Though neither of his parents had finished high school, that wasn't the catch. The family was so strapped for money that Dan just couldn't see pursuing higher education. He went to work in a local furniture factory instead. He also waited until his high school sweetheart was old enough to marry, and then he wed.

Enlisting was just a matter of time. All through high school he and a buddy had been planning to enter the army. But then his friend opted for college first and Pam didn't want Dan in uniform. It took awhile, but against even his father's advice—to join the navy, the service his father would have chosen had the army not drafted him for the last six months of World War II—Dan volunteered. First he signed up for jump school. Then he got himself assigned to a Ranger battalion. Ironically, by the time Dan was in Special Forces his high school friend was a Ranger company commander. Three other people Dan knows from high school are helicopter pilots, all of which says something about their grit.

This, too, helps explain some of Dan's disgust with the swagger and contempt projected by the black Marines, though this just gets compounded by late afternoon the first day of classes. A cabal of black MPs in the classroom also behave arrogantly. Not only do three or four (though, notably, not all) of the "brothers" (which is how the team refers to them from the first day onward) stick together but they saunter in late after every break. They never step forward in any of the hands-on training, they shirk from helping with moving the weapons off the truck into the classroom and back onto the truck, and they never ask questions. Essentially, they're not only displaying no interest but demonstrating an active lack of interest in what the ODA is teaching. By the fourth day of classes Dan and KC are openly joking with the rest of the team about these three blacks being joined at the hip, so that the challenge for the team is to separate them. KC summarizes the blacks' attitude: "I ain't workin' for the man," while Dan's favorite line is, "I'm oppressed, gimme a dollar." The general bet is that all three will manage to quit before having to spend Tuesday night in the woods, an easy assumption for 309 to make, given how many stereotypes this MP threesome has already lived up to.

Neither Dan nor KC nor any of the other team members who comment on the brothers are the least bit apologetic about their views. Nor do they speak in euphemism. They're quite open about what they think, which is really more a matter of what—given their experience—they know. None of them comes from a privileged background. Each of them has worked hard to get where he is. There's been nothing easy for them, anymore than for anyone else, in conforming. Therefore they're not about to cut whole groups of people any slack. Or if they are, it's just enough slack so that people can hang themselves. In their view this is precisely what too many blacks in the army do. Not all, of course, but enough. They opt for the less demanding jobs. They shun the woods and hard-core infantry assignments. They stick together. They act menacing. All of which runs counter to the standards of SF.

At the same time, SF's standards also require 309 members to treat these three black Marines no differently than they treat the rest of the students. No matter how much they might want to, they can't pry apart the threesome, just as they can't allow what they say among themselves to seep through to the Marines. Unlike the students, ODA members can't wear an aggressive attitude on their sleeve. Professionalism forbids it, though their standards also tell them that it's not just these three blacks whom the Marine Corps could do without. A lot of the MPs seem lazy and uninterested well beyond what their youth and immaturity would lead the soldiers to expect. In the blacks' case, though, it is their blackness—and their needing to act black together—that proves so problematic.

Cliques are bad in any unit. So is predictability. The problem is the military tends to foster both. Living on top of one another, individuals learn to detect one another's strengths and shortcomings, and people with similar interests and similar aims quickly group. This is why rank is so important in conventional units. NCOs play the heavies. It's their responsibility to stay on top of privates and keep egos, ambitions, and bullying in check.

This is trickier on teams, where there isn't such a wide spread in rank, and where soldiers are older, wilier, and know how to be more willful. At the same time, team structure assists the team sergeant in at least one regard. The natural pairing between sergeants with the same specialty is undermined by the senior/junior designation. Also, there is no special class of underlings. Team sergeants are able to assign duties to soldiers well outside their specialties, and they have plenty of lattitude in whom they can target for which chores.

SUNDAY MORNING KC AND THOSE TEAM MEMBERS HE HAS DESIGnated patrol leaders for Tuesday's field exercise—Greg, Chris, and Dan—pile into their borrowed Marine van and head off to reconnoiter the area the Marines have set aside for them. Not only do they need to coordinate locations for patrol bases and ambush sites in advance but they also want to study the lay of the land. Ironically, as KC drives the van ever deeper into the woods, the terrain looks eerily similar to Ft. Bragg's: pine trees, scrub, and imperceptible ridges.

Generously, KC steers clear of anything that looks overly swampy, although the most familiar thing about the section of MCAS New River we traverse is red. Red metallic bands ring certain pine trees; without needing to see a sign, everyone in the van knows these bands designate the clumps of trees as off-limits. They belong to red cockaded woodpeckers.

Red cockaded woodpeckers are the bane of commanders' existence at Ft. Bragg. After the birds were declared an endangered species (which they might be everywhere but on post), whole swathes of the base had to be put off-limits to training to protect the birds' habitat. In fact, before 3rd Group's new buildings were even occupied there were red bands around a number of pine trees just down the slope from Z Company's front door. Red bands are such a common sight on post that no one paid any attention to them until the company held its first clean-up day in the new area. Out came the chainsaws and trimmers and Z Company got down to serious business (all units are responsible for their own yard work). A few pine trees and a lot of undergrowth later, and the area was neat, tidy, and substantially thinned out. The joke was that if KC, who brought a chainsaw from home, had kept at it another half hour, not a single tree would have been left standing. Though that wasn't the only joke.

Not long after the soldiers were back in their team rooms, mission accomplished, two woodpecker people showed up in the B-team area. Apparently someone from another company had made a phone call to sound the alarm: Z Company was tampering with habitat. Now Major Geoffries and everyone else on the B-team was being reprimanded, until it dawned on someone that the name of the officer who allegedly reported them belonged to a captain long gone from the battalion. Then the forestry officials realized that they hadn't put up any red bands in the area; of course they hadn't, or buildings wouldn't be there. Instead, someone in the battalion must have girdled the trees with red bands as a joke, just as all three companies were moving into their new quarters.

Now, seeing the same red bands on MCAS New River, more than one hundred miles from Fayetteville, everyone in the van is further convinced the birds can't possibly be endangered; how many stands of pine do they need in North Carolina?

While KC, Greg, Chris, and Dan are on tour, Sam and Steve visit the air station's arms room, where the team stores its weapons, just as it must at Ft. Bragg. Their task is to clean the M-14s that team members shot on the range yesterday, when the MPs finally got to fire the machine guns they studied on the first day of classes. After the students finished practicing with the crew-served weapons and had each tried out an AK-47 and other exotica Special Forces soldiers have to be familiar with, it was the team's turn to get in some shooting. For about an hour team members blazed away. All sorts of weapons were fired with all sorts of degrees of seriousness.

While Chris and Steve, the team's two weapons sergeants, zeroed their sniper rifles and then wound up shooting against each other in a five-round match, Greg and KC engaged in their own friendly competition. Whatever target Greg aimed at, KC also aimed at. KC's goal was to hit the target out from under Greg. As for Chris and Steve, Chris managed to put three shots into the innermost black ring of the target, but his grouping was wider than Steve's, whose shots were more off-center. This made Steve less unhappy than Chris, but neither was satisfied; no one won. By contrast, Greg and KC regarded their competition as having been highly successful, especially because each came away convinced he could have out-shot the team's two weapons sergeants.

With Sam and Steve thus stuck scraping away the residue from yesterday's shooting, Mark is the only team member who manages to escape a Sunday morning chore. Maybe this is because he spent most of Saturday unsuccessfully trying to send a radio transmission. Also, nightly, he's been outside with his satellite dish as part of the overall exercise. More often than not he never manages to raise Ft. Bragg or get a clear signal through. But this never seems to faze him. His identity is all wrapped up in being the team's sole communications sergeant (since Carl has been away at school for months). Also, Mark doesn't doubt his abilities. Out of 106 other would-be commo sergeants who started Morse code training with him, only 16 graduated the Q course, and because there are always dozens of things that might interfere with a message going through, Mark can still think well of himself; he is still integral to the team.

As is everyone for the next activity: IV training. Everyone has to participate; it's on the training schedule for midday. Plus it's important.

As medic, Greg's aim with this Sunday afternoon, team-only class is to refresh everyone's memory on how to stick one another, though Chris and Dan take him literally. Once Dan has acted as Greg's guinea pig (largely because he doesn't trust anyone else on the team to put a needle in him), he insists on being allowed the entire bag of ringer fluid to himself as refreshment; he claims he wants to be rehydrated. Chris too wants a whole bag, as this odd round-robin of inserting catheters continues.

What's important about IV training is that it renews a perishable skill. Everyone has been taught how to insert IVs before; the rule is that every SF soldier carry one ringer bag in his rucksack. The purpose of this is not only to make sure team medics have an adequate supply but to give team members a fighting chance if medics aren't around in an emergency. Even in an emergency situation, without having been periodically reminded about the order in which to insert the needle, open the bag, and get the fluid flowing without introducing an air bubble into a vein, no soldier is likely to remember this particular perishable skill on top of all the others he's learned.

In that sense this is a serious class. In another sense it can't possibly be. There's too much blood spattered up and down people's arms as the order of when to turn which knob and open which valve gets accidentally reversed on victim after victim. In fact, with every bloody arm Dan looks smarter and smarter for having volunteered faster than anyone else to serve as Greg's demonstration subject. At the time no one envied him; Greg's hands were shaking far too much, the result of his addiction to strong, unadulterated coffee. But at least Greg didn't hesitate. He poked his needle right in, unlike everyone else who pauses before jabbing.

This counts as one of those funny contrasts. Allow these soldiers to think about what they are doing and they can easily equivocate, like anyone else. There is as much nervous laughter during IV training as there was when Chris was flailing about in the swamp. Or as there is right before a jump. It's amazing what a little bit of peer pressure cum peer coercion can do, though it's not just bravado that impels everyone to commit to leaping out of planes and plunging in needles, with the rest of the team looking on. It's also not wanting to face self-recrimination. In this regard everyone on 309 may be a little more like Greg than they might care to think. Or at least, almost everyone.

MONDAY MORNING IT'S BACK TO INSTRUCTING THE MARINES, AND the team gets down to the business of explaining patrols, ambushes, and operations orders. This is preparatory for heading out into the field on Tuesday. Already, too, it's clear that the team bet right; the three black Marines they found so problematic are gone, though two blacks and one lone female still stick with the class.

Meanwhile, Monday afternoon Mark once again tries to send commo but fails. This time he tries outside the classroom (rather than the barracks) and decides there's too much interference from the air station antennas. Then, classes over, it's back to the barracks to pack. KC goes over patrol procedures, radio contacts, and other details with his patrol leaders. The patrol leaders in turn brief their assistants, which means Chris talks to Mark, Dan fills in Steve, and Greg speaks with Sam. It's all done formally and according to the book for no other reason than that it should be and because the team is still taking this mission seriously. And no one more so than Chris.

This is more than obvious Tuesday morning, as each of the patrol leaders assembles his squad of MPs. Soldiering through the woods is Chris's bailiwick. With Mark acting as his assistant, Chris's goal will be to supervise and cajole the Marines into putting into practice what 309 has just spent the better part of a week teaching them. The plan is to conduct patrols, set up ambushes, and spend the night in the woods. But so far this is not a very enthusiastic bunch of Marines. They act as though this is just one more day of military drudgery.

To try to get the MPs moving as they grudgingly plod along, Chris sets off an artillery simulator behind them within the first hour of the first patrol. On hearing it the Marines at least react properly. They drop. And then Chris yells, "Platoon leader, let's get moving." The platoon leader responds by shouting "two hundred meters twelve o'clock" and everyone runs for two hundred meters. This seems to exhilarate the MPs somewhat.

A little more awake now, the platoon continues walking. There's a quick lunch break during which the highlight turns out to be a rotten MRE (Meals-Ready-to-Eat) package. Fortunately, the Marine who opens the vacuum-sealed brown plastic envelope is hit only with the awful odor. It gets tossed, contents and all, not buried. Although the woods feel empty, there is scattered evidence that they do serve as mock battlefields. Most often discarded thick brown MRE plastic is the giveaway, although occasionally we come across old foxholes and earthworks. Twice we pass by still-occupied camps, which we skirt, a brief reminder that we aren't just out on a jaunt; the woods are potentially full of troops. Under only slightly different circumstances they could be the enemy, though the MPs never seem to believe this. They certainly don't act as though they have any sort of imagination. Or if they do, they aren't lending it to this exercise.

Actually, KC is supposed to be the enemy. He's scheduled to drive by the designated ambush site at 1530. His van is the target on an otherwise unremarkable dirt road. Before we even reach the road, though, the squad is confused. So far they've done well walking on an azimuth, crossing danger areas, and, essentially, land navigating. But now they're noticeably less sure of themselves. There are a number of parts to an ambush and Chris again explains to them about objective rally points (ORPs). He then sends the platoon leader with three men (and Mark, as monitor) to survey the ambush site. As they reach the treeline edging the road, Mark, too, has to remind the MPs what to do. He then instructs the platoon leader to leave two of his men on guard before returning to the objective rally point, where packs get left, to round up everyone else. Once the squad has been reconstituted, the Marines deploy for the ambush.

So far so good. In fact, the ambush—shooting with blanks and all—proves to be the easiest part of the day so far, and once begun is over in no time. The Marines burst out of the woodline, surprise and then neutralize the enemy, and simulate destroying the van. Their only egregious mistakes are to fail to search one of their captives and to take down enough information; they didn't record what they found in the van.

The after-action report is conducted on the spot, with KC still in attendance. Chris is pleased to learn that Greg's squad did worse.

Then it's back into the woods to reach the location of the night ambush site. A new platoon leader is designated, though he plays no real role. Everyone just strides along in silence. No one is really patrolling; instead, this is more of a hike than a simulated movement. Again, to stir up the MPs, Chris lobs a noisemaker. This one is supposed to sound like a grenade, which prompts Chris to yell "Ambush." However, most of the patrol hears the detonation but not Chris and assume they're being hit with another incoming round. As a result, they throw themselves down, get up, and run—this time with even less energy.

Not much further along Chris halts the group. This is where he wants the patrol base to be set up for the night ambush. He keeps everyone still and silent for five minutes, to simulate the thirty minutes of listening an actual patrol would conduct before making camp. Then two Marines are sent out on a reconnaissance.

They're meant to circumnavigate us one hundred meters out. But they're gone so long that Chris has to shout them back to camp. They report that there's a road, then an intersection, not far away. Chris doesn't like this. He explains that with a road so close the patrol base is too vulnerable, because if the enemy had any indication we were in the area, they could get troops to us too easily.

But we don't move; this is only a learning exercise. It's also chow time.

As the light fades the Marines begin to loosen up, a bit. Also, once everyone's broken out his MREs, Mark becomes the most animated he's been all day. The Marines have heat packs for their food; he and Chris have never seen heat packs before, although the chemical packets designed to warm up entrées clearly impress Mark more. The Marines offer him one, while he busily trades away portions of his meal. At lunch he traded away his chicken à la king. Now he swaps jelly for cheese spread and a brownie for a maple nut cake.

I've never seen this side of Mark before: his keen interest in food and the ease with which he essentially demands what he wants. But I shouldn't be so surprised. Like Sam, Mark is a creature of comfort. And, quite transparently, food is a definite comfort while the woods are not. Also, like Sam, Mark grew up in New York City. Perhaps this explains their affinity for music no one else on 309 can stand (big band for Mark and jazz for Sam). But there their similarities end. Mark is a worrywart. He worries a lot about himself. Which is surprising, at least at first glance.

At well over six feet, Mark is the tallest man in the company. He's also one of the better educated, with an advanced degree in music performance. But despite his conspicuously large SF ring, which is a knuckle-sized silver unit crest, and his obvious interest in radios, he seems far less comfortable with all but the trappings. Part of this may have to do with how Mark came to SF. He was thirty-three when he went through the Q Course and had been in the army only a couple of years. His first stint in the military was with the air force. Reenlisting, and just prior to the Q Course, he served as a legal aide in the Judge Advocate General's (JAG) office. He had virtually no experience as an infantry soldier, nor was he at ease in the woods.

Mark applied for SF because three people he admired in the JAG's office were all SF-tabbed, and they suggested that SF might cure his midcareer/what career? doldrums. My hunch is that this challenge by them, rather than SF as a challenge, appealed to Mark. I say this because Mark's focus on 309 was always KC. For some reason KC's approval was absolutely critical to him. This had nothing to do with how KC may have been able to help or hurt Mark's career. Mark wasn't plotting to become a command sergeant major or reach a rank loftier than that of master sergeant (E-8), if that. Rather, what he seemed to be seeking the most was confirmation of his identity. What seemed to drive him was identifying himself as a member of an A-team, as if he had to have a place to belong, or else. This was in sharp contrast to his teammates, whose confidence and drive to excel came from deeply within.

Throughout the patrol Mark defers. Over MREs it's Chris who holds center stage. He treats this day and night out with the Marines as an extended opportunity to teach. Chris wants the MPs to learn as much about patrolling through the woods as they can, not only because it's his job to teach but because the mission is relatively realistic foreign internal defense. One day soon Chris may find himself teaching actual non-English speakers these same techniques, just as one day the MPs might find themselves in a situation where they have to deal with intruders (never mind insurgents) at an actual site. Thus, this is all serious business. Chris doesn't joke around. He demands the MPs' attention and their respect.

To do so he makes liberal use of illustrations. These come mostly from lessons he himself learned when he went through Ranger School, not the Q Course. They catch the Marines' attention because they are about impressively miserable conditions. The MPs are feeling pretty miserable on a whole different plane. During dinner they make it clear why they're less than enthusiastic. Most are disillusioned with the Marine Corps. No one in this squad plans to reenlist. They especially resent their NCOs, who, they claim, make them work like dogs then treat them as if they're idiots. Obviously, Chris and Mark are unlike NCOs they've dealt with before, although what precisely they make of Chris and Mark isn't so easy for me to figure out. This squad reminds me too much of a misplaced cast from *Lord of the Flies*—slightly overweight, too glum and soft, but cruel. I wouldn't want to be in the woods alone with them. Still, there's no grumbling whenever Chris urges everyone back to his feet.

With nightfall it's time to rehearse the night ambush, which means first stumbling along a slight ridge to the site, which is, again, a dirt road.

With packs dumped, a new platoon leader is appointed who turns out to be the most energetic yet. He belts out his orders so compellingly that by the third run-through of the ambush he's managed to get most of the squad shouting with him. This pleases Chris no end. Two more walk/run-throughs and Chris deems the squad ready for dress rehearsals. The difference now: the MPs get to rush the road from the woodline in some modicum of light. Chris fires off a star cluster flare for each of two dress rehearsals; Mark is fireman. Often the bright white flare hasn't quite burnt itself out as it drifts back to Earth, so sometimes it will set dead leaves and brush ablaze if no one stomps on it soon enough. But there is no such drama during our dress rehearsals, only another opportunity for Mark to comfortably stand aside.

Once the two dress rehearsals are done, more than an hour remains before the ambush is to take place. Chris calls KC over the radio to see if he'll move the start time forward. Chris claims the Marines are likely to lose their edge if they have to wait another hour, though whether this says more about Chris's lack of confidence in the MPs or his own stake in the subtle competition going on among instructors I can't tell.

KC accommodates, although it's actually Captain Tucker and Hugh (the assessor) who drive up in the van. Again, the ambush is fast. The grenade simulator meant to initiate the attack doesn't go off. Yet the Marines still do everything they're supposed to: charge out of the treeline, stop and surround the van, secure the area, inventory the van's contents. Captain Tucker and Hugh are impressed. This makes Chris and Mark happy and in turn seems to bring out the best in the Marines.

The final task for the day/night is a one-thousand-meter patrol that, now that everyone is pumped, is essentially just a single-file walk—not a tactical maneuver—to a predesignated campsite. All "predesignated" means is that we can be located on the map exactly where Chris agreed with KC we'd wind up. On the map there's no way to tell that we'll be spending the night in the midst of crackling underbrush. Just putting a foot down gives us away. With every move people make there's noise. Still, we're supposed to simulate being tactical once we reach the camp. No one's allowed to turn on a flashlight. And once we're right on top of the exact spot that matches the coordinates for where we're supposed to be, Chris imposes another five minutes of silence to stand in for the thirty minutes of stand-to that a real mission would require.

This time no one gets sent out on recon. Instead, Chris simply describes how the Marines would set up a night patrol base before turning over to them the process of deciding who will stand watch and when, in one-hour intervals.

Midway through all this, there is a racket out in the woods. Something is crashing toward us. We're silent. So is whatever is moving through the woods. Then it starts up again, and finally appears. Greg.

Greg's goal is to persuade Chris to venture back into the woods with him. Wouldn't Chris like a hot drink? Greg's on a mission to round up the Three Compancheros for a social visit to base camp, in the meantime proving that he possesses formidable night land navigation skills. But Chris can't be budged. After a short visit Greg crashes back through the branches and dead leaves to find Dan (who does wind up accompanying him to base camp for a hot drink). Which makes for a fairly striking contrast. There Greg goes, tracking down teammates through the woods in the dark. Here are the MPs, all bunched up, practically lying on top of one another, although as it turns out by morning, almost none of them sleeps— which may also explain why they stay so compact. They're freezing.

Either because they didn't want to carry anything heavy in their rucksacks, or because they really didn't know any better, or because they thought—as Marines—they really could tough it out, few of the MPs have quilted nylon poncho liners, fewer still have sleeping bags, and a handful have only their uniforms to sleep in. And this after 309 warned them to bring plenty of snivel (cold weather) gear.

Chris and Mark both started off in poncho liners and then graduated to sleeping bags. Having started off in a sleeping bag, I have only one complaint about the night—chiggers; they clearly realize I am warm, which it definitely isn't when Chris wakes to issue the first order of the morning, in pitch dark. This is that everyone should eat MREs preparatory to moving out in forty-five minutes. Great, I can stay warm in my sleeping bag for at least another thirty-five. But once Chris is standing and realizes the extent of the Marines' misery, he decides we'll move on as soon as everyone is packed. This is when these Marines really lose my respect, especially because, as we start to walk, they compete with one another over who was the most miserable, doubtless a bonding experience for them.

Significantly, not one Marine admits that not bringing heavier clothes or more gear wasn't very smart. In contrast, when we reach the base camp, where the Marines in Sam and Greg's squad are already warming themselves around two crowded fires, all Sam has to say, and he does so at great length, is how stupid he was. He, too, was cold, not freezing but cold. And why? Because he'd been an idiot. He'd brought a poncho liner but not a sleeping bag. How could he have been so stupid. . . .?

This serves as yet another pointed contrast between these young MPs who are full of apathy and ODA members who can't stand making mistakes.

AT 0800 IT'S CAPTAIN TUCKER'S SHOW. HE'S TEACHING PLATOON defense. As usual when it comes to being talked to, the MPs don't seem engaged. However, this could be for any one of a number of reasons. Most likely it's because the hardest part of the week—and the highlight—is over; everyone has passed through the night in the woods. "Platoon defense" is too much like more make-work. First there's Captain Tucker talking. Then there are the three squads deploying just through the treeline. Through the trees adjacent to the base camp is an old bunker site, and each squad is sent to the top of a different bunker to organize its imagined defense.

Shortly, Captain Tucker strides from squad to squad, huddles, makes suggestions, and moves on. The Marines have only so much time before they have to present their finished project—of sketch map and explanation—to him. But few seem to take the task very seriously.

It's curious that this morning's class *is* platoon defense, given the emphasis yesterday on patrols and ambushes at the squad level. I can't figure out why the team doesn't clinch yesterday's training by building on it and reworking it into a new scenario this morning. Some team members agree that consolidating yesterday's training would make more sense. But this is also to ignore the team's goal, and Captain Tucker's in particular.

The training 309 is doing at MCAS New River is as much for 309 as it is to provide the Marines with new skills. Captain Tucker needs to demonstrate to higher command that the team is versatile. This means covering as many forms of major "action"—patrols, ambushes, platoon defense—as possible in ten days. And he also has to find out the team's deficiencies. For instance, this morning's exercise has convinced him that 309 needs more practice teaching platoon- and company-size operations. Part of what convinces him is the flatness of Steve and Dan's squad. They are the last group Captain Tucker checks in with. When he examines them is telling: all the other Marines are already on the bus, ready to head back to quarters by the time he strides over to their hillock. This makes Steve and Dan's squad antsy. They know they, too, have seats on the bus. Captain Tucker's attention is just pro forma, just a final ticket punch. Ultimately, it's inconsequential, which is what Captain Tucker than misreads as their attitude toward training, when actually this has been the liveliest of the three squads throughout the day and night.

For one thing, Steve and Dan's squad has a different makeup than the others, comprising the sole female MP and the only blacks still in the course, as well as the only Marine to admit he's thinking of making the corps his career. It's a successful mix. There is much more camaraderie in this squad, much more levity, and fewer overweight Marines. Dan as instructor makes a big difference, too. He clearly has motivated the squad and helped it achieve esprit through humor. There is no trace of Dan as he has sounded off in the mess hall. His humor is professionally, not personally, targeted, and he leads by jabbing and prodding much more than by tugging; tugging is Chris's method, moving everybody by sheer dint of his wanting them moved.

Again, the differences in personal styles and leadership techniques among ODA members is significant. Even in the pairs assigned to instruct the MPs, it was obvious that Chris had more to say than Mark, Dan than Steve, and Sam than Greg, but this was also fine. In Chris's and Dan's cases it was a matter of who had more expertise; they simply knew more about small-unit tactics in the woods. In Sam's case it was a matter of rapport. By reminiscing about the Gulf War, he was better able to strike a bond than Greg was, especially since some Marines in their squad had also served in the Gulf. Greg hadn't. Moreover, Greg, like Steve, gave the appearance of being too close in age to the Marines. He was young, fit, and competitive. The MPs didn't particularly impress him, and this made him standoffish. If they weren't interested in him, he wasn't interested in them. Nor was he about to entertain them. For Sam, though, the Marines represented a new audience.

Something else notable about the way in which KC paired team members was that these definitely didn't represent couplings by (or of) choice. If team members had been able to choose whom to work with, Chris doubtless would have gone off with Dan, Sam and Steve would have joined up, and by default Greg and Mark would have wound up together. It is significant that this didn't work out yet all the pairs still worked.

ODA 309 may have had a hard core but it didn't have cliques.

IN THE BROADEST SENSE THE TRIP TO MCAS NEW RIVER HELPED RE-
iterate this, serving as yet another bonding experience for the whole
team. Conceivably the only person with any doubts about how well
the trip went was KC, who was perturbed for days that the commem-
orative plaque the ODA presented to the Marines at the conclusion of
training was smaller and cheaper than the plaque the Marines gave
him. Otherwise, even he had to be pleased. The letters of commenda-
tion he and Captain Tucker received from the Marine commanders
who oversaw the team's mission were positively glowing. This surely
had to raise the team's status in the battalion commander's eyes.
Equally important was how much carryover there would be back in
the team room. The current dynamic was a good one. Dan, Chris, and
Greg—the Three Compancheros—made for a strong core. Too bad
then that there were all sorts of news awaiting them at Ft. Bragg.

Special Warfare School assignments had come down. Mark,
Chris, and Rob were slated to be transferred out of the company to
begin their four-year instructor rotations within weeks. There was
also a rumor that KC was going to be asked to become the battalion
first sergeant (in the Headquarters and Support Company).

The reactions to so many changes all at once turned out to be
quite revealing. For instance, while Mark lamented that this would
render the team one of the weakest after having been the strongest
(in his view) in the group, he was clearly happy about his own
prospects of being able to teach in Phase 2 of the Q Course. Chris,
on the other hand, was in a tailspin. While he was genuinely
pleased for KC—becoming first sergeant would virtually guarantee
KC a shot at making sergeant major—just thinking that he might
have to teach officers in their Phase 2 segment of the Q course
(which is what he was slotted for) depressed him. He didn't want to
leave the team at all, but to have to teach officers was a real affront.

Rob was still in Africa so no one was sure how he would take
this. But Steve, who wasn't going anywhere, was positively elated.
As far as he was concerned this amounted to a coup. Virtually all of
the team's senior members would be leaving, including (he was

sure) Dan, because Dan was bound to try to go elsewhere once Chris, Rob, and KC went. Steve, Sam, and Greg would form the new-old core of 309, and although Sam and Greg were hardly as ecstatic as Steve, they didn't seem perturbed by these departures, either. This may have been because Sam still intended to try out for Delta Force and Greg had recently begun talking about scuba school (which hadn't yet crossed Steve's mind), but it likely also reflected a more deep-seated ambivalence about the teammates who would be leaving and what the team was or wasn't losing.

So much for a stable, cohesive team.

Still, it was KC who reacted the most interestingly of all. If he told the story once, he told it a dozen times, to anyone who was curious. When the command sergeant major interviewed him and asked why he wanted to be a first sergeant, KC decided he wasn't about to play the sergeant major's game. After all, he'd been selected—he hadn't volunteered for the interview. So he responded by answering that he wasn't sure what a first sergeant did from day to day. He didn't even know what a sergeant major's job consisted of.

"What does a first sergeant do, sergeant major?"

The sergeant major's response at the end of the interview was, "Well, I have four or five other people to consider," which was either the truth or KC's spin on his own spin of the process.

While KC insisted that toying with the sergeant major would cost him the job—suggesting that he wasn't really interested—everyone in the company continued to assure him he was a shoo-in, which had to have flattered him on several levels. Obviously he was popular, and everything he heard suggested he had respect from above as well as below. Maybe he should become first sergeant. The team he had worked so hard for was about to dissolve; within two months, 309 would be radically different. There would be a new set of people to meld together. Even worse, Captain Tucker would also be moving on. His stint on an ODA was almost up. Without a replacement officer 309 could almost be guaranteed no missions abroad. And even if the team did get another captain right away (which was unlikely, given the current shortage of captains), did KC want to start all over again to break in another officer?

At the same time, there was still the rest of the team to think about. While KC would have made some personnel changes if he could, he didn't regard any of the soldiers left to him as a dud, not even Steve. Wouldn't he be better off continuing to work with them in the woods than suddenly being responsible for a battalion's worth of administrative headaches concerning other peoples' teams in the woods?

And KC was approaching the twenty-year mark. Already other team sergeants and E-8s in the company were putting in their retirement paperwork. Among his peer group the general feeling was that SF just wasn't what it once was, and wasn't worth reenlisting for. No one who was eligible was trying to become a sergeant major (E-9). Should he?

If KC had walked up to the B-team area, the place in the company most rapidly losing people, he would have been told in no uncertain terms not to be sentimental about SF, not that he would have let on that he was. He had all sorts of financial considerations, namely, children, one of whom is handicapped. It's also likely that one of the company's smartest, most homespun sergeants would have simply offered KC his own litmus test: was KC having as good a time in SF as he should have been having?

Joe, who wasn't close to retirement but only wished he was, regarded Saudi Arabia as the last good time he'd had. He was there seven months, went for fifty-two days with no bath, had the shits for the first two and a half months, never enough toilet paper, too much goat and camel to eat, but still enjoyed it. Even when things were bad they were funny. As far as he was concerned, that was always the best part of foreign internal defense—it was foreign. And foreign was fun. Of course, fun could be had elsewhere, but never in garrison. And garrison was where 3rd Group was spending way too much time. *Was* KC having fun?

Not getting abroad or far enough away or not getting to work as a team alone was what Joe regarded as most debilitating. This is why even trips to places like MCAS New River could help, somewhat. Sometimes they could even hurt *and* help.

10 Operation in the Desert

In December, ODA 304 was in the desert with ODAs 308 and 305, and the B-team. While 309 was on the North Carolina coast with much of the rest of the battalion, three of Z Company's teams were participating in a much larger operation on the other side of the country. Their particular mission: special reconnaissance (SR). Each team was being deployed to watch a designated airstrip and note any activity. They'd been briefed: drug runners were known to use these airstrips, and drug runners were usually armed. But because this was special reconnaissance and not direct action, the soldiers' mission shouldn't endanger them. They were not supposed to give themselves away, to alert the enemy that anyone was watching, or to apprehend a soul.

It should have been simple.

Three hide sites were selected by 304. Two men would stay in one hide site for seventy-two hours straight. They would be replaced by a second pair of team members who would go to the second hide site. A third pair would go to the third hide site, and the rotations would continue for the full fourteen days of the mission. Whoever was not in the hide site would remain at the mission support site (MSS). This is where communications were coordinated. The two team members in the hide site would be able to talk to the rest of the team in the mission support site, while the mission support site would relay information to and from base camp.

Each of Z Company's three teams was in a different location and had drawn up its own plan for setting up reconnaissance. Because 304 was located farthest from base, which itself had been set up in the middle of nowhere, 304 made two decisions that were different from the other teams'. All of 304's members would stay at the mission support site for the full fourteen days, and because of this 304 requested to keep two of the unit's vehicles at its site, in case there was an emergency or the team needed to evacuate quickly.

However, the company commander was skeptical of 304's intent. Maybe the team was planning to use the vehicles to seek a little R&R in addition to performing reconnaissance. It's not as though that would have been beyond certain of 304's members. Also, if 304 was allowed two vehicles, that would cut down on the total number available to the rest of the company. This was the argument Major Geoffries used on 304's leaders—he had only so many vehicles—although no matter how much sense this made from a commander's point of view, the team read him as not trusting them enough. In part this was inevitable. Every team believes the universe should revolve around only it, while a company commander, responsible for six teams, can't take such a blinkered view. Logically, the major felt he had to limit 304 to one vehicle, which it had to camouflage and use only in an emergency.

This irked 304.

Still, it wasn't all that relevant once the team was actually at the site, at least not initially.

On first arriving at the site ODA 304 faced four pressing tasks: recon the site, establish security, camouflage the site, and make commo. The first three were easily accomplished. However, Charlie, the team's communications sergeant, had a hard time establishing communications with the relay station that would transmit his messages back to base. In fact, he never did raise anyone, although he made the attempt a number of times.

Meanwhile, two sergeants conducted a recon of the route to the first hide site. The original plan was for these two soldiers to move into the hide site that first night. Once they saw how rough the terrain was and that the slope they'd have to climb was nothing but rocks, however, they decided they could wait until just before first light the next morning. That way they would minimize the chances of twisting an ankle or wrenching a knee.

Before first light meant waking at 0430, when it was frigid, even if this was the desert; it was high desert and excuse enough for a good long pause for coffee. Rucksacks had to be repacked with sleeping bags, pads, and everything else that had been used to make the frozen ground feel more comfortable. With no particular reason to rush, it wasn't until about 0530 that Rick and Clay were finally ready to head off. But at 0535 headlights suddenly rose above the horizon from the direction of the airstrip—exactly the kind of movement they were supposed to be watching for.

Because it was still dark, the headlights gave the intruding vehicle away but also made it impossible to tell whom the vehicle belonged to.

Clay, the team's sole medic, and Rick, the assistant operations sergeant, moved out of the site to get a better look. Both sergeants crouched behind some scrub, which provided concealment but not cover. Clay scanned with binoculars.

For obvious security reasons the site had been situated in a draw. To get a better view, Clay and Rick had no choice but to move above and beyond their teammates. And a good thing, too, because whoever was in the vehicle was behaving suspiciously. At irregular intervals, first a red light then a bright white beacon would flash from the truck.

Clay watched through the binoculars and relayed to Rick, "Three guys. Just got out of the vehicle. Two have weapons."

No sooner did he say this than the white light panned in their direction. Clay immediately lowered the glasses. The light turned off. Clay raised the glasses again. Back came the floodlight. Then at least one weapon barked.

Neither Clay nor Rick had time to hear the discharge before feeling its impact. Clay first.

"I'm hit, I'm hit."

It was Clay yelling as he scrambled back down the side of the gully. At the same time Clay was being checked over by his teammates in the mission support site, Rick was moaning 150 meters away. He, too, had been hit.

Later, Rick described how he knew he was hit. He was enveloped by a loud ringing noise and felt something definitely wrong with his mouth. Indeed, by the time Clay—who, it turned out, had been hit only by bone fragments blown out of Rick's jaw—was back at Rick's side with his medic bag and another team member, Rick had a good idea that something was badly wrong. He had lost feeling in his upper left side but knew that he could push his right hand—Nomex glove and all—somewhere *inside* his neck. He could also hear the blood pouring out and puddling. And his throat was filling up; it was growing hard to breathe.

That's when the team dropped all pretense of maintaining security and turned on its own white flashlights. Rick was the focus of everyone's attention. In the after-action reports no one mentioned seeing the vehicle drive away, though it must have, before the flashlights even came on. Clay got to work. At the same time that he packed superabsorbent Kerlex bandages into the gaping wound in Rick's neck, he reassured Rick in as calm and reasoned a tone as any victim would want to hear that it was nothing, just a scratch.

But Rick knew better. Clay was just doing his medic thing. Rick also knew that, medic thing or not, to help Clay he had to remain as quiet as possible. He couldn't thrash around or scream. However, it didn't help that the second man to reach his side couldn't keep *himself* from proclaiming, "Holy shit, he's fucked up bad."

Clay told John to shut the fuck up and then began cursing Rick in turn. Once he felt he had the bleeding marginally under control and knew the full extent of the wound—Rick's external jugular vein had been completely severed, there was a tremendous amount of muscle tissue damage, and Clay could see about four inches of exposed carotid artery pulsing away—all he wanted was for Rick to pass out.

"Pass out, motherfucker, pass out." The last thing he needed was for Rick to go into shock.

Meanwhile, back at the site the team leader, DJ, was doing his own yelling to the commo sergeant, Charlie, to get commo up. However, Charlie had been unable so far to get word in or out of the site.

Realizing no help could reach them without their making radio contact first, DJ yelled to get the camouflage net off the hidden Jeep Cherokee. They had to get Rick out of there.

In the back of the Jeep Clay clenched Rick's head between his legs to maintain pressure on the wound. Already he had packed the hole in Rick's neck with five rolls of Kerlex over which he'd stuck an abdominal dressing. Blood still soaked through. It took another dressing and an ace bandage to somewhat staunch the flow.

Tim, another teammate, was holding the IV bags. Because all SF soldiers are trained to administer IVs, this was one less thing Clay had to be distracted by as he worried about Rick's vital signs. Also, because all SF soldiers carry IV bags for contingencies like this, Clay had plenty at his disposal. Two were already dripping into Rick and the rest were warming up on the jeep's defroster. Even so, Rick later could recall how cold the liquid felt as it flowed into his arms.

In fact, Rick began to regain feeling just as the jeep was beginning to pull out of the wash. That meant intense pain. Afterward he said it was as if a switch had been turned on. But because he had what was technically a head wound, Clay couldn't give him anything to stop the pain. DJ urged Rick just to yell or scream. And then Allen, another teammate, started to drive.

The nearest town turned out to be twenty minutes away at seventy or eighty mph. At times Allen attempted to drive even faster, until DJ reminded him they'd all die if Allen crashed, which wouldn't help Rick at all.

During the drive Clay continued suctioning blood from Rick's mouth through an improvised syringe. Despite his best efforts, the entire back of the Cherokee was soon dripping red.

As for the three team members still at the mission support site, DJ's parting instructions had been to pack up the team's equipment and prepare for exfiltration. For certain they'd been compromised, not that they yet knew by whom or why. However, not more than thirty minutes after the jeep hurtled out of the wash, a vehicle rose over the horizon and seemed to be making a beeline for the site. Then it stopped. Three unarmed men emerged and two of them began walking straight toward the hidden soldiers. When

they were only ten meters away, John suddenly emerged to confront them. John's two teammates remained hidden, covering him.

Before even finding out who the intruders were, John warned
them they were in a military training area and had to leave immediately. One of the two civilians then asked John who he was and
how many soldiers there were. This, of course, made John more
nervous than he already was. Again he ordered them to leave the
area. After what must have seemed like ages, the civilians finally appeared to get the message. How could they not, with John in camouflage fatigues and combat boots, gripping an M-16? They
apologized and turned back toward their truck. However, John was
also curious now. What were they doing there? What were they
looking for?

Their answer: game they had shot earlier.

John asked whether they had been in the area that morning.
They answered that they had, about an hour previously. John asked
if they had a red-and-white searchlight on their vehicle. They did.

Clearly, John realized, these men shot Rick.

Maybe they were still armed.

John realized he still didn't know who they were or what they
were up to, nor did he want anyone else on the team to get hurt.
Given the civilians' long coats, which could easily hide weapons,
John decided they had to be searched. And now that he knew they
were Rick's shooters, they had better be detained.

John ordered the two civilians nearest him to drop to their
knees and place their hands on their heads. His teammates
searched them as he moved on to frisk the third civilian, still standing by the truck.

Once John determined no one else was in the truck, all six men
moved back to the mission support site to wait—both sets of three
no doubt wondering what the hell was going on.

Yet, as nerve-wracking as the situation was for the three soldiers
left in the desert, it was positively brutal for those still standing by
Rick.

First, they had to find the town's hospital. This took stopping at a
convenience store—where DJ got out, weapons and all—to ask for

directions, only to have to stop again later to ask someone else. When they finally got to the hospital, it was not only closed but locked. It took a lot of banging on the doors and yelling at windows to rouse the duty nurse. The team members later said they wondered what must have gone through her head as she faced these blood-spattered men in camouflage fatigues, two of whom still carried M-16s.

At that hour there was no doctor in the hospital so she had to call one. Clay and Tim took Rick into the emergency room, where they waited at least ten minutes for the ER doctor to arrive. In the interim Clay informed an ER nurse about Rick's injuries, presented Rick's vital statistics, and described what he thought was wrong. To a person, the team members who were present later recounted how overwhelmed the nurse, then the doctor, appeared.

Indeed, as Clay continued to apply direct pressure to the wound, with Tim still monitoring IV levels, one of the first things the doctor wanted to do, once he finally arrived, was rip out all the IV lines Clay had put in and replace them with his own. Clay responded in no uncertain terms, "Over my dead body." Then the doctor doubted Clay's medical descriptions of the severity of the wound. He asked to see it. Clay, who knew he had to continue applying direct pressure, refused. He did manage to show the doctor about an inch of the injury, to which the doctor reacted, "It's more than I can handle!"

That was the last straw. Twenty precious minutes had already been wasted in this so-called emergency room.

Clay knew Rick was deteriorating and needed a civilian life flight or a military medical airlift immediately. But apparently no one in the area would fly helicopters before 0900 hours. It was now about 0725; almost an hour and a half had elapsed since the shooting. DJ kept working the phones, trying to find some way out for Rick.

Again, the doctor attempted to take charge. He had the hospital staff change the IV lines Clay had put in and replace the pressured IV bags with unpressured bags. Rick was also intubated and X-rayed.

It was 0800 and still no med-evac. Now Clay was told that none would fly owing to "fog." His response: Rick needed to be flown out on anything. That's when a twin-engine fixed-wing craft was offered. Clay didn't hesitate: "Let's go for it."

About 0815 the doctor returned to Rick's side to announce he was going to insert a chest tube, "just in case." Meanwhile, Rick's blood pressure had dropped dangerously low. Having checked his chest cavity every five to ten minutes, Clay knew Rick didn't have any breathing problems a chest tube would help. Because Rick was not doing particularly well otherwise, Clay felt the last thing Rick needed was another painful procedure. After Clay somewhat forcefully convinced the doctor not to insert the chest tube, the plane and air crew arrived.

Rick was not out of the woods yet. Clay was still monitoring his vital signs, and they were suddenly alarming. In fact, for the first time, Rick's eyes were rolled back in their sockets and a sternal rub elicited no response.

Clay alerted the doctor, but his nonchalant reply was that Clay was probably standing on one of the IV hoses. Clay checked. No one was standing on a hose. Clay then acted. He dropped the head of the trauma bed and one of the recently arrived flight nurses put pressure cuffs on the IV bags. Within ten minutes Rick was semiconscious again. In another fifteen they could be airborne.

Rick remembers much of this. He remembers all the profanity Clay had to use to get through to the hospital staff and how his tone of voice would completely change depending on whether he was talking to Rick or dueling with the doctor. He remembers growing tired at a certain point. He also has dim memories of one of the nurses saying, "Oh shit, we're losing him." And he definitely remembers telling Clay—once it was time to get on the air ambulance—"You can't leave me, you can't leave me, these assholes will kill me."

Clay wasn't about to leave Rick.

With DJ's permission, Clay traveled on the air ambulance to the trauma center. He was even invited into the operating room by a trauma staff, which immediately impressed him with their concern for Rick. That's when Clay knew Rick was going to be OK, and he could relinquish control.

So much for routine training.

According to the police investigation, the shooting from beginning to end was an accident. The three civilians were varmint hunters. The lights they operated were meant to locate then blind coyotes and other game. Somehow they had caught Clay's binoculars just long enough for one of the men to think he had seen an animal, which is when he fired, which is how Rick got hit. The hunters then drove off, knowing they wouldn't be able to find their kill until daybreak. After dawn they returned. It was all just a matter of routine for them.

Of course, none of this was quite so routine for 304. As the incident unfolded, no one had any idea what was happening. It was conceivable, given the area they were in, that they were coming under real attack. They knew that the airstrip might attract drug runners and that drug runners can be armed. This the team had been prepared for. But nobody had said anything about varmint hunters, or drug runners posing as varmint hunters.

AND EVEN LESS HAD BEEN SAID TO SUE, RICK'S WIFE, BEFORE RICK left on this deployment.

Sue had a long flight across the country before she knew just what condition Rick was in. And she was lucky. This was a peacetime accident in the continental United States. She could be at her husband's side in a matter of hours, and the company and battalion staffs made sure she was. So did Major Geoffries's wife, who didn't hesitate to take in Sue's two small children. But Sue was also fortunate for a second reason. Though Rick had come as close to dying as he'd probably ever want to, he was still very much Rick. He'd have a series of surgeries to go through, a ragged scar, and residual pain for the rest of his life, but as soon as he was back in Fayetteville and had regained enough strength to bull his way into the team room, he was there. Had he not been, he would surely have driven Sue insane.

Certainly no one who knew Rick expected him to stay put at home simply because doctors told him that's where he belonged. No self-respecting SF soldier listened to doctors anyway, and particularly not when the medical advice was public knowledge and intended to lay an individual low. Lying low wasn't the SF thing to do unless you were hiding. In Rick's case all of this was compounded. His nickname was Sergeant Fury. No way could he be laid low. Plus, he was integral to his team.

That 304 was Z Company's HALO team automatically made it special. As far as 304's own members were concerned, the team's status also made them special. As far as other teams were concerned, this was just typical HALO team nonsense. In their view 304 wasn't any different from any other team before Rick's shooting. And the team remained no different afterward. But 304, which had been having a rocky time before the accident, did emerge from the desert a different team. The accident made for an amazing bonding experience. At least it did so for those members who had shared in saving Rick, and as time would rapidly tell, there were also bonds within bonds. Clay and Rick became virtually inseparable. How ironic that only a few short months before, Rick had barely been able to stomach 304's newest member.

304 DIDN'T HAVE A CAPTAIN WHEN CLAY JOINED THE TEAM. AND the warrant officer in charge never seemed particularly committed to his ODA. Thus, the running of 304 usually fell to the team sergeant. The problem was, 304 didn't have a permanent team sergeant either. As the highest-ranking NCO on the team, Rick was filling in as the acting team sergeant the morning Clay sashayed into the team room.

Clay came to the team a cherry. He was a medic fresh out of the Q Course. Being a medic automatically tagged him. Just passing the grueling Phase 2 portion of the Q Course signified he was smart. Everyone agreed that medic training was the most difficult of the SF specialties. On top of this, Clay had also gone to Arabic language school, another indicator of intelligence, because only 3rd Group designees who scored the highest on SF's language aptitude tests went on to learn Arabic, not French.

So given this background, Rick could already assume certain things about Clay. Still, none of this figured so prominently as where Clay had served prior to SFAS: with the Golden Knights. *This* was the kiss of death as far as Rick was concerned. Golden Geeks (as they are mockingly referred to) are members of the army's competition freefall parachute team. This team competes all over the country, which means its members get to spend the bulk of their time sky-diving, not humping through the woods. The team is pampered beyond an infantryman's wildest dreams. Rick was convinced Clay would know nothing about tactics, fieldcraft, or soldiering.

Worse still, two of Clay's Q Course classmates dropped in to visit him his first day in the team room. Both visitors were obnoxious. They were not only loud but, worse, woofed a lot of shit. And Clay joined right in.

Ideally, no SF soldier should woof. Few of those who do are liked. Even if a soldier does possess some special talent his teammates find useful, this doesn't give him license to brag or boast. Loudmouths are barely tolerated, let alone loudmouths who have only just been minted by the Q Course. This is what got Steve on 309 into so much trouble.

Thus, Clay had a number of strikes against him at the outset. In Rick's view, here was this woofer who would lord his parachuting abilities over the rest of the team. Normally, Rick's reaction would be to try to make sure Clay's reception stayed cool. But being the de facto team leader, he couldn't stay cold forever. As acting team sergeant, it was his responsibility to get to know Clay.

This was fortuitous, because it is not as though Rick himself had the most orthodox SF background. Most of Rick's SF career had been spent on a special projects team. Special projects teams are classified. Some SF veterans still refer to them as "long hair teams" (team members operate in plain clothes, without giveaway military haircuts). However, many of the more recent arrivals to SF had never heard of such teams and doubted they exist. Officially the army maintains that any SF soldier assigned to such a team, which isn't listed on any nonclassified organizational chart, is temporarily removed from SF command and transferred to some other department of defense agency. Technically, these men are no longer SF soldiers. Nevertheless, Special Operations (under which SF is housed) probably does incorporate some SF soldiers on its "dark-side" teams to help perform security-related tasks. Someone has to test the security at American embassies and other sensitive U.S. government installations. Someone also has to scout for potential danger before ODAs themselves are deployed. Finally, there is SF's own internal security. (Of course, about much of this I can only guess.)

Whatever Rick did for eight years (which still remains classified), it became clear to him in his eighth year that it was time to move on. If he remained on this special projects team much longer, he was not likely to progress careerwise. Also, Operation Desert Shield was about to turn into Operation Desert Storm, and Rick was still more soldier than security operative. He decided in high school, after liberating the school library's copy of Robin Moore's *The Green Berets,* that he would become a Special Forces soldier. No way was he going to miss this war.

After pulling every string he could find, Rick succeeded in rejoining an ODA. He arrived in Saudi Arabia only weeks after 3rd Group deployed but before the ground war started. And once back on an ODA, he stayed. Before long, thanks to his rank—and despite his lack of conventional ODA team time—he was also acting team sergeant.

Although Rick hadn't served on an ODA in years, 304 viewed the teamwork he was used to as a boon. He had become particularly skilled in the arts of deception and persuasion, and was especially persuasive when it came to talking to officers all the way up the chain of command. This, said the men on 304, was because he had to deal with so many different kinds of people while on the special projects team. As a result, he was unusually good at blowing smoke. Blowing smoke, like currying favor, meant he could get the team all sorts of opportunities, the opportunity of choice always being to jump.

What more could a HALO team ask for in a team sergeant?

Just as Rick finally had the team beginning to click the way he wanted, along came Clay. Getting someone new is always potentially disruptive. Clay could have been anyone. The idea of any new warm body was bound to rub Rick the wrong way. But because Clay was a newby, Rick couldn't find out much about him. Beyond the fact that Clay looked as though he could have been a Golden

Geek—he was slight and wore glasses—Rick had no other information for sizing him up.

CHANCES ARE CLAY WOULD HAVE HAD A HARD TIME ON ANY TEAM the first few weeks. Moving from the Q Course to an ODA isn't easy. It usually helps to already know someone on the team or to report with a buddy from the course. But that isn't always possible, and it could be worse yet if a soldier didn't realize he was being sized up and didn't know there was a certain impression he should be making.

At least Clay recognized he was being studied and tested and that Rick was making his acceptance difficult. What is less clear is whether Clay knew what Rick was holding against him, although it almost didn't matter. Service with the Golden Knights had taught Clay the incomparable value of good public relations. He knew how to be ingratiating. Thus, he later said, it took him only two weeks to turn Rick around.

Rick, on the other hand, credits himself with the beginning of his thaw toward Clay, which occurred when the team was on an out-of-state HALO train-up. Because it was a train-up, 304 was able to spend the better part of every day jumping. With every jump Clay proved he not only *could* help but was already helping team members improve their HALO skills. Nor was he obnoxious about his expertise. This is when Rick began to realize Clay might turn out to be a real asset. The clincher, though, came over beer.

It was during an evening drinking session that Rick realized how much he and Clay had in common, including lots of people they knew. The more beers they drank together, the more Clay proved, just by drinking, that he probably did have more in common with Rick than most of 304's other members.

It also turned out that Clay had field experience. He had spent four years as a paratrooper in the 82nd before joining the Golden Knights. Also, he had initially wanted to be an engineer, not a medic. Rick had trained as an engineer. There were lots of connections.

More then got made when, on their return to Ft. Bragg, the team was assigned a bona fide team sergeant, who outranked Rick.

Rick was no longer in charge of the team, which was a wrench on one level—he liked the responsibility. On another level, it meant he could go back to socializing with his teammates. There was no longer any reason for him to maintain distance to preserve respect, and there was no question that Rick liked to socialize. He and Clay were just beginning to become running buddies when the mission in the desert came up. Then Clay saved Rick's life.

Perhaps providentially, Rick had long had a theory that men's friendships are stronger and deeper than women's, especially when men are put together in dangerous situations. But once Rick was back in the team room—after his recovery, more surgery, and more recovery—it was hard to tell which way his friendship with Clay really ran. Gratitude, gratification, and responsibility all seemed to merge. This was bonding on a whole new level for both soldiers. It also altered the nature of the team.

Basically, Clay and Rick were both more chief than Indian. Clay was used to being smart, knowing a lot, and shooting from the hip but still being right, and he played this cerebral/smart-ass role to perfection. Rick, on the other hand, was an action junkie. They egged each other on. Much as Rick initially suspected, their chemistry probably should have led to a disastrous relationship. But as with Chris and Rob on 309 (though in a completely different way), Clay's and Rick's egos were just complementary enough to keep them from competing. Also, I think Rick regarded Clay as a sort of guarantee. So long as Clay would go along with whatever Rick suggested, they could both push the edge of the envelope further than either one would have dared to do on his own. Rick was probably the more irresponsible of the two, but Clay may have actually been more devious. It was hard to tell. They operated as if they were joined at the hip. This wasn't particularly healthy for the team.

It especially wasn't good for ODA members who joined 304 after Rick's shooting, as the team underwent major personnel shifts. The new soldiers would never be able to break into the circle of those who had been in the desert that morning. And there was an even tighter inner circle—of Clay and Rick—which meant there were also orbits within orbits. Even with DJ as team sergeant, Clay and Rick still dominated the team. DJ was too relaxed; he was essentially "retired on active duty" (ROAD). And because he rarely exerted the sort of energy Clay and Rick were capable of, too often the two of them pulled the entire team in their direction. Just as a twosome they made the team's critical mass. Everyone new had to curry favor with them, nor could anyone take them on. They had had this unique experience and were untouchable. They had a combat attachment.

YET ALTHOUGH 304's ORDEAL IN THE DESERT WAS THE CLOSEST any team in the company had come to combat since 3rd Group was reactivated, every SF soldier who serves long enough will know at least one person who will die because his parachute malfunctions, or a helicopter crashes, or a live round of ammunition accidentally pierces flesh. Just training can be hazardous.

There are two types of risk SF soldiers perpetually face as they train: catastrophic and routine, with costs running from death to disability. Contrary to what one might think, catastrophic risks do not occur just under the guise of foreign combat or exotic disease; any training exercise can prove lethal. More common, though, are the cumulative threats that mount into disability. These come from jumping and jarring knees, backs, and ankles. Or from marching with tremendous loads in uncomfortable rucksacks while wearing nothing more supportive than combat boots. Also, bones begin to permanently ache from too many nights spent on cold ground, or from too many days spent mushing through cold rain. Nor does it help long-term stresses on the body that physical training (PT) is performed five mornings a week—at dawn, if not before—often for twenty years or more. While this weekly regimen of running, sit-ups, and ruck marches keeps soldiers fit enough to hump their heavy loads over long distances, it doesn't give a body any letup. And none of the younger soldiers stops at the bare minimum, so wear from this accumulates, too.

Training doesn't cause physical trauma alone. There are also social impacts. There is the deployment risk to marriages and family life. A soldier can be called away at any time with no warning, for any length of time. Long deployments cause marital strains, but so do long gaps between deployments, when wives feel they need a break because their husbands are getting antsy being stuck in garrison so long. From practically any angle, training has to be viewed as a serious business with lots of repercussions. It costs even while it benefits, and can all too easily wreak havoc on body, soul, ego, team.

Certainly 304's experience in the desert tested all this, and then affirmed the worthiness of the team—sort of. Whether the team really came through with such flying colors depends. From a strictly tactical standpoint, 304 team members did what they never could have done in combat. The team dropped all its security measures to make a heroic effort to save one soldier's life. In doing so the team quite consciously jeopardized its mission. Also, the threat 304 faced (though team members would have argued they couldn't have known this at the time) was minuscule. Everything went to hell over one intruding vehicle. In an actual combat scenario, 304 wouldn't have had any of these luxuries.

But even if 304's members were aware of this in their self-examination after the incident, by the time the team was back at Ft. Bragg all perspective had been lost—*if* 304 had had a realistic perspective in the first place. While later Clay would say he was sure that completing the Q Course less than a year before made all the difference, with his medic training still fresh, there may have been an even bigger lesson the team was missing in reliving the drama of this one momentous event.

It *was* just one event. And as impressive as Clay's efforts were, extricating Rick was simply too easy a success. For the team there was a real danger in taking this one incident of high drama so to heart. In a sense, such self-(re)assuredness only paralleled the kinds of expectations the public, and policymakers in particular, have of SF and of special operators' capabilities. Heroics can be skewing. Training, more missions, and real-world deployments are the only cure.

For soldiers, though, not their wives.

11 Wives and Other Women

ALTHOUGH PERHAPS THERE SHOULD BE, THERE IS NO Q COURSE for wives. Nor is there any survival, evasion, resistance, or escape training. This is certainly to SF soldiers' advantage in one regard. Some manage to get away with all sorts of nonsense without their wives being any the wiser. However, it may not be of much long-term benefit, because numerous SF marriages end in divorce.

Even at the best of times there is nothing easy, glorious, or remunerative about being an SF wife. Just a lot of turmoil and worry shot through with pride, when the marriage is stable. But SF can virtually guarantee that it won't be.

For instance, even though you have been told the phone will ring some time in the middle of the night and you know your husband will have to get up and go in to the company for a simulated call-up, it's still annoying. It's annoying because every time the phone rings and it's the army on the other end, he will all too willingly do whatever the other end of the line asks or suggests. It doesn't matter whether it's serious or not, mandatory or a favor. If he's a good soldier, it doesn't even matter whether someone needs him specifically or whether anyone else would do. Too often he'll just volunteer.

Probably the most debilitating long-term challenge military wives face is the mental one of wrestling with the differences between duty and devotion to army and family. That's because it's not always clear which is regarded as duty and which as devotion. No matter how many times a husband demonstrates his affection, he always seems to be demonstrating it more to the army. Nor is it enjoyable being reminded that essentially the army *is* his life and you are just a wife—and conceivably not even a first, or a last.

Reminders are everywhere. They are perhaps the worst when he is packing to go away. Even if it's only a matter of shoving MREs into a field ruck for nothing more than a routine exercise that has been on the training schedule for months, it is hard to watch him prepare without feeling jealous, worried, sure that already you occupy only the back of his mind. There is a whole parade of concerns that, no matter how many times they recur, you never grow comfortable with: *he's* going away, *he's* going to have fun, but what if he gets hurt, what if the kids get sick, what if the car breaks down, what if his parachute doesn't open. . . .?

Not all trips are just field exercises you've known about for weeks. All sorts of things come up unexpectedly. As a result, no matter how secure the marriage, it is impossible to remain on an even keel all the time. This is probably a truism, but the military has an added arsenal for throwing wives off balance: it can cancel vacations for you, give your husband forty-eight-hour notice he's being assigned to temporary duty two time zones away, not keep accidents from being talked about on the grapevine, or not prevent infidelities from occurring.

Also, the bureaucracy is bigger than everyone. So what that your husband has been scheduled for voluntary surgery, which he's already had to cancel twice. The army needs him to stay two states away for five months and he has to leave tomorrow. On the other hand, the frenzy of getting shots and visas and powers of attorney can be all for nought. Sometimes the bureaucracy changes its mind and retracts its decisions. Sometimes it can even be challenged and convinced that there is a better man for the job. However, when you hear of this happening, it only makes it worse when, later, your husband claims he can't find anyone to replace him on an assignment. Is that true? Has he really tried hard enough? Or does he want to go away for awhile, even as he's telling you he doesn't?

There are lots of little voices that grow very good at asking lots of nagging questions.

It's also unclear on whom absences are harder: wives with children or wives without. Without children women can more easily throw themselves into work, career, independence. But this also means they have that much less in common with wives who are mothers, so that when the team is away their concerns tend to be different, their needs never quite the same, and the team not as much of a team among wives.

Mothers have at least three burdens: disciplining their children, making ends meet, and maintaining stability. Within the military at large, the here-again, gone-again nature of fatherhood poses all sorts of problems for wives who one week must act as sole parent and the next are demoted to being only second in charge. Often the returning father doesn't even know exactly what he's returning to: who did well in school, who's been acting up, why one sibling isn't speaking to another, how the bank account has dwindled, why he's now in debt.

And none of this is something the military can address as well as it would like to. Rather, it's much like team room dynamics. Every team is set up the same way, yet each is different. No matter how carefully the military tries to organize the lives of its members with support systems in place, other realities always intrude.

In SF most families seem to manage without ever availing themselves of all the family support groups and services the army provides. In most army units chaplains are busy people. Not so in 3rd Group, where, if the chaplain does begin counseling a couple, it is usually at the wife's insistence, not the husband's.

Most SF soldiers are just too private. Also, they are all fully aware of how small the organization can turn out to be. As much as the rhetoric claims SF is tight-knit, that really means that rumors and hearsay have less far to travel. In fact, one way some teams ensure that rumors can't fly is to minimize socializing. The thinking is that the less wives come to know each other, the less they'll gossip. A far stronger unwritten rule is that there are some things that go on among the men that no wife should ever find out about. This is based on the assumption that once one wife has been told, the rest will quickly find out. Taken together this means that women can be fairly effectively shut out. Even worse, from a wife's perspective, this also ensures that she may never find out if her husband cheats.

But this may be good as well as bad.

As one team sergeant described it, the reaction to temporary duty assignments is virtually mechanical. Put an SF soldier on an airplane that he doesn't have to jump out of and he has an erection. This might be overstating it but even I could never be sure. After a year and a half in team rooms, the only thing some soldiers still tried to keep me in the dark about was their extracurricular activities. Others were more than open, but several who knew I knew they were married would try to explain away conversational slips with "she's just a good friend, that's all," as if I would believe that they had time for close platonic relationships. This was the flip side to silence, which my husband assured me was so sacrosanct that no matter how much time I spent in certain team rooms with certain team members, none of them would tell me whether he strayed. I didn't believe him. But when I asked I was reassured; he was right—which was hardly reassuring at all.

It was never hard for me to imagine how the possibilities didn't tug too hard, especially when teams were away. Nor did it matter where they were sent. Anywhere could offer just the right mix for an unsettling sort of compartmentalization: with attention focused on the mission, not on home, on the here and now, not the future, on results, not consequences. Then, too, all the tension built up in preparing and executing the assignment . . . why not celebrate afterward? Add alcohol, and with everyone potentially egging one another on, how could even the most happily married soldiers not succumb on occasion? Especially when, if they did go out drinking while they were away, it was usually in bars that were either familiar SF stomping grounds, which meant they attracted women interested in Green Berets, or to places that never saw Green Berets, which made team members all the more alluring.

How could any wife, hundreds or thousands of miles away, possibly compete?

In one sense the battle was lost before it was even begun. In another sense, there was no contest at all. The same compartmentalization that allowed men to be swept along by the moment meant that whatever woman was involved during that moment really didn't matter. When soldiers were away on short trips, or even long exercises with limited opportunities for R & R, the women they met in bars became objectives, targets, diversions, distractions, and stuff for stories. For the SF members I knew who routinely fooled around, love never came into the equation of conquest. They separated sex from affection, and love was felt only for wives and children, not for one-night stands or even long-term extramarital relationships. They really did compartmentalize. This didn't exonerate their behavior and would never pass muster with their wives, but sex did serve a number of purposes quite apart from anything involving sentiment. No SF soldier told me this in so many words, but between all the words it seemed fairly clear.

WITHOUT DOUBT THERE IS INTENSE PEER PRESSURE ON TEAMS. TEAM members themselves tend to deny this, but the denial, too, is rooted in peer pressure cum SF culture. SF culture values individuality. SF-the-organization requires conformity. Most soldiers will abide by the ethos of their team; this is, after all, what conformity demands. If the ethos is to be faithful, team members stay (or at least act) faithful. If, on the other hand, a critical mass within the team favors nightlife, the whole team can swing—at least temporarily—in that direction.

The same company could easily have two teams at opposite ends of the spectrum. On one, socializing after-hours might be nonexistent, even on deployments. Enough team members are good family men that the activities of the few members of the team who are single or divorced, or aren't so upstanding, have little impact. If these three or four partyers don't socialize together after-hours, this also means no critical mass develops to sway the rest of the team to party with them.

But on one team I was familiar with, the biggest partyers were married men. It took only a few to get the rest going. From the perspective of these ringleaders, a team that socialized together after work was a real team, and the way to foster team spirit was through spirited behavior, or so the rationale went. But to listen to the instigators describe their exploits, it was the exploits themselves, and the challenge of not getting caught—the illicitness and adventure all combined—that made them want to expand the game, to include others, to add complications, to up the ante. Their chief goal was to involve the entire team; the content of what occurred along the way was almost incidental.

These soldiers themselves cited parallels between chasing women and practicing fieldcraft, but again, this is their rationalizing. More likely another dynamic was also at work: their wives represented one thing to them and other women represented a host of other things, and they were too undisciplined to choose between them. Also, SF didn't make them. Instead, SF sent them traveling, into the field, away from home, under cover. Ultimately, the team code of tacit silence provided them with their greatest protection. Their own wiliness did the rest, as they straight-facedly told their wives they had to be away suddenly on a field exercise, or when they glibly ad libbed alibis for one another.

Whenever teams traveled, soldiers had opportunity handed to them. Not only did being away offer them plenty of latitude but, as the partyers I knew put it, they could also work in packs. They could wrap themselves in the mystique of being security consultants. And the fact they were in good physical shape always made a difference, particularly to the women they liked to target, professional women who, in their words, were used to Joe Suit-and-Tie. In fact, when describing their exploits, it was always important to highlight who these women were and what they did for a living: pilots, tax assessors, lawyers. The ideal often cited was of six-figure girls, women who would buy these soldiers drinks, loan them their cars, and otherwise pamper them. Obviously, fantasy played a big role in all of this. The men could easily play up to whatever the women wanted to think security consultants and Green Berets were, while the response to their presenting themselves as mysterious operatives had to win these soldiers the kind of flattery and infatuation their wives were long past paying them.

At the same time, it wasn't just to satisfy their own egos or sate their own individual lust that soldiers would indulge in skirt chasing and barhopping. No matter which clichéd explanations they offered about challenge, trophy hunting, doing-the-warrior-thing, it was evident that on some teams there was nothing the least bit subtle about expectations. On long deployments tallies might be kept. Alternatively, for tight teams five or six men all having sex with the same woman wasn't completely unheard of, and even if an individual soldier didn't think he wanted to participate, he simply stopped thinking.

On the few teams where such things occurred, the justification was that messing around was good for the team. Obviously, too, the instigators on such teams wanted everyone to be culpable together. But on most teams, soldiers simply talked a good game and didn't break nearly as many rules as listening to them could suggest.

One could be crude and claim that talk about sex offers penis-positive proof among males that they are males. It certainly seems critical to male bonding. In fact, unsubtle talk about sex serves all sorts of subtle purposes on teams, where males do have to bond. Not only does sex serve as the great equalizer and great individualizer; it is also the one thing team members can exaggerate about without risking anyone's being able to prove them wrong. Two things about how males on teams bond have to be borne in mind. ODA members never reveal everything about themselves to one another, but they also can't live a provable lie. Given the presumption that everyone is heterosexual, an interest in females becomes the least common denominator team members share. This is more than apparent when teams are away from home. It's as if it is incumbent on anyone who sees an attractive female anywhere in the vicinity of the team to alert the rest of the ODA—"blond, three o'clock"—regardless of whether his teammates will agree she's worth looking at. Differences in taste are critical and yet another reason why the topic of sex (and even women as sexual objects) is so useful. Within the rubric of keen heterosexual interest, different preferences allow for all sorts of insignificant but consequential posturing.

For instance, anal sex was a favorite topic on several teams. The explanation for this on ODA 304 was that young soldiers like T & A,

SF soldiers like asses. Jokes ran dirty and they ran deep. Before 307 went into Iraq during the Gulf War, soldiers prepared 8-by-11-inch American flags to sew into the insides of their otherwise insignia-free shirts, which would then serve as recognition panels for U.S. helicopter pilots if the team needed rescue. Scrawled across the white stripes on souvenir copies that team members also made were their names preceded or followed by monikers that were variations on an anal sex theme, as if this is what each of these soldiers routinely engaged in. Yet because there was never any way to find out for whom this was fantasy and who really indulged in it this was a perfect subject for banter.

Soldiers could talk tough about what they were capable of in or out of the bedroom, and allude to all sorts of prowess, and no one could call them on it. Tellingly, this wasn't true for anything else related to being men or to soldiering. Basically, there was nothing else as important to all team members they could discuss so graphically ad infinitum. If everyone on a team fished, maybe fishing could have been a substitute; fish stories lend themselves to exaggeration just about as readily as sex does. But fishing is the only prototypically male activity that at all approaches sex as a topic. Hunting can't work; it involves shooting. Shooting is a skill no SF soldier can boast about without being able to publicly prove he can back up what he says. The same is true for any type of fieldcraft.

Ironically, soldiers may be among the few groups of men who can't get away with simply talking tough to be macho. Most normal things males boast about to validate their maleness teammates already do together. Only sex with women, which is held in common but still allows individuals to define themselves separately, according to their preferences—redheads, blow jobs, legs—doesn't challenge individual integrity or risk group cohesion.

Being revealing about sex also allows for self-ridicule, which in turn permits team members to set themselves up in various ways. For instance, there were at least two different running jokes on one of the teams happily played up to by the soldiers the jokes were aimed at. It was widely known that one team member was never allowed to look at anything remotely pornographic at home. He ad-

vertised this, which then gave him license to run to the adult section of any magazine stand and leaf through smut quite contentedly
whenever the team was outside of Fayetteville. As for the second
soldier, he got kidded every morning about whether his wife had
allowed him any the night before. He was known to get cut off, so
that he always had a ready-made excuse for his morning moodi-
ness. If he hadn't had sex in a while, the team would give him latitude and forgive him his bad mood, and if he had there was always
the chance someone else hadn't and he could make them jealous.

Interestingly, this isn't at all how that soldier's wife presented
their marriage whenever team wives got together. In the company
of other women she always portrayed her husband as a continual
tease and not as someone she would ever want to deny sex to. It was
hard to know whom to believe. However, the real contrast wasn't so
much in what was said but in how much was revealed and to
whom. There is no way the other wives would have recognized this
soldier had they only been told what their own husbands were.

There was never any way to guess, from meeting the wives of
team members, the team member to whom any particular wife was
married. Had I been put to the test after all the time I spent with individual soldiers, I would have failed miserably. I would not have
paired up the battalion's craggiest womanizer with a woman who
looked twice his size and strength, or the NCO with the most biting
wit with the most neatly put together and politest wife. Meeting
wives never seemed to shed any light on their husbands. Never
once did I meet a wife and—knowing her husband—think, ah,
they're so much alike. Not physically, not in terms of temperament,
not even when it came to hobbies or interests. While the SF wives I
knew complemented their husbands by being calm or flamboyant
or simply domestic, and were stabilizing in this sense, few would
have proven an asset on the teams, where soldiers have to be in
good physical shape, stay somewhat cognizant of world events, and
maintain more than just a passing interest in things military. These
are not domains that seemed to appeal at all to most wives. Nor did
any of the wives I know live vicariously through their husbands. I
never heard any of them voice a desire to live in the woods or train

foreign soldiers, although often they would have liked to see some of the foreign places their husbands got to visit.

PARADOXES ABOUND IN THE AGE-OLD RELATIONSHIP BETWEEN HUSbands and wives, just as they do in the relationship between love and war. But paradoxes even surface in the domestic business of whom GIs marry, which often has to do with how GIs go from a lack of love to blind love, and then find themselves in a mistaken marriage.

For unmarried soldiers everywhere the availability of women is critical. If young enlisted men can't meet marriageable women, they can't marry. But usually there is a pattern. Young enlistees fool around. Then they get serious. The catch comes in where they happen to be and whom they happen to be with when the urge to be serious strikes.

Though soldiers most often complain about the dearth (and girth) of local women, whom they euphemistically refer to as "corn-fed," type is actually the real sticking point. Too often the bars and clubs that GIs frequent attract women a lot of GIs would prefer not to marry. But, as they put it, what are their options? Where are they likely to meet nice girls? Not where they're likely to go in any numbers. Also, the competition around bases is always stiff and the ratio skewed. Worse yet, women have the whole range of men in town to choose from. Enlisted soldiers have officers and civilians to compete with.

GIs face a slew of handicaps.

Of course, by the time most soldiers go through the Q Course and enter SF, they're already well beyond this point. Ranking E-4 and higher, the majority have already married. But this business of whom they did marry—as younger GIs once upon a time—is still pertinent. SF lore has it that ODA members have a higher divorce rate than other soldiers. Although Special Operations psychologists deny this, claiming that SF's statistics are really no different than the army's while the army's are not much different from the civilian world's, older SF NCOs hotly contest this. They remain convinced that one badge of being in SF is having gone through at least one divorce—usually from a wife too casually met.

A number of team members married their high school sweethearts. Others married sisters or cousins of their military buddies or their wives. These marriages seemed to last, although actually more critical than how a couple met was attitude. To endure as an SF wife meant not minding either the military (which is often why military brats made the best spouses) or poverty.

For many SF wives their first home was a single-wide trailer. And though, as E-6s and E-7s, most Z Company soldiers did eventually wind up owning houses, having two or three children and a mortgage payment didn't stretch their money any further. During the winter some team members turned on their heat only at night. Others heated with wood they chopped themselves. Some would even joke about how their wives could qualify for Food Stamps and AFDC.

Consequently, many wives tried to work. But there have long been two problems with enlisted wives seeking employment, especially if they married their husbands young and never managed to advance beyond a high school diploma. First, prospective employers often assume that military families are constantly being moved and thus aren't willing to train individuals they presume won't stay. And, second, without a skill acquired either through school or on-the-job training, many NCO wives find nothing better than low-end, minimum-wage employment. Too often this won't bring in enough money to pay for child care. Therefore, they remain unemployed outside the home. They also wind up trapped. If they can't work they often can't afford school. Nor is money the only sticking point. Again, there is the matter of whom they can get to watch their children. Husbands certainly can't be counted on because they don't have regular schedules. This means that some wives, whether they want to or not, stay housebound.

But not all wives. In contrast, some not only work but bring in good money. Team members married to women who had licenses of various kinds—in nursing or real estate, for example—often joked that their wives earned more money than they did, and this created its own tensions. Most often soldiers who waited to marry or were on second wives found themselves in this position. But essentially wives ran the same kind of gamut as the soldiers. There was no single type in terms of ambition, temperament, or style.

There also wasn't much common ground among team wives,

except that they were team wives. And this represented a significant change. It is another reason given for why teams in 3rd Group weren't socializing the way teams used to. According to veteran SF NCOs and their wives, team parties used to be regular occurrences. Now they were few and far between, and when team members and their wives did get together, the lack of casual socializing tended to show. It usually took several drinks before everyone loosened up.

Some of this had to do with distance. Ft. Bragg was a big post and military personnel lived in pockets throughout Fayetteville, which itself was spread out. There was nothing to compel or even encourage team members to live near one another. Then, too, the larger society made for all sorts of drift, not just in terms of which wives worked and which didn't, or where people lived, but in terms of what women thought. In the past it was simply expected that a military wife would be willing to sacrifice everything for her husband's career. Not only was this out of fashion by the 1990s but for many women who grew up under the influence of the woman's movement, it was out of character too. If they didn't like their husbands' colleagues they didn't have to spend time with them; if they didn't spend time with them they had no way to determine whether they might have liked them or not.

Changes in society's attitudes toward domesticity—especially concerning who should be helping whom with what—also put a squeeze on military marriages. For instance, with child rearing no longer considered an exclusively female occupation, all sorts of demands greeted the SF soldier when he came home at night. After spending all day in the team room, his duty was hardly done. Husbands' time had become an ever more valuable (and controllable) commodity, which extended right into weekends. And while such togetherness either worked well or it grated, even many husbands' attitudes had changed. This was partially a function of demographics. Whenever SF has admitted only sergeants, the average age on teams has risen. This means many soldiers, like Roger Harmon on 307 and Mark and KC on 309, were already well into or through their first marriage by the time they made it onto teams and—older and more mature—they were also much more serious when they committed to second marriages.

But some changes, too, the army helped foster. The decreasing tolerance for alcohol abuse and the extent to which a reprimand could damage even an enlisted soldier's career signaled clear changes in military culture. If not yet unacceptable, partying was no longer expected. The army helped undermine the need for teams to socialize by also stepping into the breach and making available a whole array of family support services. Team parties used to help wives get to know one another. Now, prior to any deployment, SF wives are routinely informed; they are told whom, in the chain of command, within Special Forces, and on the base they can turn to. This has meant that unless there is some special danger, there is no real reason for wives to *have* to interact.

But two different sets of circumstances could still bring wives together: accidents and isolation. With an accident the coming together is automatic. Rick's wife was overwhelmed with people offering help once word spread that he'd been shot. Fortunately, accidents are not so common. Unfortunately, neither is isolation. Undoubtedly 3rd Group companies and Z Company's ODAs would have had a different kind of social life had 3rd Group been situated on a smaller, more remote post. The sprawl of Fayetteville and Ft. Bragg often made people nostalgic for smaller bases like Ft. Devens (the former home of 10th Group) or wherever they may have been stationed abroad, when families depended on one another for company and entertainment. But isolation wasn't entirely unknown at Ft. Bragg. Real-world events did occasionally manufacture it.

Loneliness tended to surround wives whenever there was a real-world deployment, when, suddenly there went the other adult in the family. More to the point, there also went the reason a woman was stuck being a military wife. Unless a wife's relatives or close friends had likewise experienced the continual worry of having a husband in potential danger, they couldn't know what this absence felt like. They couldn't help quell all her fears. Who could, when the one person who could help the most was the person deployed?

Certainly this was the problem during the Gulf War. The wait until 3rd Group soldiers knew for sure they were going to the Gulf was agonizing. Team members were keyed up and then let down on what seemed to be a weekly basis. They'd be about to leave, told they weren't yet going, then called up for a twenty-four-hour departure, only to be stood down again. That much of this occurred between the Thanksgiving and Christmas holidays didn't help. Nerves were stretched thin as vacations had to be canceled for nought. Then came the even more nerve-wracking business of watching the air war begin on television without knowing whether there would have to be a ground war, but with word already filtering back about the missions that 5th Group soldiers were performing behind enemy lines. These too were classified, nonpublicized missions, so that while learning about them heightened the anxiety team members were already feeling—about getting to the Gulf, having to go there, what they would face once there—this wasn't information they were supposed to share with their wives. Talk about undercurrents. Yet even when this information was shared, it didn't help bridge the gap, which, on a daily basis, was only widening as team members increasingly focused on the war and mentally couldn't avoid drawing back from spouses, who couldn't help but be increasingly clingy.

Then once 3rd Group was sent, the strung-out nature of not-knowing and having no control over what would next transpire automatically intensified. It was under these conditions that the lack of solidarity among wives completely altered. In fact, whenever teams are sent on real-world, long-term, and/or combat missions, wives have to draw together not only for the kind of mutual support impossible to find elsewhere but also for the back-channel sources of information.

When husbands are away, they self-admittedly hold to one of two philosophies. Either they write letters (and telephone) as often as possible or they write as seldom as they think they can get away with. Those who don't write or call claim that thinking about home makes being away worse and distracts them. Of course, this also could be a convenient excuse. Still, wives share whatever information they do get, and usually this helps, because team members have little more to write about than life as lived by the entire team. Wives quickly clue one another in.

Meanwhile, something unspoken that also draws wives together seems to be the notion that if they behave as though they, too, are a cohesive unit, the ODA will return home as a team, intact, with everyone alive. The descriptive term for this in anthropology is "sympathetic magic." What such behavior also suggests, though, is that wives do recognize, on some level, the extent to which they occupy a parallel universe, something husbands already know and often worry over.

WHAT HUSBANDS THINK THEIR WIVES ARE DOING AT A DISTANCE CAN affect them tremendously. The army knows this, ergo family support services. But though the army might step in with financial, health care, and morale assistance to tide the wives over, it can't prevent or control everything. This is significant because during the Gulf War the flow of information wasn't just from the Gulf back to the States; rumors flew in all directions, and just enough stories reached Saudi Arabia about wives messing around at home to give enough husbands pause. Some team members insisted they knew of soldiers who received videotape proof of their wives engaging in sex acts with other men. Others circulated stories about wives who used their husbands' absence to financially clean them out before vanishing. Stories like these tend to surface on every long deployment and are largely apocryphal. Even so, something about them still grips the men long enough to turn them leery. No wonder so many wives are encouraged to go home to their parents when their husbands are away. This addresses all sorts of needs in one fell swoop.

For working wives, this was no option during the Gulf War. Then, too, there was the tug of staying close to Ft. Bragg, where everyone was on the same emotional roller-coaster. Sometimes being around military personnel who know more about the military than reporters do is helpful; it can allay fears. At other times, a little bit of knowledge is dangerous and wives would get worked up for no good reason.

One thing the Gulf War did make clear was that being a wife rather than a girlfriend or fiancée does make a difference as far as the military is concerned. I wasn't a wife yet. I also wasn't at Ft. Bragg. In general, benefits accrue only to those the army can safely classify as dependents—spouses and children. Much the same can be said for information. Anyone falling outside these bounds exists only by the grace of whatever goodwill he or she can elicit. Officially I wasn't part of the flow of information, although a very forthcoming captain's wife did keep me well informed. This may be one very practical but unheralded reason why there is always a flurry of marriages on the eve of war. Only marriage automatically plugs women in. With war they also plug into one another.

After war, though, disconnects recur. For instance, it was never apparent how much of a team remained among wives once husbands returned from the Gulf. Teams certainly didn't socialize anymore. Maybe most wives felt they didn't need to, because if nothing else they now knew just how fast they could count on one another when they had to. Usually there was enough to occupy them when their husbands were home anyway. Particularly around the holidays.

APPARENTLY WIVES ON 309 SPOKE TO ONE ANOTHER DAILY DURING the Gulf War, and, while some had fast friendships before the war, most husbands believed they all remained friendly afterward. Steve knew better—he was aware of tensions among some of 309's wives—which is why his volunteering his house without first consulting his wife about hosting a team Christmas party a year after the Gulf War made little sense. It also turned out to be a huge mistake. As Steve had to admit to the team a few days later, she had too much else going on that weekend with her own office Christmas parties. Although as Steve was explaining this, he was also warming up to a new marital crisis, which prompted Greg to intercede. What about his house? Obviously, parties were *not* common events for ODA 309.

But the logistics were easy. The theme was potluck and BYOB, although it was also evident that Greg's wife had spent the better part of the previous day preparing. Whatever room was left in the refrigerator was reserved for beer, while as guests arrived bearing food, dishes soon were everywhere. It was a salad-and-casserole feast. It was also quite the gathering: kids were encouraged to watch movies in a back bedroom, and at least while everyone was eating, husbands, wives, and infants stayed together in the living room. It was also incredibly sedate.

Conversation revolved around domestic issues. Only when everyone's interest in food had finally waned did the men move outside with some of the older children, while most of the wives gravitated to the kitchen.

Conversation outside, in between horseshoes and batting balls around, was boring: shoptalk. Worse, it was stilted, as if wearing slacks and nice shirts was too constraining. Normally there was nothing awkward about these men when they sat around the team room in fatigues discussing all these same subjects. By contrast, nothing was restrained about their wives' conversation in the kitchen.

Once again these women were discussing sex. The only other time I had been at a gathering of 309 wives, at a dinner organized by KC's wife, sex wound up as the topic of choice by the end of the evening. The talk was even racier now. A little bit of what the wives were engaging in was obviously one-upmanship about whose husband was the most insatiable, when (early morning?), and where (had anyone tried the top of the dryer? one wife swore by it). But this was also bonding. What had brought these women together wasn't really a Christmas party but the men outside. These wives had no interest in their husbands' principal interest—soldiering—but they all had an interest in soldiers, and quite specific soldiers at that.

In contrast to how sex was discussed in team rooms, where husbands never talked in any sort of detail about their wives, the foibles that the wives shared in the kitchen were their husbands'. Some were also of the sort I was not so sure I wanted to hear. I definitely didn't want to remember all the details when I was back in the team room. As it was, I didn't see how I could look at some of these women's husbands without smiling. But whom would I be smiling at? On my own, knowing who liked to do what was fairly useless information, and it wasn't likely to do me any bonding good with the team.

It did tell me something more about bonding, however. Just the fact that these wives were being this personal, and far more personal than their husbands ever were, was revealing: of course the women could exchange information like this. Unlike their husbands, the wives didn't have to work and live with one another. They also didn't have to worry that details they divulged today might boomerang as ridicule tomorrow. There was no immediate tomorrow for the teamful of wives.

At the same time, the lack of real intimacy among the wives as a group meant that whenever they did get together, they needed to ensure they still had certain fundamental things in common. The ultimate shortcut to this was sex talk. The humor in the mock risqué helped prevent anything serious or divisive from coming up, and certain unspoken sentiments could be shared without other subjects ever needing to be broached. No religion, no politics, no hot-button issues. In this regard the women operated exactly like the men. But then, it was because of the men that the women found themselves in such a situation to begin with. And within the rubric of remaining SF wives they also had much less choice than their seemingly freewheeling can-you-believe-he-does-this conversation in the kitchen suggested.

This is because the allusions were completely hollow. Yes, the talk was suggestive and made various men sound quite appealing. But it was also meaningless. Disarming perhaps, but nonthreatening for sure. Unless specifically invited, team members won't mess around with one another's wives.

Not-messing-around within the team is the corollary rule to not telling wives about messing around outside marriage. And among SF soldiers this is as binding a rule. Nor is its purpose the least bit hidden. Soldiers know they had better stick to it if they want to maintain order and protect trust.

12 The Specter of Change

In SF there are rules and then there are rules. Not sleeping with a teammate's wife is on a completely different order of magnitude than having to participate in routinely military, but still ritual, events.

SF, like other units, holds a ceremony whenever there is a change in command, though just how fancy this is usually depends on the rank attached to the position being filled. Consequently, majors in charge of companies and lieutenant colonels in charge of battalions have nothing on group commanders, who are full-bird colonels. Changes of command at the group level can be truly impressive. Certainly 3rd Group's was, though the sight would probably have been more stirring still had I not known that all those bulging rucksacks were stuffed with newspaper.

There stood the whole group, all three battalions and a battalion's worth of support staff in formation, fully decked out, on the Pike Field parade ground. The uniqueness of this occasion was hard to miss. For two mornings running, team members had been up at 0300, yesterday to practice and today to perform the real thing. At 0400 they drew their weapons: M-16s with bayonets now fixed.

Although this entire event seems uncharacteristically formal for SF, it's completely army, with the 82nd Airborne Division band, a color guard, and a twenty-one-gun salute. The reviewing stand is full of guests who sit under a specially erected awning, having been escorted to their seats across an unfurled red carpet. But even with all the pomp and circumstance—befitting the changeover from one full-bird colonel to another—there are still indicators that this remains an SF ceremony after all. For one, there are mod demos to the side.

Mod demos are SF's stock-in-trade when it comes to self-promotion. Generally whenever SF participates in any kind of event open to the public, or whenever visiting dignitaries are being sold on unconventional American know-how, SF organizes a modular demonstration. All newly appointed U.S. ambassadors, for instance, are treated to mod demos. There used to be an entire team (the Gabriel team) devoted to promoting SF in this fashion. Now any team might be called on to cough up a commo sergeant to stand behind his tools of the trade: radios, antennae, battery packs, all the things a commo sergeant might carry and use in the field. Or an engineer to stand behind rolls of det cord, blasting caps, and wire. Or a medic to display the neat packages of bandages, surgical instruments, and drugs normally carried in a medic bag. Or a weapons sergeant to answer questions about any one of the dozen or so foreign or domestic weapons arrayed in front of him.

Presumably the mod demos set up at this ceremony are meant for visitors from Fayetteville and other civilians. Certainly neither the outgoing nor the incoming colonel is new to SF. Nor is the general who officiates. All three have known one another and served in SF for years. And each represents a slightly different phase in SF's evolution. The general was born in eastern Europe just before World War II and exemplifies the type of soldier SF initially recruited. The outgoing colonel, an ROTC graduate, served in Vietnam and Central America. His chest is full of combat and combat-related decorations. In contrast, the incoming colonel missed serving in Vietnam, instead spending tours in Germany and Panama. A West Point graduate, he probably best epitomizes the direction in which SF is moving. Since being commissioned he's attended all the right schools, and increasingly these seem to be what count toward advancement.

By design, though, this ceremony belongs less to him than to the outgoing colonel, whose intention has long been to show off SF to advantage. Thus, there is a HALO jump in addition to the mod demos. The event plan calls for one of the group's HALO teams to jump out of a helicopter, then land on the parade ground in front of the reviewing stand. However, where the team actually winds up is well out of sight in the tree line on the far side of the field, leading to all sorts of ribbing of all HALO teams afterward, and belying the co-ordination it took to order this helicopter in the first place, and a second one to shortly follow.

Between the two helicopters comes the ceremony proper. The outgoing colonel reviews the troops by walking around all four bat-talions. The group flag then passes hands. The general presents the outgoing colonel with the Legion of Merit, and his wife with the spouse's equivalent for meritorious service. He also presents battle streamers to 3rd Group as a whole, and First Battalion in particular for service in Desert Storm. In his speech he remarks on First Bat-talion's performance in Desert Storm and hails Second Battalion's recent deployment to Cuba's Guantanamo Bay to help with Haitian refugees. This nicely alludes to the range of the group's capabilities. He also generously praises the outgoing colonel, who, at this point, literally becomes outgoing.

The second helicopter now swoops in over the pine trees, then hovers in a corner of the field, affording the colonel just enough time to jog toward it and strap himself into a harness at the end of a long rope. The helicopter slowly rises, with the colonel still at-tached to the rope, dangling below its belly. This is STABOing, an uncomfortable maneuver but one that allows him to wave to the crowd below as he demonstrates a final SF capability. His wife is later teased for not choosing to exit alongside him.

Formally the group now belongs to its new commander. In his speech, which he makes from the reviewing stand and not from the field, the new commander sounds a bit nervous, not nearly so self-confident or colloquial as his predecessor or the presiding general. But he's brief. Then, still not walking onto the field, he conducts his review of the troops from the reviewing stand, as they march past us. The band plays and the battalions stride past within feet of the guests. Staring straight ahead, weapons rigidly held, rucksacks bulging behind, legs synchronized, the ODAs look as though they have been at this for far longer than just two mornings, which is either a testament to SF soldiers' sense of discipline or to how well marching was drilled into them before they turned SF. Of course, this is done with gritted teeth.

All the teams have been grousing. And to a person the soldiers have sounded the same litany: one reason they came into SF was to escape just such parade ground nonsense.

But I wonder which is worse, this or the new group commander's self-introduction to the group a few days later when, to accommodate all fifty-four ODAs, as well as support staff, his briefing has to be held in the unair-conditioned main post theater. Even then the auditorium is full. It's a daunting sight, and in some regards more impressive than seeing all fifty-four teams stand to attention and present arms on the parade field. Here there are no guests or women, just seat after seat of camouflage-clad soldiers. From the back everyone looks completely interchangeable: a head of hair above shoulders smeared green and brown.

In true briefing fashion the lights are dimmed and slides are projected onto a screen front and center. These outline the colonel's talking points, which are so self-evident they require little explanation. Nevertheless, the purpose of the talk is to go through them one by one so that the colonel can familiarize "his men" with his dos and don'ts and give them a sense of what he expects.

He begins by describing how he—like all other SF officers—would much rather have his own ODA than command fifty-four teams. He summarizes his experience: as a team leader, a company commander, and a battalion commander. He notes that his most recent posting was as a "staff weenie"—his term, though this is also a calculated expression to signal to the NCOs that he knows how they think, understands them, and even appreciates their attitudes.

Next, he touches on the buzz topics that all officers of his rank seem to have to address: the importance of quiet professionalism and family support. He points out that family support is what SF detachments have been doing from the beginning, before there was such a fancy term for it, and he pays proper lip service to team members' wives as the people who really support the soldiers.

Finally, he moves on to the soldiers themselves. He cites his preferences: for split detachments full of soldiers who really want to be in SF rather than full teams rounded out with men who don't. He admits that it's sometimes difficult to criticize or counsel soldiers who just shouldn't be in SF, but admonishes everyone that now is the time to do a better job of moving inappropriate personnel out of the unit so that duds don't just get shuffled from team to team.

Then it's on to training. As he points out, the teams have to be prepared to go to war and to win. To do this they must train. Consequently, he wants to see real training, not just a dog and pony show whenever he comes for a visit. If a team is planning to do something interesting in training, he wants to be apprised of it. In his view— and because this is how his ODA operated—Monday should be a preparation day for going out to the field on Tuesday. Friday is the day to come back from the field, clean weapons, and take care of general maintenance before heading home for the weekend. Training should always be as realistic as possible. All training should be conducted as if all exercises were live-fire exercises, while all live-fire exercises should be conducted without fire-control officers. There are no fire-control officers in combat. Everyone has to be a safety officer. Everyone is on duty twenty-four hours a day. . . .

A secondary theme he sounds is that he won't favor any one battalion, any one company, or any one team. He intends to spread the wealth evenly. . . .

No wonder his audience is bored. In mouthing all the correct platitudes the colonel is actually saying very little. Even when he comments that he doesn't like the idea of Green, Red, and Amber cycles, which means they're now history, this only stands to reason. Rubbing lemon juice on why he might dislike this arrangement: this was his predecessor's system; of course, he'll have to revamp it to set himself apart.

Otherwise, the audience isn't left with any real sense of what their new commander wants. Does he favor training for direct action or does he prefer focusing on foreign internal defense? He doesn't mention where he sees the group going, nor does he indicate in which direction he sees himself pushing it.

From the teams' perspective the only purpose the briefing has served is to remind them who's in charge. The colonel has simply introduced himself as the new honcho at the top of the group hierarchy. He has no more compelled them to want to follow him than any other officer. The same distance yawns as when he reviewed them from on high out at Pike Field. Nor, in their review of him, do they believe anything substantial is likely to change in their favor.

As proof of this, just hours later, once everyone is home for the night, the calling starts. Word comes down the "tree" from battalion staff that the colonel is planning to visit Z Company for PT in the morning; everyone needs to be sure he is wearing the right uniform. Everyone in the company consequently gets a call. So much for the colonel's having convinced those who will be executing his orders that he really is committed more to real training than propriety. Either they don't trust his self-presentation or they already know more about him than he has chosen to reveal. The ODAs take their cues from this.

Within weeks there's more. Suddenly, Gargoyle sunglasses are no longer allowed. The new group commander wants to see more conservative, more uniform eyewear on his soldiers. Then there's a new policy about posters in the team rooms. No more T & A. While this makes sense in light of the Tailhook mess and may well have been mandated from on high, the teams blame the colonel, especially because he's also made it clear that he doesn't want team rooms looking like living rooms. No more couches.

The teams' comfort does not seem to rate very high with their new boss. Yet another change has to do with web gear. The new order is for vests to replace these gear-laden suspenders. The problem with vests is that they are infinitely hotter. And as some team members complain, it's taken them years to get their web gear arranged just right, with canteens here, signal mirrors and flares there. From the ODA perspective the demand that they wear vests is just one more indication of how much higher command is trying to standardize them; the vests will be that much harder to personalize. The message here is twofold: image is everything and conventionalization is truly underway.

JUST A FEW WEEKS LATER, OUT NEAR THE COBRA GUNNERY RANGES well away from the main post, the entire battalion prepares for a field training exercise (FTX). This is the battalion commander's idea. He wants the teams to prove they can teach an entire infantry company (which can run anywhere from 120 to 160 men) how to attack and overrun a position. In other words, this is foreign internal defense training, and should act as both a refresher and a reminder at the same time: that infantry tactics can be complicated.

Marines take part in the exercise. On a ridge some miles away from the SF encampment, they operate 155 mm. howitzers that will initiate the attack, along with 4.2-inch mortars manned by fifteen SF soldiers located elsewhere. At the exercise area itself there is a razor-wire-enclosed ammunition supply point (ASP), where stored ammunition requires a twenty-four-hour guard. A mess hall, which is a trailer under camouflage netting, sits some distance away from Z Company's location. Tents house battalion and support staffs and a command-and-control center. A generator whines as soon as it is dark. Without question, this is the most elaborate SF exercise I've seen so far on post.

It's also one that has everyone extremely disgruntled. Z Company's very first maneuver doesn't help. This is a platoon-sized attack on a position defended by support and headquarters personnel. Two problems immediately arise. The first is having to wear MILES (Multiple Integrated Laser Engagement System) gear. The soldiers hate it. Festooning themselves with sensors means having to carry weight on their helmets and junk across their chests. With MILES the aim is to simulate actual casualties. Soldiers are supposed to be able to electronically eliminate one another with well-placed shots. Alarms should sound whenever a sensor has been hit. However, SF soldiers have long since figured out how to rig the strings of sensors so that even the best-aimed shots won't activate the alarms. Consequently, they regard having to fix adapters to their gun muzzles as an unnecessary waste of time, while tugging on the sensors just adds up to more aggravation in the mounting heat.

Problem number two is more substantial. The range—a set of scruffy clearings amid scrub oak—is too small to accommodate the entire company. This means the soldiers bunch, a real worry considering the live fire version to follow. Also, they make a few serious mistakes. The lead element, for instance, walks into the objective before halting to do a leader's recon.

Still, when the switch is made from the ineffective MILES gear to deadly live rounds, no one gets hurt. The second attack is far more successful than the first, though as a lot of soldiers comment afterward, the first couldn't have been much worse. This sums up the tone for the day.

Lunch follows, though before anyone has time to begin the great MRE entrée swap, Major Geoffries orders Z Company to pile into trucks to make way for the next company due in the area to practice the same attack. The schedule calls for Z Company to learn about mortars at the range where ODAs 306 and 309 have set them up.

At this new range, which is set under cooler pines, the company finally falls out to eat. This also gives KC (from 309) and 306's team captain time to vent to Major Geoffries. Apparently the mortars they're responsible for shooting off were ordered without fuses, or came without fuses from battalion, and can't be fired. The battalion colonel has also been by and chewed out everyone present, but especially 306's captain, innumerable times. Earlier he caught the captain in his humvee without a helmet on. Then he was dissatisfied with who was manning the mortars. In his view the composite team shouldn't have been drawn from 306 and 309, each of which is understaffed at the moment, but instead should have been comprised of all the weapons sergeants in the company. In other words, what was the rationale for having just any old set of Z Company soldiers in this position? There couldn't have been any. . . .

In yet another sally past the mortar range the colonel yelled again at 306's captain, this time because his team had roof racks on its vehicles. Apparently someone higher up in the chain of command said he no longer wanted to see roof racks on humvees (never mind that they had been bolted on for Desert Storm to carry extra water and fuel canisters). Why weren't they off yet?

After hearing all this Major Geoffries decides the company can learn about mortars sometime later in the week, back in the company area. Better that his teams should eat and E & E (escape and evade). One of the reasons 306 and 309 have caught so many ass-chewings is that they're right off the road leading into the exercise area. Obviously the battalion commander is spending the day driving up and down this road. Z Company might as well go straight up to the Marine position for classes on the howitzers. In the tangle of roads to get there the hope is we won't run into the colonel. Just in case, everyone is instructed to put on his helmet. This, then, becomes fodder for a new round of complaining, which is actually growing quite old. Traditionally, SF standards have been looser than the rest of the army's; SF soldiers never used to wear protective kevlar in vehicles, and only rarely wore helmets at all. From the teams' perspective, all the new edicts forcing them into these steel pots (mockingly called "domes of obedience") offered further proof that galloping conventionalization was well under way. Helmets are a million times worse than MILES gear.

At least no one has to wear a helmet at the Marine position, a bare nob in the blazing sun. Otherwise brains would boil. The Marines give three short classes on their function as forward observers and how they will respond when the battalion calls for artillery fire. It's so hot that no one really cares. And Rick, who probably shouldn't be on this exercise (he's supposed to be recovering from his latest surgery), looks decidedly ill.

After the washboard ride back to camp Rick is hustled into the military ambulance on station there and the medics crank up the air conditioning. Once his temperature drops they'll drive him back to Fayetteville. The combination of his medicine, the heat, and doing too much too soon has wiped him out. Before heading home he gives away his pop tarts and sunflower seeds and invites me to stay under his poncho, where he has a Thermarest sleeping pad and pillow laid out; I just have a sleeping bag under mine, in the middle of a nest of seed ticks. But there's no resting yet. A brief water break later it's time for the next activity on the training schedule: a short shuffle down the road so the company can practice squad-sized tactics, yet another component in the full battalion attack tomorrow. But with no air stirring, Major Geoffries is realistic. He sees no reason for the squads (ODAs 307, 308, and a combined team of 304 and 305) to move around much. That he sends them into the woods out of sight means they don't have to.

While the teams might gripe about Major Geoffries and what they perceive to be his lack of leadership skills, his wishy-washiness, and his seeming inability to stand up to the battalion commander, he is actually far more committed to them than they realize. Major Geoffries knows how hot it is. He knows how everyone is feeling about this "required" exercise. If anything, he more than agrees with the NCOs. The planning *has* been abysmal. The company wasn't given any sort of direction in the attack this morning. Nothing seems to have been worked out fully, let alone imaginatively. The training value approaches zero. All he can see teams getting out of this is time away from Fayetteville. There's not even enough mingling between companies for any sort of solidarity to build across the battalion. Over dinner, teams—not even companies—stick together. The hot meal of meat, potatoes, and green beans does nothing for group morale. Nor is there any more mixing the next morning when, although this is a battalionwide exercise, each company still sticks to itself, and within companies teams also stay fairly separate as they work toward the battalion attack.

THE ENTIRE BATTALION WILL ONLY REALLY COME TOGETHER TWICE: just prior to launching into the woods for a run-through of the full-scale joint attack and for a live-fire repeat. The walk-through for the battalion attack is scheduled for 1230 (Day Two), with the live-fire version to take place the following morning (Day Three), all of which probably seemed perfectly reasonable when it was first put together in the air-conditioned comfort of Ft. Bragg. However, by midday on Day Two it's hard to tell which is the more insufferable: the heat or the humidity. Immediately after the full-scale walk-through a number of soldiers look as if they are ready to pass out. Fortunately none does. Luckily the walk-through is deemed a success.

This is auspicious because word comes down from on high that the group commander is heading out to the exercise area and will be bringing a general in tow. Today. Which inspires the battalion staff to rejigger the schedule and move the live-fire exercise forward. So much for the group commander's purported desire to see training as it's really done.

At first the teams are told to get ready to run through the entire exercise immediately. Then it's decided instead to feed them an early dinner. This in turn suggests to cynical team members that the battalion staff intends the live-fire exercise to be a dog and pony show, which is why they'd prefer the men fed: they'll grumble less.

In fact, moving up the live-fire exercise promises one reward: the battalion won't have to wake at 0400 to stage it.

As with most exercises, getting everyone into position takes longer than the live-fire assault itself. There's a lot of standing around before all the men are on the road leading into the free-fire zone. Then comes the short walk through the woods before teams reconfigure themselves as squads, preparatory to zigzagging from bush to tree to bush in the rush toward the objective, the far edge of a long clearing.

The first two signal flares meant to initiate the attack both hit trees, but scattered bursts of rifle fire signify that the squads still know to bound forward under the combined light of illumination flares and dusk. Lulls in the shooting reveal men working to stay in line with one another. Harsh-tasting smoke billows just above the ground as smoke grenades get popped. From where I am, just behind one of the forward-moving squads, it all seems real but unreal at the same time. Key battle sounds, like screams, are missing, though the noise is still so loud that it becomes physical. Ear protection only helps rearrange its effects. Then it's over. With no opposition, the event has to end almost as soon as it begins; forward elements are on top of the objective in no time. In fact, the mad minute after the ceasefire, when soldiers stand in line pointing

their guns into the same (safe) distance, blazing away with whatever ammunition they have left, proves the most dramatically satis-
fying moment of all. It turns out to be much easier to empty
magazines this way than to return unexpended ammunition,
which provokes at least one soldier to grumble, "I thought there
were budget problems"—itself perhaps the best commentary on
the real drama in the exercise.

Still, no one has enough energy to get too worked up about the
waste tonight. With the attack behind them no one even seems to
mind that the group commander never showed up. Nor was there
a visit from a general. The battalion commander doesn't stick
around to conduct the after-action review. Instead, the teams have
to be told they did well by one of his underlings. So this portion of
the exercise is also considered a major success. But to what end?

Some team members come out of the field with poison oak.
Others wind up with thirty to forty tick bites. These are hazards that
come with the territory this time of year. Luckily both are treatable,
if not preventable, by eating garlic or swallowing match heads, mixing sulphur and talc, wearing flea collars around ankles, using
army bug juice, keeping sleeves rolled down. Or relief will come
later in baking soda baths. If only there were similar cures for other
effects of the exercise.

SF VETERANS CONTINUALLY LAMENT THE DAYS BEFORE SF WAS
made its own branch, when team members taught one another,
teams were more responsible for their own training, and, so long as
they didn't wind up in trouble and could perform to standards, they
weren't nearly so leashed. Often in the recent past ODAs could head
off on cross-country mountain ski trips or attend civilian schools
where they learned skills like rock climbing or mule packing. The
philosophy was that any training proved valuable because it kept
soldiers versatile. Implicit, too, was the idea that creative-minded
training made for creative-minded soldiers. Now teams were having
to prove that any special training they sought made sense in the area
of the world they were oriented to, while commanders seemed less
and less open-minded about what this should include. For instance,

mules are important in Central America but absent in most of Africa. Soldiers from 3rd Group wanting to attend mule-packing school couldn't fit themselves into the right criterion (officially known as METL—Mission Essential Task List) no matter how hard they tried. Commanders just didn't seem to care that what worked with mules might also work with camels. Imagination, increasingly, was losing out to standardization and control.

Forget the heat, humidity, and bugs; these changes in what constituted training were the most enervating. According to soldiers who had served most of their careers in SF, too many individuals were also being sent to too many schools too often. Seldom did teams hold their full complement. Certainly, on paper, ODAs still looked impressive, full of highly trained soldiers who *had* attended all the right schools. Further proof came in the form of results from certification, recertification, and validation, though to many NCOs having to continually retake so many skills tests likewise focused too much attention on individuals, rather than teams. Team members weren't supposed to run through land navigation courses together, and target shooting challenged men only individually. While veteran NCOs understood the principle behind the incessant need to demonstrate this kind of readiness, they still didn't approve. Again, they blamed the fact that SF had become its own branch; officers occupying all the new layers of command had to know whether teams were deployable or not and, since tests made for easily measurable means, tests were administered. Some veterans even recognized that from the perspective of SF command, tests and standards, and the ability to show all these off on paper, *were* critical to their being able to present SF as a legitimate and viable branch of the army, and to sell conventional commanders on the worth of SF soldiers.

Still, too many decisions that influenced training were being made at God level, which is how soldiers commonly refer to realms inhabited by generals and high-ranking staffers. There were altogether too many echelons, all seeking to exert control; with way too much distance between them and the teams, decision makers at

God level didn't seem to appreciate that teams might have their own training needs.

As for newly arrived NCOs and captains, they quickly absorbed all these gripes and then added some of their own. Naturally, they came to the teams eager to perform. Long-time SF members recall feeling equally impatient when they were just arrived, though what they remember being the most anxious about was learning all the fieldcraft their elders knew. Every time they went into the field, they were reminded how much more experience the old-timers had, how much wisdom this lent them, and how much depth this granted teams. In contrast, the battalionwide exercises, the seemingly endless recertification in basic soldiering skills, the need to demonstrate to higher command just how many hoops they could jump through wasn't generating this same sentiment among younger soldiers. If anything, such practices only served to reconfirm younger soldiers' sense that they were just as good, and quicker, stronger, maybe even better than older SF members. And they probably were better at much of the conventional stuff. But were they also as flexible, as wily, as mature? Without more unconventional tests or better team training there was no good way to find out. Nor was this what commanders, ultimately, seemed interested in determining. Commanders operated under their own constraints and suffered their own preoccupations. Always, too, they were answerable to higher authority. So to higher authority then, on behalf of veteran NCOs: is it really superior soldiers who make SF special or superior soldiers in well-trained teams?

Conclusion: SF and the Future

ON THE SURFACE, IT IS EASY TO SENSE HOW THE LACK OF A DRAFT, the turbulence from downsizing, and the end of the Cold War have squeezed the army, and, in turn, affected SF. On top of this there are AIDS, the demise of smoking, the curtailment of drinking, and the army's own emphasis on education to consider. Add to this the sheer weight of the new branch hierarchy and bear in mind that initially SF was run by a single colonel. Now colonels are a dime a dozen and generals aren't particularly rare, and team life has had to become more restricted. Yet not everything has been lost or reconfigured. An SF soldier who served on a mobile training team in El Salvador in the 1960s would still recognize a foreign internal defense assignment today. This is because at least two things continue to anchor SF. The first is that SF remains institutionally young, with enough founding members alive, committed, and influential. Behind the scenes they fight to keep SF unconventionally oriented, while the second source of consistency resides in SF's team-level organization. Structurally, the ODA remains an unsurpassed invention.

As evidenced by all the mobile-training and technical-assistance field teams that have never attracted attention, teams obviously *do* police themselves. So much anonymity suggests most soldiers *have* behaved professionally. In fact, given the wide range of circumstances under which teams have slipped in and out of other countries over the years, we might conclude that the key to SF's success must reside in team structure even more than in specific personnel. Although how personnel are selected also guarantees that the structure *can* prevail. The Q Course is critical. And it, too, is quite ingenious.

However, not everything connected to SF works as well as it could, nor is it fair of SF NCOs to blame all the changes they don't like on officers and higher command. Contradictions may also be inherent in SF's design, some of which date to the founding of the organization, which weaken its stability. The direct action/foreign internal defense divide is one. Another is the inadequate acquisition of local expertise. Finally, there is the familiar bogeyman of SF's image. All weigh heavily on SF's future.

WHILE ITS FORMAL MILITARY PEDIGREE DATES SF'S FOUNDING TO 1942, 10th Group was officially created (as SF's first group) a decade later. All SF groups now share a genealogy that links them to a deactivated unit with a glorious past: the 1st Special Service Force, a joint Canadian-American organization activated in 1942 but disbanded in 1945, seven years before 10th Group was born. As a unit, the 1st Special Service Force saw a lot of fighting in World War II but never actually engaged in unconventional warfare. Instead, it specialized in Ranger-type actions.

Historically, U.S. Army Rangers have served as shock troops, trained to fight behind enemy lines and/or in advance of regular infantry and artillery units. Their primary mission is to be a direct-action vanguard for a more massive conventional onslaught. While Rangers are exceptional conventional fighters who, like the Special Forces, fall under the Special Operations umbrella, and undergo some of the toughest training in the world, they are not schooled to be unconventional. They are not meant to remain clandestine for long. Instead, they are supposed to act fast, decisively, and without seeking extensive local involvement.

Unfortunately, as distinct as this should make Rangers from SF, it is a difference that SF's borrowed history has tended to blur. The distinction between the two organizations is also not helped by the fact that SF soldiers have to be capable of exactly the sorts of direct action missions Rangers train for. Combine slippage here with SF's own organizational need to survive (as an entity in the army) and the rationale begins to build for why some SF commanders have gone out of their way to encourage their teams to train harder for the Rangeresque components of warfare. Their reasoning is that they are just being practical; SF will continue to be funded so long as it proves itself useful.

We have already seen some of the effects of this emphasis on direct action. As with ODA 309, teams don't become familiar with the full range of situations they may face when they deploy. Nor do Rangeresque skills enhance regional expertise. They certainly don't acclimate soldiers to anything foreign.

Despite each SF group's being assigned a different region of the world, with individual teams responsible for clusters of specific countries, acquiring deep local knowledge has rarely proved easy. One structural assumption has long been that commanders are interchangeable. Starting off in 7th Group, an officer may well wind up heading 3rd Group. Never mind the differences between Latin America and Africa. Command and control is command and control, and the same approaches are presumed to be applicable everywhere. From the top down, then, little regard develops for the significance of cultural differences, which may not matter to most direct action missions but always matters in unconventional warfare.

Even language training receives more lip service than serious attention. Whole teams attend language school and/or refresher courses together. But unlike virtually all other schools SF soldiers attend, this learning is classroom only. Unless a team is deployed, it receives no practical foreign language training; it isn't immersed. And although SF language teaching itself may be more sophisticated than what high school students receive, the results aren't much different. The soldiers do well enough to pass tests, but a month after school has ended most wind up suffering what they graphically describe as a memory dump. The language never gets locked in. In groups like 3rd Group the statistics that suggest most soldiers are language-proficient mislead. Team members are the first to admit this, and they know they are even less knowledgeable about local history, politics, and culture. Soldiers in 3rd Group weren't receiving any formalized training about their area of operations and weren't being offered incentives to educate themselves.

In this regard 3rd Group will never live up to the standards set by the original 10th Group, which, oriented toward Europe, was full of soldiers of European extraction. Clearly, 10th Group's achievements haven't been duplicated in many of the groups; 5th Group soldiers can't pose as North Africans or 1st Group soldiers as Thais no matter how hard they might try. The only group to have come close to SF's ideals is 7th Group, where Spanish has proven to be an easy language to learn and practice for soldiers who are not already native speakers. Notably, too, 7th Group has managed to attract and retain a Hispanic critical mass. Also, Latin America is close and, through the 1980s, 7th Group ODAs were spending considerable time on the ground in Honduras, El Salvador, and elsewhere in Central America.

In this regard, 7th Group has been fortunate. Not all teams get to their area of operations more than once, and some never get there at all. Regions invariably include countries that are politically off-limits, such as the entire Eastern bloc for the duration of the Cold War. Or budgetary constraints keep teams on base. But sometimes the deployment problem can directly relate to conventional commanders' control over SF soldiers operating in their theaters.

Since its formation in the early 1950s, SF has raised a series of troubling issues for military and civilian leaders concerned about covert operations and a democratic government's role in fostering them. Conventionally trained and minded commanding officers tend to have doubts about where SF fits into their bigger picture. Vietnam explains much of this, though intraservice rivalry for funding further justifies conventional commanders' doubts. More deep-seated still are suspicions fed by philosophical differences concerning how wars should be fought. Special Forces teams are not designed to directly or immediately take and hold ground. Yet, for many military leaders, taking and holding ground is what war always boils down to. Therefore, of what use is SF?

The quick answer is, SF soldiers secure trust.

More reflective answers depend on how one thinks future wars will unfold, what they might pertain to, and whom they will involve. Either the Gulf War was an aberration—as many argue today—or it is a harbinger of quick, decisive victories to come. I favor the former view. The Gulf War can represent the wave of the future only so long as battles take place on open terrain and the enemy fights according to conventional standards: in militarily recognizable units, away from civilian centers, using familiar weapons, and in order to seize some thing. Only a handful of countries can afford to fight us as Iraq did. Yet there are many places where people still want to fight.

Armed conflict currently rages on every populated continent except Australia. And as the world's sole remaining superpower, the United States figures prominently in each of these, whether or not we send troops or covert aid. All sides strive for us to side with them, dollars reach into every foreign crevice, and our mixed-up strategy of seeking stability some places and liberty for some peoples *is* interference, whether or not we are willing to acknowledge the significance of even our nonintervention.

Taking the long view, humans will never know a future without war. War has been with us as far back as the archaeological record extends. Anthropologists may debate the origins, causes, and functions of war. Military historians may argue about the impacts of the development of nuclear weapons. World War III may no longer seem likely. But war has hardly been outmoded. Nor has it been very well contained. It does not belong to just one type of society or one strain of people. At ground level, Bosnian farmers, Dinka herders, Ecuadorian soldiers, and Tamil shopkeepers shoot or are shot at with comparable bullets and with much the same aim: to right perceived wrongs or defend gains already made. Otherwise, the current euphemism for such strife—ethnic conflict—too often obscures more than it reveals.

Dubbing conflicts "ethnic" signifies that those doing the labeling—in battle-free western Europe and the United States—consider wars being fought today to be different. In typical inter-European fights, blood was shed over territory and conquest required that at least some victims live. Today's wars, in contrast, are described as viciously tribal, designed to determine who deserves control, and who should be "cleansed." "Ethnic cleansing" itself, of course, is another euphemism: for local, total dirty war. But, then, war can never be clean so long as arms races price the latest weapons out of some parties' reach.

Wars have to be dirty whenever the disgruntled and dissatisfied can't afford what those in power possess: international legitimacy, extensive resources, uniformed armies. Opposition groups have little choice but to behave illicitly and, often, indecently. When they oppose legitimate governments, they turn to neighboring states for shelter. Or they turn to wealthy rogue states, like Libya and Iran, for funding. Commonly, they politicize the populace by undermining the government's ability to protect innocent civilians. They also tap into, and twist, local feelings about injustice. Suicide bombers represent one extreme result, the constant threat of random violence another—the full range of which becomes hard to counteract, especially because there is no technological solution. Justice demands equitable distribution, exemplary government behavior, a more inclusive morality, or complete autonomy. No missile system will ever be able to deliver this. Only a societal reorganization can.

The issue, then, that continually confronts decision makers is whether a long-term commitment to restructure society is what the United States *should* engage in when confronting others' wars. Unfortunately, in our system, politicians' responses only have to be short-term, and all depend on which way the domestic and international winds blow. Even Realpolitik tends to be ignored. Realistically, what the United States can throw at dirty war is quite limited.

Essentially, there is only SF.

SF's design predisposes it for dirty war. This does not mean SF soldiers are dirty fighters, but that they are clever and cunning, able to adapt themselves to local conditions and fight or train others to defend themselves. Self-sufficient and self-contained, SF teams have the ability to act independently yet dependably over long stretches of time—which is exactly what dirty wars demand.

No other military unit has these long-range, long-term, ground-dwelling capabilities. Nor does any other organization exist that is so impressively low-tech.

Yes, SF soldiers get issued expensive Goretex raingear and top-of-the-line sleeping bags, have night-vision goggles, and learn high-speed helicopter insertion techniques. But they can also move through the woods at night with no visual aids, sneak to any area on foot, and work just as competently soaked as dry. Experientially SF soldiers know that patrols don't have to be high-tech to be effective, standard operating procedure shouldn't be complex if it is to remain fluid, and nothing needs to be computerized, though everything had better be well planned. Staying flexible is key.

Thanks to their design, teams *can* be flexible. With so much redundancy and duplication built in, teams can be swift and mercurial, hard to pin down in the woods, hard for the enemy to grasp, able to regroup instantaneously, then fall back apart and be equally effective. Hands down, a team is smarter than any smart weapon. Teams can guide themselves if they have to; they can improvise, survive unsupported, fail and still succeed. And though one might think SF soldiers deserve credit for much of this, all good teams are greater than the sum of their parts. Indeed, no design could be more effective. The interchangeability of teams keeps all teams jostling to be the best, while their closed nature twists relentless inter-team competition into unremitting internal pressure.

Accordingly, the soldiers SF selects for must be self-confident just short of stubborn, self-possessed but not egotistical, able to focus and compartmentalize, to adapt and conform. Teamwork itself requires males who can bond. Indeed, if teams are to remain effective, bonding is the one convention that must be upheld. For better, not worse, all team members have to be men who think enough alike that, without thinking, they inherently recognize those arenas in which they can and cannot compete with each other. And as counterintuitive as it may seem, some amount of posturing *is* integral to bonding, while bonding ensures cohesion.

Not only do the twelve men on an ODA have to know they can

trust one another, but they must project trust to win locals over, showing themselves to be powerful, ethical, selfless, team-oriented people, the very lack of which incites local fighting in the first place.

Conventional rhetoric might contend that wars are fought for ground, which they are, but it is also important to note that they are fought by people who, if they care enough, aren't easily beaten. SF soldiers have been carefully trained to break or bolster such people. They can aid partisans in toppling a government or protect allies from insurgency. These are two opposed, yet parallel, jobs, both of which require that soldiers know how to establish rapport. Rapport is SF's stock-in-trade. With it, SF soldiers constitute the military's most potent weapon for building, boosting, and sustaining local morale.

AS THE FORMER SOVIET UNION DISSOLVES AND COUNTRIES ELSEwhere collapse, divide, and reunite, ODAs should become busier. They have the versatility and range to protect U.S. interests in foreign nations, whether in capital cities or the hinterlands. SF soldiers are able to act as dispassionate combatants or compassionate humanitarians. No other set of Americans can switch gears so effortlessly and effectively; no other military unit has so many mature and adaptable soldiers.

But regardless of these qualities, certain realities persist. SF soldiers are only as capable as politicians allow them to be. Ultimately, it is politicians who dictate policy, which officers orchestrate and soldiers execute. At worst, politicians risk their careers by supporting mistaken foreign ventures. At best, soldiers risk their lives. Often, they sacrifice a healthy family, too. And while every unit in the army can boast career soldiers who will respond above and beyond the call of duty, SF soldiers routinely dare more than others do.

Team life demands uncompromising commitment, unwavering allegiance, and what does it offer in return? There is always the promise of exotic travel and adventure, but even dramatic foreign engagements, when they occur, tend to be too fleeting. SF members need something more than future possibilities to get them through so much mundane training and routine. On a daily basis, being one among a peerless few, belonging to an elite, holding membership in a closed, select society would seem to help. But when everyone spends most of his time with others who wear the beret, the SF tab, and a group flash, how much do these really signify? They can't mean all that much. Within the company, being in SF is superfluous. Instead, what counts there is being indispensable, on *the* best, most capable, hottest, and finest team.

ODA members would be the first to point out that teams, and not just teams' missions, make Special Forces unconventional and unique within the military. This is why the current preoccupation with individual skills, overinflating soldiers' singular abilities and selling teams as super-conventional assets, poses a genuine danger. It is the team, not the individual, that drives SF and makes this small elite America's most significant repository for unconventional warfare capabilities.

Consider the kind of world we live in today. Somalia, Haiti, Bosnia: the twenty-first century has only just begun. And our track record so far? Dare we ask the Kurds? What about the citizens of Panama? When the U.S. government makes broad, sweeping promises, it usually tries to live up to its word, at least initially. Often, large airlifts and small teams of men get sent. And they try. Operation Provide Comfort, Operation Restore Hope, Operation Uphold Democracy. But then come other crises-of-the-moment. Television audiences shift their focus. Policymakers' attention wavers. Funding dries up. SF itself experiences much the same sort of treatment. And it shouldn't.

As globalization redefines loyalties and glaring inequities provoke increasingly indiscriminate violence, we need a flexible, unconventional force. To have, if not to use. To not misuse.

Acknowledgments

F<small>IRST AND FOREMOST</small> I <small>THANK THE</small> D<small>EPARTMENT OF THE</small> A<small>RMY FOR</small> granting me permission to be an anthropologist among the men of 3rd Group. And to 3rd Group, thank you for allowing me to hang around.

While NCOs, not officers, have been the focus of my attention, there are two officers to whom I owe deep, deep gratitude. Colonel Peter Stankovich and Major Gregory Discavage gave me unquestioning support. My fieldwork would have been doomed without them, and nonexistent without the active support and encouragement I received from everyone in Z Company.

I must especially thank William Bender, James Johnson, Terry Corner, Paul Bandurraga, Bruce D'Amours, Mike Pellegrino, Anthony Minor, Dave Schell, Alex Stallone, Jay Cashion, Daniel Molesky, Michael Pevler, Richard Dwaine, James Carver, Larry Colley, William MacPherson-White, Joe Donaldson, Ernest Brown, and Wayne Jenkins.

And Jerry Morman, Clifford Nelson, Kevin Cleveland, Cassius Williams, Harold King, Kenneth Hartsfield, Bruce Ward, Edwin Goodwin, Kevin Tillman, William Dolasky, Keven Wright, Jeffrey Wright, Steven Wood, Keith Ducote, John Terzian, William Berkey, Charles Everson, Barry Williams, Samuel Makanani, John Turnmire, Sidney Brown, Joseph Self, Creston Hooks, Dave Lafountain, Daryl

Shanks, Wayne Colombo, William Jennings, Steven Whitmarsh, and Phillip Wyllie.

Elsewhere around Ft. Bragg, and at SWCS, in the battalion, and 3rd Group: Lieutenant Colonel Parker; Majors Schroer, Martinez, Roland, Banks, Marlin, Barta, and Pierce; Chaplain Boatwright, Captain DeSilva, Chief Warrant Officer Swanson, and Sergeant Major Griffith; Sergeants Bellis, Snow, Rosado, Gaspar, Offhaus, Johnson, Zimmer, and McKay; and Joe Lupyak, Skip Poole, Jim Grastie, and Fred Fuller.

Also, Diane Discavage, Kim McHale, Lori Johnson, Kimberly Schell, Monica Corner, Marsha Minor, Cindy D'Amours, Debby Pevler, Peggy Cashion, and Linda Nann.

Thank you, too, Kerry Allen, Henry Williams, and Dave Scott.

Unfortunately, with all the turbulence in the team rooms, and ever-changing rosters, some names may not appear above. I apologize but am not to blame; as the former company operations sergeant, my husband is. In all fairness, though, he is not responsible for any other errors, but does promise to protect me.

Preceding authors, whose works helped educate me about SF, include: Aaron Bank, John Cook, Donald Duncan, W. E. B. Griffin, Hans Halberstadt, Francis Kelly, Bob Mayer, Robin Moore, Ian Padden, Alfred Paddock, James Rowe, Al Santoli, Charles Simpson, Shelby Stanton, Jeff Stein, and Ian Sutherland.

Jennifer Taw and Rebecca Simons both made the attempt to save me from cryptic writing. They each plowed through the manuscript in record time. Jenny also introduced me to Lieutenant Colonel Will Irwin, who deserves a medal for closely reading the text not once but twice. Every writer should be able to have a reader like him, though (again) all opinions and any errors are mine, not his. Also, Dr. David Marlowe, Andrew Marlowe, and Lou Marano graciously dealt with later writing worries. Mary Powers, as ever, listened to all my worries. So did Florence Simons. And wherever the late Howard Simons is, doubtless he heard me too.

Mitch Horowitz prodded me to a better book, though the book itself is really the result of Jeff Tulis's incredible salesmanship. And

Jeff's not even an agent, just a conceptual genius who happens to be a political scientist, too.

Finally, there is John. Usually authors thank their spouses for living the book with them. But John really did live this. Had he not I wouldn't be writing these words.

Index

Personal names of soldiers are fictitious, as are numbers of ODA groups.